PAUL CROOK

INTELLECTUALS & the DECLINE of RELIGION

ESSAYS AND REVIEWS

Published by

Boolarong Press.

655 Toohey Road

Salisbury Qld 4107

Australia

www.boolarongpress.com.au

National Library of Australia Cataloguing-in-Publication entry:

Creator:	Crook, D. P. (David Paul), author.
Title:	Intellectuals and the decline of religion : essays and reviews / Paul Crook.
ISBN:	9781925522525 (paperback)
Subjects:	Intellectuals in literature.
	Religion and science.
	Anthologies.
	Essays.

Cover Design: Boolarong Press

Cover Image by design36, used under license from Shutterstock.com

Printed and bound by Watson Ferguson & Company, Salisbury, Brisbane, Australia.

Contents

Preface

In recent years I have been exploring the response of British intellectuals to one of the momentous historical changes of the twentieth century: the rise of secularism and the corresponding decline of religion throughout the western world. This is of course a massive phenomenon, multi-faceted and irregular if relentless. We live today in this secularised world. I have penned a number of brief reflective essays on writers who have attracted my attention. These pieces have so far appeared only as posts on my website (dpcrook.wordpress.com.), with the hope of provoking debate and discussion.

The people range from John Henry Newman in the nineteenth century to Joseph Needham, who died in 1995, with the writings clustering mainly from the end of World War One to roughly the 1960s. I had expected more sustained analysis from my "public intellectuals" of the deep and underlying causes of expanding unbelief. For that you will have to go to modern historians. But the authors presented here did give some intriguing commentaries and opinions on what was happening and what they considered to be the social and cultural consequences for humanity (western humanity mainly, it should be said). Reactions ranged from mild complacency to prophesy of the death of civilisation. Confidence in organised religion was notably limited. Fascinating balance sheets were drawn up about the historical achievements versus failings of Christianity. And there were gleams of hope for a revivification of faith and spirituality amidst what Alec Vidler called "secular despair".

What I found of especial interest were the mystical experiences, a sense of the transcendental, of a merging with the universe and feeling of pure being, that many authors reported. C. S. Lewis and Malcolm Muggeridge are only two examples. Joseph Needham pointed to the obvious parallels with Buddhism. Both he and Arnold Toynbee (and others) explored the possibilities of a "higher religion" embodying the universal spiritual truths of the world's great religions.

Many of the writers in the Contents table are hardly household names today, sadly. I have cast my net more widely than a specialised focus upon ideas, giving the story (however briefly) of their lives, in the belief that this will add interest and make their commentaries and world-views more meaningful. Much of what they said is perceptive and, I would suggest, of relevance to us today. They wrote in an age of total war, horrific violence and ideological intensity and conflict. It was an age also of emerging mass media, advertising, rapidly evolving information communications and popular culture. This is all very familiar, if evolving dramatically faster now than ever. How Chesterton would have relished Facebook!

The second part of this book simply prints reviews I have done of books that attracted my attention, appearing in the admirable *Australian Journal of Politics and History* (*AJPH*) between 2001 and 2016. They are brief, around six hundred words apiece, and cover territory from ancient Egypt and the Habsburgs to Charles Darwin and modern America. I have permitted myself the liberty of including also a longer review article, plus some miscellaneous writings that may be of interest.

Acknowledgments: Of the many people to whom I am indebted over the years, I would particularly like to thank Margaret Higgs for her valued friendship and for helping me to obtain library resources, often rare and very difficult to obtain. Boolarong Press, and especially Dan Kelly, have been most helpful on the publishing side. Finally, I would like to express deep gratitude to my beloved wife Ann for her meticulous formatting and proof-reading of this text, and, most of all, for her unfailing love and support, a priceless gift.

I dedicate this book to the memory of my son Daniel.

* * *

Essays 1-10 have not been published before. Essay 11 first appeared in the online journal *This View of Life* at evolution-institute.org (6 September 2015). The reviews all appeared in *AJPH*. Here are the references. Review 1: 47, 3 (2001), pp. 453-454; Review 2: 49, 1 (2003), pp. 141-142; Review 3: 49, 3 (2003), pp. 465-466; Review 4: 51, 1 (2005), pp. 144-145; Review 5: 52, 1 (2006), pp. 161-162; Review 6: 53, 1 (2007), pp. 160-161; Review 7: 54, 1 (2008), pp. 135-143; Review 8: 54, 1 (2008), pp. 166-167; Review 9: 54, 3 (2008), pp. 504-505; Review 10: 55, 1 (2009), pp. 151-152; Review 11: 55, 3 (2009), pp. 472-473; Review 12: 55, 3 (2009), pp. 473-474; Review 13: 58, 3 (2012), pp. 471-472; Review 14: 59, 1 (2013), pp. 253-254; Review 15: 59, 1 (2013), pp. 157-158; Review 16: 59, 3 (2013), pp. 490-491; Review 17: 59, 3 (2013), pp. 499-500; Review 18: 60, 1 (2014), pp. 145-146; Review 19: 60, 3 (2014), pp. 484-485; Review 20: 61, 1 (2015), pp. 152-153; Review 21: 61, 1 (2015), pp. 153-154; Review 22: 61, 3 (2015), pp. 482-483.

1. Was Newman's Theory of Development Darwinian? And Other Thoughts About It

John Henry Newman's theory of development of Christian doctrine has often been compared to Darwin's theory of evolution. That is because he seemed to be saying that Church doctrine had developed over the ages as historical conditions had changed. This can look, at least superficially, as if the Christian tradition had evolved by adapting to the environment, rather as Darwin's theory proposes that evolution occurs as the result of environmental pressures causing natural selection. I have made the parallel myself, in passing, in lectures. However as Newman scholars, such as Ian Ker, Sheridan Gilley and Avery Dulles, have been at pains to point out, the parallel is ultimately misleading. Newman did emphasise the changes that had, inevitably, occurred in mainline Christian thought over great time, but he did not see this as a sort of knee jerk Darwinian reaction to changing historical circumstances and challenges. He was in fact writing to defend Christianity against the sceptics who asked: "how can you believe in a church that has changed its mind so often, shifted its doctrinal grounds so often, has seen so many heresies, wars between sects, and the corruption and decay of the early faith of the fathers?" Newman, it seems to me (no theologian), is saying that the essential truths proclaimed by Christ and the early church have in fact been preserved; but also "developed" to bring out truths that were latent in early commentaries. As John Cornwell says:

> Such developments as occur, Newman argues, must be shown to be in accord with the Christianity of the Apostles, and antique Christianity.... He asks that developments should be such that the Church would remain recognisably the same to an Early Father who returned to earth.... Far from the Church being changed by the cultures it encounters, it is the Church that assimilates and transforms cultures.[1]

John Henry Newman (1801-1890) was a massive figure in nineteenth century English religious thought, and he continued to be influential (some of his ideas were implemented in Vatican II). He was a founding father of, and major inspirational force behind, the so-called Oxford or Tractarian Movement, which aimed to revitalise Anglicanism. In an age of indolence and ignorance of its historical traditions, the

Church of England seemed to these reformers to have lost its way. Newman, John Keble, Edward Pusey and others sought to restore its sense of spirituality and sense of connection with its Christian past, disrupted by the Reformation. This caused a storm of opposition, and the movement was accused of trying to restore a hated Catholicism (see my essay on Alec Vidler for more details). Newman tried in the Tracts and other writings to defend the "middle way" of Anglicanism, but after much agonising he finally decided that the Anglican Church was in schism, and he converted to Catholicism in 1845.

An Essay on the Development of Christian Doctrine was published in the same year. Newman wrote it before he actually converted in order to clear his mind of any doubts or difficulties that might still cause him to hesitate about such a massive, and for his family and many friends, such a painful move. He still had, as he said in Development, "vague misgivings" about "accretions and additions" (such as Transubstantiation) that had been added to the early Christian faith. Were these illicit, as anti-Catholics accused, or justifiable and reasonable developments of Christianity? He worked out seven tests to show whether or not changes in dogma had been in accord with Christianity at the time of the apostles. We needn't go into these often abstruse and difficult tests just now. Suffice to say that by the time Newman had got far advanced on his book, he resolved to be received into the Catholic Church, and to allow the work to be published unfinished. He "half re-wrote" and greatly rearranged the book for a second edition in 1878, which is now regarded as the standard text. Quotes below are from this text.[2]

Newman had a great feeling for history (not surprising given he spent so much of his life studying the early history of the church, the fathers, and the early heresies). He preferred to view Christian faith through the lens of history, rather than using the rigidly theoretical dogmatic systems of the scholastic school and others. So he resented the assumptions of the sceptics that history proved Christianity to be a fraud. Was it logical to work from this assumption? He thought not. It was not self-evident and needed proof. So far that had not been forthcoming. The critics assumed that there was no real continuity in Christian doctrine and beliefs, again a problematic assumption. More "natural" was "to consider that the society of Christians, which the Apostles left on earth, were of that religion to which the Apostles had converted them; that the external continuity of name, profession, and communion, argues a real continuity of doctrine". It was not a "violent assumption", Newman argues, but rather good sense, "to take it for granted, before proof to the contrary, that the Christianity of the second, fourth, seventh, twelfth, sixteenth, and intermediate centuries is in its substance the very religion which Christ and His Apostles taught in the first, whatever may be the modifications for good or for evil which lapse of years, or the vicissitudes of human affairs, have impressed upon it".[3]

Interestingly, Newman starts to use a relativistic concept of human perceptions about phenomena in general, and sets of ideas and ideologies in particular. Nothing is set in concrete. Definitions themselves are difficult when it comes to encompassing the whole reality or range of characteristics and qualities of (say) organisms in biology or (say) theories or doctrines in philosophy, politics, economics or religion. Things change over time. Definitions change as more and more people mull over (say) ideas. Ideas, whether real or not, have life, or at least live in the minds of those who are impacted by them. In his eloquent (if sometimes ponderously Victorian) style, Newman puts it thus:

> ... when some great enunciation, whether true or false, about human nature, or present good, or government, or duty, or religion, is carried forward into the public throng of men and draws attention, then it is not merely received passively in this or that form into many minds, but it becomes an active principle within them, leading them to an ever-new contemplation of itself, to an application of it in various directions, and a propagation of itself on every side.[4]

He lists such doctrines as the divine right of kings, the rights of man, "the anti-social bearings of a priesthood", utilitarianism, free trade or the philosophy of Epicurus. Such ideas had their history of initial confusion and inadequate expression, misconceptions and conflicts between adherents, new insights, accumulation of judgments and teachings, modifications and expansions and combinations with other ideas until some sort of more organised understanding of the doctrine emerged, all related to the changing circumstances of the times in which the ideas flourished. A doctrine:

> … will be interrogated and criticized by enemies, and defended by well-wishers.... It will, in proportion to its native vigour and subtlety, introduce itself into the framework and details of social life, changing public opinion, and strengthening the foundations of established order.[5]

It can grow into an ethical code, a system of government, a theology or ritual. But it is after all the representation of an original idea "being in substance what that idea meant from the first, its complete image as seen in a combination of diversified aspects, with the suggestions and corrections of many minds and the illustrations of many experiences".[6]

In a striking metaphor he compared the development of an idea with a river. It was not, as some said, clearer near the spring, but in fact "more equable, and purer, and stronger, when its bed has become deep, and broad, and full". Its beginnings were no measure of its capabilities. Its goes through trials and difficulties. It meanders, sometimes fails, then it strikes out in one distinct direction.

> In time it enters upon strange territory; points of controversy alter their bearing; parties rise and fall around it; dangers and hopes appear in new relations; and old principles reappear under new forms. It changes with them in order to remain the same. In a higher world it is otherwise, but here below to live is to change….[7]

Newman's "Tests"

The first part of *Essay on Development* sought to establish, by detailed analysis, an historical argument in favour of the essential continuity, the "oneness", between the teaching of the Apostles – the early church – and "the body of doctrine known at this day by the name of Catholic, and professed substantially both by Eastern and Western Christendom". He then turned to the "only question" that still could be raised, "whether the said Catholic faith, as now held, is logically, as well as historically, the representative of the ancient faith". We move from the historical to the logical.[8]

It was in this context that he ventured to propose seven "tests" (called Notes in the second edition) by which legitimate developments of the ancient faith could be discriminated from illegitimate changes, "healthy" and faithful developments distinguished from corruptions or perversions of the truth. These tests were not proposed as definitive but rather as Newman's best effort, based on his extensive studies of church history, to show whether later doctrines were in accord with early Christianity, whether they were authentic or not.

Here, in Newman's succinct summary, are the tests of an idea:

> There is no corruption if it retains one and the same type, the same principles, the same organization; if its beginnings anticipate its subsequent phases, and its later phenomena protect and subserve its earlier; if it has a power of assimilation and revival, and a vigorous action from first to last.[9]

This is just a short commentary on Newman's theory. So I will just give some of his reasoning on one of the "tests", namely that of "Chronic Vigour" (number seven). He is essentially arguing that a truly evolving, authentic Christian doctrine will exhibit great historical resilience and power to survive, even in the face of terrible difficulties and challenges. On the other hand, corrupt doctrines lack this survival power. They may have their day and flourish for a time, but their essential weaknesses will ensure that they ultimately decay and die. Corruption tends to become dissolution. Thus "duration" is an important test of a faithful development.

Newman goes as far as to allege:

> The course of heresies is always short; it is an intermediate state between life and death, or what is like death; or, if it does not result in death, it is resolved into some new, perhaps opposite, course of error, which lays no claim to be connected with it.[10]

Only in this way can heresies persist. Newman seems to wriggle at times on this issue, given the obvious difficulty that many heresies did seem historically to have a fair life span. Such heresies persisted, he argues, out of social habit and fashion, links with political institutions, and so on. But they tend to collapse under challenge, under "the first rough influence from without". This was what happened to classical paganism, to heretics such as the Nestorians and Monophysites; and such too "is that Protestantism, or (as it sometimes calls itself) attachment to the Establishment, which is not unfrequently the boast of the respectable and wealthy among ourselves".[11] This was, of course, a rather unkind swipe at his former Church of England. It was also an historically problematic verdict on nineteenth century Protestantism generally, given the strength of the Nonconformist churches in both Britain and the United States.[12]

Newman finalises his case for the ultimate sustainability of the Catholic faith in his concluding chapter. Here perhaps is some echo of "the survival of the fittest":

> When we consider the succession of ages during which the Catholic system has endured, the severity of the trials it has undergone, the sudden and wonderful changes without and within which have befallen it, the incessant mental activity and the intellectual gifts of its maintainers, the enthusiasm which it has kindled, the fury of the controversies which have been carried on among its professors, the impetuosity

> of the assaults made upon it, the ever-increasing responsibilities to which it has been committed by the continuous development of its dogmas, it is quite inconceivable that it should not have been broken up and lost, were it a corruption of Christianity. Yet it is still living, if there be a living religion or philosophy in the world; vigorous, energetic, persuasive, progressive... it grows and is not overgrown; it spreads out, yet is not enfeebled; it is ever germinating, yet ever consistent with itself.[13]

There have been widely ranging theological reactions to Newman's theory of development. You might like to follow them up, if interested, in the reading below. But certainly the theory has been of major significance. Much of it was tentative and has been "developed" since. Newman would have approved. The "tests", for example, are seen now, as Avery Dulles says, as "rules of thumb" rather than "a set of laws".[14] Moreover the problems that Newman sought to resolve in theology are still with us. As Gerard McCarren observes, Newman's articulation of doctrinal development retains its influence:

> … not merely for its enduring place in Christian intellectual history, but because Newman's "difficulty", despite recent theological advances, and indeed all the more because of such progress, remains a theological challenge today. Newman's statement of the problem continues to demand attention because the problem still calls for solution, and because his answer to it, whatever its shortcomings, promises assistance to theologians who strive to explore the issues and venture viable solutions.[15]

---

[1]John Cornwell, *Newman's Unquiet Grave: The Reluctant Saint* (London, New York, Continuum, 2010), pp. 85-86.

[2] John Henry Cardinal Newman, *An Essay on the Development of Christian Doctrine* (1878). I have used a modern reprint (Indiana, University of Notre Dame Press, 1989), with a Foreword by Ian Ker. All further references are to this source.

[3] *Ibid*, p. 5.

[4] *Ibid*, p. 36.

[5] *Ibid*, p. 37

[6] *Ibid*, pp. 38.

[7] *Ibid*, p. 40. As Sheridan Gilley says: "Thus Newman has been wrongly taken to justify any and every kind of change, when his whole point is that development, properly understood, has its own laws, by which the idea of Christianity unfolds itself in every form of intellectual and institutional expression, making the

Church ever more itself": in *The Cambridge Companion to John Henry Newman* (Cambridge, Cambridge University Press, 2013), p. 12, in Ch.1 "Life and Writings". (On a personal note Sheridan was long ago a student of mine at the University of Queensland).

[8] Newman, *An Essay on Development,* p. 169.

[9] *Ibid,* pp. 169-171.

[10] *Ibid,* p. 204.

[11] *Ibid*, p. 205.

[12] For a critical account of Newman's embedded anti-Protestantism (and of the Tractarian movement in detail) see Frank M. Turner, *John Henry Newman: The Challenge to Evangelical Religion* (New Haven, London, Yale University Press, 2002).

[13] Newman, *Essay on Development*, pp. 437-438.

[14] Avery Dulles, *Newman* (London, New York, Continuum, 2002), p. 79.

[15] Gerard H. McCarren, "Development of Doctrine" in *The Cambridge Companion to John Henry Newman*, pp. 129-130, and generally.

Further Reading

This is in addition to the works cited above.

Ian Ker, *John Henry Newman: A Biography* (Oxford, Clarendon Press, 1988).

Ian Ker and Alan G. Hill, eds, *Newman After a Hundred Years* (Oxford, Clarendon Press, 1990).

Nicholas Lash, *Newman on Development* (Shepherdstown, WV, Patmos Press, 1975).

2. Maude Petre: A Modernist Martyr

Maude Petre (1863-1942) was an amazing woman, a woman of great faith, a strong woman of indomitable character, and a scholarly woman dedicated to the pursuit of truth, however inconvenient this search might prove. She was a key figure in the English Catholic Modernist Movement that flourished for a time from the late nineteenth century. The "movement" was to have long term influence within the Catholic Church, despite being virtually suppressed by the papacy by 1910. Its lasting impact can be discerned in the radical changes implemented by Vatican II in 1965. Despite the wording of Pius X's encyclical *Pascendi gregis* in 1907, condemning the errors of modernism, Catholic Modernism was neither an organised school nor doctrinal system, but rather a loose group of people who essentially wanted Catholic teachings to come to terms with modern Biblical scholarship and modern science. The church, they said, needed to adapt to modern thought, but without abandoning its core tenets of faith. As Alec Vidler said of the modernists,

> ... they had felt bound to use scientific and historico-critical methods of study and to follow the argument wherever it led.... What they had attempted to do was, while remaining sincere and loyal Roman Catholics, to forward such a revision and fresh presentation of the Church's teaching as would acclimatize it in the modern world.[1]

Maud Petre would have said a hearty Amen to that!

Brief Life

Maude was born into an old aristocratic English Catholic family. She was fortunate to be well connected and financially secure, which gave her a certain degree of protection against church authorities, but she was by no means immune. She published widely (fourteen books and over ninety articles), becoming essentially a publicist for English Modernism, a saga described in her illuminating autobiography *My Way of Faith* (1937), a book that is unfortunately very difficult to procure these days. (Let's hope that some enterprising publisher will bring out a reprint.)

She was born in Coptfold Hall, the family estate in a village in Essex. One of her ancestors, much revered by the family, was a Catholic activist in the 1820s. Maude wrote a biography of him entitled *The Ninth Lord Petre: Pioneer of Roman Catholic Emancipation* (1928). Her father, a gentleman farmer, was a son of the thirteenth Lord Petre, and her mother (a convert) was a Howard, fifth daughter of the earl of Wicklow in County Donegal. (The eighth earl of Wicklow was to become a close friend of the Catholic novelist Evelyn Waugh.) As her biographer Ellen Leonard makes clear, Maude early set out on a spiritual journey, describing herself as "passionately religious" and "innately sceptical", not a recipe for a quiet life:

> When she was twenty-two, at the suggestion of her confessor as a remedy for her religious doubts, she studied scholastic philosophy [especially Aquinas] under private instruction in Latin from professors of the college of propaganda fide in Rome. This unusual educational opportunity for a Roman Catholic at that time did not solve her religious doubts but it provided a philosophical foundation for her writing. Although she did not consider herself a scholar she read widely and was fluent in French, Italian, and Latin.[2]

In 1890 she entered the London noviciate of the Daughters of the Heart of Mary, founded during the French Revolution and notably more emancipated than traditional women's orders: civilian clothes, mixing in the local community, keeping their own names (instead of saint's names). She was appointed local superior in London in 1896, provincial superior in England and Ireland 1900-1905, and made provincial councillor from 1905-1908. She looked set to become a ranking nun in Britain, but her writings on religion intervened, making her suspect to the hierarchy. She advocated "spiritual liberty" in her book *Catholicism and Independence* (1907) and for this was forced out of her order in 1908. Pius X had just condemned modernism. Its leading advocates included the French theologian and biblical scholar Alfred Loisy, his English friend Baron Friedrich von Hügel and the Irish-born Jesuit scholar George Tyrrell. Von Hügel was a long-time friend of the Petre family, so family connections played a role in what happened next. Von Hügel introduced both Tyrrell and Maude to the revisionist ideas of Loisy. As Alec Vidler summarised:

> Loisy had in effect turned the tables on the Liberal Protestants [such as Harnack and Sabatier], and shown that

> an objective and even radical historical criticism of Christian origins could be held to justify, not a reduced and attenuated version of Protestant piety, but the full and rich corporate life of the Catholic Church. But, in doing so, he had of course given up the traditional view of biblical inerrancy and the scholastic system of Christological orthodoxy. No one expected the Roman authorities officially to endorse the new apologetic forthwith, but there were many who hoped that they would allow its further exploration. What Rome did in fact was to condemn it out of hand, simply because it was sacrilegious to suggest that traditional teaching required any modification or revision whatever.[3]

In an age of cultural crisis and turmoil generally in Europe from the 1880s to the Great War, the church felt threatened, as did many conservative thinkers, and reacted – it now seems – with inappropriate rigidity and defensiveness. Repressive measures included the appointment of councils of vigilance in every diocese, and the imposition in 1910 of an anti-modernist oath on all clerics. The Bishop of Southwark, Peter Amigo, refused Maude the sacraments in his diocese in 1908 (after her book appeared), and she was forced to take mass in other parishes, causing her great distress. Amigo became a perennial scourge to her, later requesting that she take the anti-modernist oath (even though she was not a cleric). She refused to do this, writing in her memoir that "if one's life did not bear testimony to one's faith an oath would not do so".[4] She lived, as Leonard remarks, in a state of "partial excommunication" thereafter. Tyrrell was excommunicated at about the same time.

George Tyrrell (1861-1909) was an immense influence upon her.[5] He and Maude became deep lifelong friends, soulmates. One could say that theirs was one of the great love affairs of the time, although celibate and essentially spiritual. After his death from Bright's disease at forty-eight, Maude became his literary executor, publishing his writings posthumously, including a two volume *Autobiography and Life* in 1912, which, predictably, was placed on the Vatican Index of forbidden books.[6] Maude's own books were placed on the Index in 1913. She got some revenge by writing a history entitled *Modernism: Its Failures and Its Fruits* (written 1914, published 1918). In it she deplored the church persecution of modernists.

Although continuing her devotions and writing, Maude nursed wounded soldiers in France and England during World War 1, set up a branch of the Labour Party in Storrington, was active in municipal government and the Women's Institute, housing and hospital projects, and, later, in ecumenical movements (such as the World Congress of Faith). Wikipedia makes the relevant point that, "She is important as the only English Modernist to write on social and political matters". (R. H. Tawney would have approved, as he constantly chided the churches of the time for not being openly enough committed to social and political reform.).Her works include *Reflections of a Non-Combatant* (1915); *Democracy at the Crossroads* (1918); *State Morality and a League of Nations* (1919) in which she rightly forecast the intractable problems facing the newly-founded League; and her internationalist plea for peace; *The Two Cities, or Statecraft and Idealism* (1925).In her last years she returned again to her modernist friends, writing *Von Hügel and Tyrrell: The Story of a Friendship* (1937) and *Alfred Loisy: His Religious Significance* (1944).

She moved to London in 1939 and was soon busy fire-watching during the Blitz:

> She died suddenly in her home [in Kensington] on 16 December 1942. A requiem mass was celebrated at the Assumption Convent, Kensington Square, London. At her request she was buried in the parish churchyard of St Mary's Church, Storrington, in the same plot as her friend George Tyrrell.[7]

As Ellen Leonard sums up her writings and life, they reflected "a critical approach to authority, an insistence on spiritual independence, and a respect for pluralism".

My Way of Faith

Maude's *My Way of Faith* (1937) may be described as an account of her spiritual journey. She denied that it was an autobiography, but it does contain large chunks of autobiography. She stops off within a loosely narrative framework to discuss in more detail certain themes that loomed large at certain times in her life; and throughout she recounts her wrestlings with religious doubts and scruples. Certain themes recur: her ambivalence about the Thomistic scholasticism that she was educated in at Rome; the issue of church authority; Modernism and her role in it; and her love for George Tyrrell.[8] She herself felt towards the end of her life that she was a relic of the past, a woman of faith in a pagan world, "a negligible survival of a former civilization.... It is as though one were marooned on an island of the past: a past which has no part in the present".[9] Her book was an effort to explain how she had managed to "keep my faith".

Scholasticism

If we look at Maude's early religious education, we detect a recurring ambivalence about scholasticism, the massive theological system associated mainly with St Thomas Aquinas and on which Catholic thought was founded. Whereas Thomism was commonly interpreted as asserting the dominance of reason over heart, of asserting that reason could provide proof of religion's truth, Maude accepted the philosophical impossibility of this claim. However she did not swing over to the other extreme, embraced by some modernists, of placing heart above head, of rejecting scholasticism altogether as simply an intellectual system empowering entrenched Catholic powers. (Tyrrell's position was more complex, basically arguing that St Thomas's original ideas had been distorted over time, but rejecting later scholasticism.[10]). Maude valued the mind, not least because it gave her independence:

> My "heart" has been ever only too ready to believe, but my mind has been ever like the snake, wriggling beneath St. Michael's foot. And I am too much built in one piece to separate the two parts of myself. With my mind I have craved for certainty – for such proof as no sane mind can deny – but this I have not found. With my heart I have desired God, and have known, through the whole of my varying life, that nothing else could content me.[11]

Maude's introduction to scholasticism was highly unusual for a Victorian woman. It was accidental in a way. Had her parents not both died when she was nineteen, as she says, she would probably have married like other women and had a normal family life. She craved affection and was, by her own judgment, probably over-sexed. But she was also passionately devout, orthodoxly so to begin with, although terrified of the doctrine of eternal punishment and never unquestioning. Her local priest suggested the "fairly crazy idea" that she might escape her doubts by studying scholastic philosophy in Rome. So, with no ties, she went to Rome at twenty-two, a lone woman studying under various ecclesiastics, totally ignorant of historic Rome (she did not even recognise St Peter's on her first viewing!). She was parked in the College of Propaganda for a time, communicated in Latin with her teachers, and had a maid companion to chaperone her during lessons.

Her spiritual guides introduced her to the great scholastic system "as a supreme and final remedy for doubt. I need not say that it proved to be no such thing".[12] She was soon immersed in St. Thomas's thirteenth century classic *SummaTheologica*, a book that became her lifelong companion. She always felt uneasy at those of her modernist friends, like von Hügel and even Tyrrell, who could be dismissive of Thomism as simply a "method of spiritual compulsion". She accepted that St Thomas,

> … did indeed aim at rendering religious truth impregnable according to human reason. His building was sound – good bricks, good mortar, good beams - but then you must come inside it, and this is what the anti-scholastic refuses to do.[13]

She accepted their point that faith should be free and spontaneous, but she wished to combine a free and unifying faith with a spirit of vigorous rationality.

What Maude found in Aquinas was an exhilarating spiritual system that aimed at the whole of nature. It was broad and all-encompassing, if overambitious in its ultimate philosophical goal. It ought not to be pigeonholed away in a particularistic manner. She compared his thought with the profound sense of misery in Pascal:

> There is in St. Thomas, on the contrary, an abounding hope and optimism. He believed in human nature, he believed in the human soul and in the human body. He believed in the great material universe as he believed in the world of pure spirits; he believed in nature, as he believed in supernature. The human reason was, to him, a magnificent instrument for reaching out, beyond its own limits, to the threshold of a Truth before which it surrendered its arms. His philosophical system presents a glorious hierarchy, from inanimate, through animate and sentient, to the intellectual and spiritual world. He leads us through all nature, from a stone to the Throne of God.[14]

And - a clinching emotion for an English countrywoman - St. Thomas was a friend to the whole animal kingdom, allowing it space within the universal hierarchy

Whereas others found the scholastic process cold and rational, Maude found it "spiritually exhilarating, and full of the possibilities of prayer". Like physical exercise to the body:

> … it seemed to expand one's soul; to open the lungs to the winds of eternity… and so the faculties of the mind, being stimulated and exercised, dispose it to an apprehension of spiritual truth - of a truth beyond its actual comprehension.[15]

For Maude *contemplation* was the supreme human state or action, and was not a simple matter of losing oneself in love for God, but had "more of the character of perfect knowledge than of perfect love… above all a fullness of knowledge with which love is incorporated".[16] She saw herself as a born Platonist, mentally rejoicing in scholasticism, but morally she was with thinkers like Augustine or Pascal.

She came to believe that it was the principle of unity that underlay the quest for faith. In its metaphysical character faith was the recognition of unity, to be sought with head and with heart – a recognition that the squabbling schools would do well to mark. Through the notion of being:

> … we come to a sense of the unity of being, and thence to the sense of supreme unity and being. And thus the search for unity becomes the search for God…. In so far as we are contented we are at one with something, and that something is, for us, for the time that we are at one with it, our *all*.[17]

We may note here both mystical and even Buddhist parallels. It is no surprise then that Maude was drawn to ecumenical movements in her later life. Again in this she was ahead of her Catholic times.

Modernism

Maude devotes a section of her book to Modernism. She had published a more detailed study *Modernism, its Failure and its Fruits* in 1918. Here she reflects on it from the perspective of 1937 (incorporating some of the earlier work). Why bother, she asks, given the general verdict that modernism had fizzled out? Who would be interested after the world crises that had followed?

> Because there are those, after such a world convulsion as the Great War; who, in the face of world-wide movements of irreligion and paganism such as Christianity has never known, can still not forget a movement which they themselves now declare to be dead, nor the part I took in it.[18]

Although it had failed to bring internal reform to the Catholic Church so far, modernism had opened eyes to issues that still needed debate, "for many, many are the things openly said by Catholics, priests or laymen, that could never have been safely said had men like Tyrrell not first said them, and been decapitated for so doing".[19] Most significantly of all, modernism had raised the soul-wracking question "What are we to do with the articles of our religious Catechism when the articles of our scientific and historical catechism come into direct conflict with them".[20]

Maude analysed the movement under two categories: (1) inner problems that arose from the issues of character, doctrine and discipline with the Church itself; and (2) outer problems arising from the devastating new discoveries in science and history, problems which affected the whole foundations of religion, but over which the Church had no control.

One of the key inner problems was that of the rights and limits of church authority. Maude fought against the prevailing domineering ethos of papal and general church authority. The faithful, as a body, deserved a greater voice in ecclesiastical government. The church was in need of cleansing, spiritually, morally and materially:

> … the Church is sick, and her sickness can only be cured by casting out four evil spirits that have lodged in her: the lying spirit, which is the unwillingness to accept any truths but those which she regards as her own peculiar possession; the spirit of domination, which vents itself in spiritual tyranny and a dread of the interior life of the soul with God in freedom and liberty; the spirit of avarice, which results in worldliness; the spirit of sloth and lethargy, which paralyses the life of the Church and reduces her to immobility.[21]

Maude dreamed of a church that was more inclusive, open to knowledge, more expansive in its teachings, more tolerant, and more adaptive to cultural and intellectual context. Having mixed in the everyday world, Maude believed that the church should embrace the cause of social and economic reform, addressing such key challenges as poverty and inequality. She was much more aware of these issues than some of her more reclusive modernist colleagues, and wrote a good deal on the subject across the years. She was sympathetic towards the social movement of modernism in Italy and France. Democratic and socialist forces should be drawn into the church, the working class encouraged to participate in the life of the church, their aspirations recognised and appreciated.

Maude writes at some length about theological issues that not only put the modernists at odds with official church thinking, but also divided modernists themselves. One was an immanentist tendency that could go too far – in Maude's view – in reaction against the sterile scholasticism of the church. Immanentism had long been a theological bone of contention, a perennial theme in religious thought, with roots in St. Paul,

St. Augustine and Pascal. In Maude's time it was associated with figures such as Lucien Laberthonnière (1860-1932), to whose ideas Tyrrell was attracted (too much in Maude's judgment). The Frenchman's apologetic was labelled the "philosophy of action". It regarded faith "as an adhesion of the whole being, and not of mere intellect, to religious truth". In a telling metaphor in his *Essays,* Laberthonnière said that religious truth was indeed mysterious but:

> It is no abyss of darkness on the borders of which we dwell in terror; it is as the starlit ocean which washes our shore and invites us to embark on its bosom. And if it be through life that we find the meaning of religious truth, it is also through religious truth that we find the meaning of life....[22]

His school believed in religion "as primarily a vital necessity of mind and heart; a vital response to the profoundest needs of the soul". Such ideas gave great solace to Maude: "... here we were told that reason was not sole master; that it was in our very being that we found our need of God and our kinship with him".[23] The philosophy of action, along with modernism, had been condemned in the encyclical *Pascendi* as suspicious and dangerous, encouraging loose-cannon and undisciplined pan-religious ideas. Maude rejected this papal heavy-handedness. She too was suspicious of anti-intellectualism, but she had ecumenical sympathies and saw truth in Pascal's,

> ... the way of the heart – of the heart as Pascal used the term – of the heart as significant of man's intuitive nature, and of his whole being in its spiritual needs, tendencies and desires... it was charity that constituted the key-word; the sesame that could open the door at which reason knocked in vain.[24]

What of the "outer problems" facing the churches? The most menacing were those posed by advancing science and history. Darwinian evolution was one such scientific challenge,[25] Biblical history perhaps the greatest historical challenge. How had the churches responded? One response was the hard-line papal stance, which alienated both intelligent believers and non-believers. Another response came from those whom Maude labelled "mediating liberals". They were to be found in Anglican and Protestant, as well as Catholic circles. She included John Henry Newman and Wilfrid Ward amongst the Catholics, seeing them as forerunners of Modernism. They raised, but did not fully confront "the onslaught of increasing human knowledge". The modernists, by contrast, took an uncompromising attitude. All advances that challenged religion must be bravely faced up to, in the confidence that true faith would ultimately survive, indeed become stronger.[26]

Maude felt that some modernists were more willing than others to accept that science and history had their limitations, were themselves human-based and relativistic. (Relativity and quantum theory were in the air at the time, and demonstrated the uncertainty, even mystery, of physics.) Tyrrell, she felt, was too impulsive in embracing new knowledge, von Hügel more cautious. The latter "pointed out the limits of science and history; their inadequacy to present the full, living force of their object; their need to be incorporated in a greater whole, wherein all knowledge is rooted".[27]

Biblical criticism was, in Maude's opinion, the more painful test of Christian faith. This was because Christianity was, more than other faiths, indissolubly bound up with historical happenings, and with an historical Christ. Modernists faced the problems of Biblical criticism but did not solve it: "Some Modernists gave up faith for history; some gave up history for faith. Some sought a method of evasion in a philosophy of pure symbolism. Some kept both faith and problem".[28] Maude tried to illustrate the Christological problem by comparing the church to a river:

> … for the Church carries in her stream the gathered thought and reasoning of past as well as present; of a past whose questions were of a totally different order from those of our day. Like a river she accumulates soil and vegetation from every region through which she passes. And, like a river again, she must carry all that comes to her; nothing can be cast out. She cannot cut herself off from the world; to possess it she must be possessed by it. She can never accept any order from any power to leave this world alone and confine herself to the next one; and to exclude all influence of human knowledge would be to fulfil such a monstrous mandate.[29]

Summing up, Maude agreed that it had been impossible for the church not to make an official pronouncement on modernism. It emerged as:

> … a kind of supreme statement of the traditional position…. Savagely she guarded her treasure, and struck out at those she accused of endeavouring to wrest it from her. And very surely I believe, now as then, that she has

> indeed been the custodian of religious truths and values that would have perished without her.[30]

But custodianship had turned into the spirit of immobility. Modernism was in fact raising vital issues for the church and the survival of religion. Maude often used the metaphor of a tree being axed. For the hidebound church hierarchy, the modernists were laying an axe to the very roots of faith:

> For the Modernists those roots went too deep, and extended too widely to be touched by any human axe. The last answer could only be in virtue of a growing spirituality, in which all lesser questions would be absorbed. Dogma is not an absolute truth, nor is science.[31]

Maude and George

I said before that Maude Petre and George Tyrrell had one of the great love affairs of the time, albeit non-sexual. However I should qualify that. Maude's love was by far the more intense and passionate. We know this from her account of their friendship in *My Way of Faith*, and know even more from Ellen Leonard's *Unresting Transformation*, which quotes extensively from Maude's personal journals and other letters. Reading between the lines, it seems that Maude would even have been prepared to sacrifice her vocation to marry Tyrrell, to be a wife and mother, but she knew that that this dream was impossible, given Tyrrell's commitment to his priestly vow of celibacy. He himself admitted that he was unfitted to love anyone truly, and was wary of excessive closeness or "clinging dependence" upon him. Maude was herself spikily independent, but she did exert an emotional claim upon him. They had disparities of temperament and opinions, and often quarrelled. He deeply appreciated her friendship, a central feature of his later life. But he was also often irritated by her and felt a compulsion to escape her feminine needs and attention. Leonard says that Tyrrell's reaction to Maude "vacillated between affection and appreciation at certain times, and rebuff and resentment at other times". This caused Maude abiding pain and repressed frustration. But as Leonard adds: "This relationship opened for Petre a new and exciting intellectual world as well as tapping within her a depth of love which she had never before experienced".[32] Their relationship threatened scandal at times, but Maude stoically averted her eyes from such a prospect.

Recalling all this in 1937, Maude judged that she might have been able to keep her position in her order, had it not been for her "burden of fidelity" to Tyrrell. She reflected "how much better I could have done had I kept my own feelings under more control; had I been less feminine in my susceptibilities, less hungry for an affection as great and exclusive as my own". She goes on:

> Tyrrell and I were as unalike as possible in temperament and character; he was elusive, I was direct; he was rebellious, I was law-abiding; he was subtle, I was simple; he was utterly without self-regard, I was self-conscious.... It was, of course, on the spiritual side that I was, first and last, drawn to Tyrrell. He struck deep into the very needs and longings of the soul; his spirituality was intensely human; he had the keenest sense of moral problems... and wonderful daring in dealing with them; he would sacrifice conventions, in a bundle, for one reality; and, above all, he was the stuff of which martyrs are made, and in nothing did he appeal to me more than in this.... For the first time in my life I cared for someone enough to be ready to risk all in his companionship.[33]

Tyrrell helped to break down a residual aristocratic reserve and aloofness in Maude, and this stood her in good stead in her later war and social work. Her aristocratic bearing and status did help her, however, in her tussles with the Catholic priesthood. At least one priest, who had been given the task of reprimanding her, admitted that he shrunk from tackling such a formidable scion of the local gentry.

Tyrrell preached a retreat for the benefit of Maude's order in July 1900. This was the real beginning of their friendship. It was a time when Maude was exploring new ideas, and mixing with reformist thinkers such as her friends Henri Bremond and Friedrich von Hügel. Already regarded as suspect within his Jesuit order, Tyrrell fled to a quiet mission in Richmond, Yorkshire. In that seclusion their lifelong correspondence began, full of honest and candid thoughts (unfortunately Maude's letters seem not to have survived, and only some of his). Maude became totally caught up in Tyrrell's modernist cause. She was torn between sharing in his work, and shielding him from the looming threat of excommunication and loss of vocation. He was less than pliable:

> I felt, from the outset, [she wrote], that he was both great and weak, of great spiritual capacity, of dangerous daring; I wanted to share his dangers, to check his imprudence, to ensure his perseverance.... I had a feeling that my friend was capable of desperate solutions, and that the very heroism of his character, and his indifference to his own

> fate and fortune, constituted a danger. To me the continuance of his life as a Catholic priest mattered more than anything else, and I would certainly have died to secure his spiritual safety.[34]

In 1902 Maude moved to Richmond (with her little nephews, whom she was caring for at the time while continuing her role as provincial). She and Tyrrell read and studied together and met with like-minded people such as von Hügel, at that time still a major theological influence upon them. (Maude was later to drift away from von Hügel, who was reluctant to martyr himself for the cause.)

Her state of mind can be gauged from devotional essays she wrote in her little book *Where Saints Have Trod* (1903). She explored the ways in which human love was compatible with religious transcendence, although (as she knew) it could be hard:

> It is the inevitable result of love on this earth that in loving, we give to the beloved the power of paining us; the greater our love the greater also the corresponding power… Into every affection may creep from time to time, that sense of disillusion. No one is so loving as to be at no times cold and loveless.[35]

Yet it was in loving another that one found God.[36]

By 1904 Maude was in London. She had been pressured by Bremond and Tyrrell to leave Richmond, because of gossip (probably spread by the sister of Maude's brother-in-law). Tyrrell was becoming more desperate about his role as a Jesuit. He was forced to publish under a pseudonym. Maude wrote to a friend in December 1903:

> [Tyrrell is] ready to throw it all up – and God knows how gladly I would do so to be with him always – know that our *union* and our *cause* are one, and can never be separated and that to forsake the latter for the former would be to drop a treasure in order to find it. But how I love him! & how I long to be with him! – we must persevere.[37]

Tyrrell's final rupture with the Jesuit society came in February 1906, "and then he commenced a wandering existence until he settled in a cottage attached to a house I had bought in Storrington", a large eighteenth century manor called Mulberry House. Without consulting him Maude settled a life annuity upon him to secure him from poverty. She made the house into:

> … a kind of guest-house [and convalescent home for poor women], and thus rendered it more possible for him to make his home with me, as he did in great part. We had continual comings and goings, and many well-known figures appeared at my table. My own religious life was undisturbed until after Tyrrell's death, and I was able to frequent the Church even after he was deprived of the sacraments, as well as being suspended from his priestly rights.[38]

Basically Tyrrell had refused to accept the guidelines, or censorship, of his writings being demanded by Rome. Many of the modernists who formed an informal *salon* that gathered at Storrington strongly supported Tyrrell. Maude resisted all efforts by people to make her break with Tyrrell, and devoted herself to his support, and to her own writings and good works in the parish.

On 6 July 1909 Tyrrell's illness worsened. He died on 15 July. Maude went to great pains to show that he died still a Catholic, but without retracting his "heretical" beliefs. He made confessions, even when very weak, and received absolution and Extreme Unction. Because there was no retraction, Tyrrell was denied a Catholic funeral. He was buried in his surplice in the parish churchyard at Storrington, also Maude's final resting place. Friends flocked to the burial from near and far, with Bremond reading the funeral prayers.[39] As Alec Vidler was to comment, the quiet, peaceful village had become "the centre of an ecclesiastical *cause célèbre* that attracted international attention".[40]

Maude experienced Tyrrell's death "not only as a moment of great suffering but as one of liberation and revelation".[41] All uncertainty over Tyrrell was gone, all trepidations and all need to protect him. She could now focus on preserving his legacy by publishing his works.

Why I Kept the Faith

Maude concludes her book by making a quiet justification of her own gentle rebellion within the church, and then explaining why she had remained in the church.

Montalembert had once said that no soul had ever been lost by obedience. Maude both thought this profoundly true and worth dissenting from. This was typical of her ability to see all sides of an argument, and to appreciate fine shades of meaning. As she says, it is true that countless heroic souls had been martyred because of obedience to church teachings. Then she protests:

> But – but- if all acted so would the Church have held on her triumphant course through the ages? Would she not have withered by the wayside while men pursued their inevitable course, from science to science, from one material achievement to another? Have not even those who left her contributed to her life and survival? Have not those who resisted her claims, when they deemed them unjust, saved the future of others unborn…?[42]

The church was itself human and would never have survived without the human capacity to evolve and adapt, to meet:

> … the changes imposed by the growth and the progress of humanity…. Can any one even maintain that positive revolts, leading to heresy and schism, have done nothing for the purifying of the Church, and her better adaptation to the needs of her own people?... The Church, like everything else, must move or must die.[43]

Why, Maude was often asked, had she stayed within her church? Her answer, in a nutshell, was that the church was her path to God. As she said, it was not because the church was an end in itself, nor because she thought God could not reveal himself in many and various ways. When she asked herself what the church had been to her during the whole course of her spiritual life, she answered to herself: "The Church has lighted my way. Instead of struggling through a wilderness I have had a road – a road to virtue and truth. Only a road – the road to an end, not the end itself – the road to truth, not the fullness of truth itself".[44]

She went on to say, in her final statement of faith, that the church:

> … taught me why I was in this world and what I had to do while I was in it; she taught me the right use of the body, without despising it, and its subjugation to the soul; she taught me spiritual ambition, in virtue of my high destiny; she taught me to remember my own weakness and my inability to fulfil that destiny unaided; she taught me that God was my portion, and she offered me priceless help in the attainment of that portion… she spread out her sacramental system, with its visible and corporeal means of spiritual regeneration and strength and growth… she taught me what Christ was and ever has been to mankind, and she has kept His living remembrance in the Sacrament of the Eucharist; she told me of those who had almost

> transcended the bodily senses and heard words not given to man to utter, and she told me of them because to all of us are vouchsafed crumbs from that celestial table. In one word, she has taught me how to seek God.[45]

---

[1] Alec Vidler, *The Church in an Age of Revolution* (London, Pelican, 1951), p.180, and generally chapter 16.

[2] Ellen M. Leonard, entry on Maude Petre in *Oxford Dictionary of National Biography*. See also Leonard's *Unresting Transformation* (New York, London, University Press of America, 1991). Other works include C. F. Crews, *English Catholic Modernism: Maude Petre's Way of Faith* (Notre Dame, University of Notre Dame Press, 1984).

[3] Vidler, *Church in Age of Revolution*, pp. 184-185.

[4] M. D. Petre, *My Way of Faith* (London, J. M. Dent and Sons, 1937), p. 246.

[5] Tyrrell was born in Dublin, brought up in the Church of Ireland, converted to Catholicism in his youth after moving to London, trained as a Jesuit, thoroughly studying scholastic theology and philosophy, was ordained priest in 1891 and was at first "trenchantly orthodox" (*Ibid*, p.186). A prickly and stubborn character, he soon clashed with his church superiors. He was a brilliant writer with a wide circle of intellectual friends, and was soon active in modernist circles that included von Hügel, Maude, Wilfred Ward and Henri Bremond. His criticism of Vatican censorship led to his "rustication" from the Jesuit order. For a time he published his modernist writings under other names. He then publicly attacked Leo X's encyclical *Pascendi* (1907) and was finally excommunicated (something he had long expected). He continued to write fiery polemics, including *Medievalism* (1908) and *Christianity at the Crossroads* (1909), which forecast a universal religion essentially Catholic in nature. He is described in *Oxford Dictionary of National Biography* as a spiritual writer "so gifted, so reckless, and so provocative". Much of his work was eschatological, mystic and apocalyptic. As Vidler says: "at the heart of Tyrrell's [work] is an attempt to show that the 'idea'… of the Christ of eschatology whose 'work on earth was to prepare and hasten the Kingdom – to close the last chapter of human history' – the mysterious, transcendental Christ… was embodied and developed in Catholicism, and that there was no chasm between the Gospel and the Church": Alex Vidler, *20th Century Defenders of the Faith* (London, SCM Press,1965), p. 48. See also N. Sagovsky, *On God's Side: A Life of George Tyrrell* (Oxford, Clarendon Press, 1990).

[6] Sadly, despite the efforts of von Hügel and Maude, Tyrrell was denied a Catholic funeral. He was buried in the parish churchyard at Storrington, Maude's home, which had already become a meeting place for modernists.

[7] *Oxford Dictionary of National Biography* . Officious to the end, Amigo would not allow a priest to officiate at her burial.

[8] Petre, *My Way of Faith*. The reader who would like to know more in detail about Maude's life and ideas is referred to Ellen Leonard's excellent book

Unresting Transformation: The Theology and Spirituality of Maude Petre (London, New York, University Press of America, 1991).
[9] Petre, *My Way of Faith*, p. xii.
[10] See Ellen Leonard, *George Tyrrell and the Catholic Tradition* (London; Darton, Longman, Todd, 1982).
[11] Petre, *My Way of Faith*, p. 187.
[12] *Ibid*, p. 174.
[13] *Ibid*, p. 175.
[14] *Ibid*, p.180.
[15] *Ibid*, p. 184.
[16] *Ibid*, p. 185.
[17] *Ibid*, p. 189.
[18] *Ibid*, p. 207.
[19] *Ibid*, p. 208.
[20] *Ibid,* p. 209.
[21] *Ibid,* p. 214. Maude is here paraphrasing Fogazzaro's *Il Santo*, a "classic romance of Modernism".
[22] *Ibid*, p .223.
[23] *Ibid*, pp. 223-225.
[24] *Ibid*, p. 228.
[25] Maude's brother had lost his faith after reading the German Darwinist Ernst Haeckel's *Riddle of the Universe* (London, Watts & Co., 1901).
[26] *Ibid*, p. 232.
[27] *Ibid.*
[28] *Ibid*, p. 235.
[29] *Ibid.*
[30] *Ibid*, p. 241.
[31] *Ibid,* p. 242.
[32] Leonard, *Unresting Transformation*, p. 25.
[33] Petre, *My Way of Faith*, pp. 270-271.
[34] *Ibid*, p. 276.
[35] Quoted, Leonard, *Unresting Transformation*, p. 42.
[36] *Ibid.*
[37] Quoted, *ibid*, p. 35 (see Chapter 2 following for the full story). Leonard provides some interesting comments on Maude made by the lapsed Catholic poet Wilfrid Scawen Blunt, who used to visit her and her friends at Storrington. In August 1907 he described her in his diary as a young woman [in fact she was forty-four], "plain, but with a pleasant, ruddy complexion, and a look of extreme honesty… a serious, good woman, large minded, but without much humour, that was my impression of her". In January 1908, after reading her book *Catholicism and Independence*, which precipitated her departure from the Filles de Marie, he wrote: "It interests me immensely, and surprises me also, for I did not at all guess her intellectual gifts. These essays show her to be the best serious woman writer of her time. She has certain qualities women rarely possess, precision, sense of proportion, accuracy of illustration. Her psychology is

accurate and true" (pp. 48, 52). This gives insight into the gender stereotypes of the day, and helps explain why Maude was unfairly neglected as a thinker.

[38] Petre, *My Way of Faith*, pp. 283-285.

[39] Bremond was disciplined for this.

[40] Quoted in Leonard, *Unresting Transformation*, p. 62.

[41] *Ibid*, pp. 58. Her diary of 6 July reads: "GT taken ill – July 7 to 8 – First kiss! July 15 He died. July 14 knew me for the last time, threw his arms round me". *Ibid*, p. 57. In *My Way of Faith* Maude writes: "But during those ten days the barrier was smashed to bits under the feet of Death, the great liberator; and even had that liberator retired I think I should never have lost an understanding which came to me during those days. For then heart met heart in a union for which no danger any longer existed; he knew, better than ever, what he was to me, and I knew, at last, what I was to him. No! not as much as he was to me, but a great deal all the same" (pp. 286-287).

[42] Petre, *My Way of Faith*, pp. 336-337.

[43] *Ibid*, p. 338.

[44] *Ibid*, p. 341.

[45] *Ibid.*

3. The Portly Prophet: G. K. Chesterton on Religion and Society

G. K. Chesterton (1874-1936) was a high profile public intellectual of the early twentieth century. He was a journalist, author, public speaker and activist. Like today's TV personalities, he kept popping up everywhere. He was portly, witty and eccentric, a famous character of his time. He wrote novels, essays and short stories, quasi-theology, detective stories (he wrote the famous Father Brown series, churning them out whenever G. K.'s Weekly was running short of money, which was quite often), and was a respected literary critic – his book on Dickens is still highly regarded. Bernard Shaw, not a man given to praise, called him a man of colossal genius. He was perhaps best known at the time, and since, as a feisty champion of religion in a time of rising secularisation.

I would like to set down here some of G. K. Chesterton's thoughts on religious issues and how they relate to broader social concerns. I have concentrated on a few major themes in his voluminous writings; and for convenience have extracted his views mainly from Ian Ker's long and very detailed biography, which contains great chunks from his letters and papers, and extended quotes from his writings.[1] [I have given the name and date of the original work in square brackets where necessary. The reader is referred to Ker for the full details, also for original page numbers in Chesterton's books.]

Original Sin

In *Heretics* (1905), Chesterton calls the doctrine of original sin the "permanent possibility of selfishness... arising from the mere fact of having a self – almost the first thing to be believed in". This could be called "the doctrine of the equality of men".[2]

There is a close connection then between Chesterton's conception of original sin and his legendary faith in the common people and popular culture, which he constantly defended against the onslaughts of elitism and modernism. We are all equal in the fact of our original sin, the high as well as the low. However, because Christ had redeemed humanity by his death on the cross, the essential value and worth of the individual had been revealed to all. In contrast to the intellectuals, with their contempt for "the masses" and mass culture, and in contrast to the great man or hero theories of Carlyle, Nietzsche and others who worshipped power, Chesterton argued that the real heroes were ordinary people, "common men at their best". Christ had celebrated the poor, the disadvantaged, the thief on the cross who repented, the humble. Chesterton admired Dickens for finding everybody interesting and encouraging "anybody to be anything", an essentially Christian attitude (despite Dickens' lack of religious belief). However Chesterton did not subscribe to the Victorian Doctrine of Progress. Partly because of original sin, he had no faith that education was a panacea for society's ills or that humans were perfectible.[3]

In his major work *Orthodoxy* (1908), Chesterton again attacked the visionary intellectuals, whether liberal, utopian socialist or dogmatic Marxists, all holding a vision of "progress", one that took no account of original sin. The trouble with modern intellectuals (he said) was that, for them, "the vision of heaven is always changing". Progress meant "changing the world to suit the vision", not "always changing the vision", so that ultimately their vision of reality stayed the same. The true revolution was the Christian one, which meant that human reality was changed through the transformation of people's hearts and souls. To the Christian "there must always be a case for revolution; for in the hearts of men God has been put under the feet of Satan". So reality changed but the Christian vision remained fixed, a "composite", "a definite picture composed of... elements in their best proportion and relation". This picture was fixed by God's mind, for only such a mind could place "the exact proportions of a composite happiness".[4]

Finally Chesterton related his concept of progress to something similar to John Henry Newman's famous theology of development. For spiritual progress, one needed to be "revolutionary not conservative". By leaving things as they are –the crude conservative creed – you leave them open to a torrent of change. To preserve essentials and identity, there had to be change, reform, revolution. As Ker says:

> Chesterton's "theory of progress" demands, then, a constant vigilance, for it has to deal with original sin, which means that the constant danger is "not in man's environment, but in man". This is why the only political system Chesterton can trust is democracy.[5]

Democracy, as Chesterton said, was:

> … profoundly Christian in this practical sense – that it is an attempt to get at the opinion of those who would be too modest to offer it. It is a mystical adventure; it is especially trusting of those who do not trust themselves. That enigma is strictly peculiar to Christendom.[6]

The passages above illustrate Chesterton's constant use of paradox, a methodology that he defended passionately, but which infuriated contemporaries. Whilst it certainly hindered his development of a coherent body of thought, paradox could offer sparkling panoramas and valuable insights.

In *Orthodoxy*, for instance, he includes original sin as one of the unattractive but convincing creeds of a truth-telling Christian church:

> All other philosophies say the things that plainly seem to be true; only this philosophy has again and again said the thing that does not seem to be true, but is true. Alone of all creeds it is convincing where it is not attractive. Thus with original sin, it is the primary paradox of Christianity... that the ordinary condition of man is not his sane or sensible condition; that the normal itself is an abnormality.[7]

Chesterton here is not being pessimistic, rather the opposite. Original sin is central to the human condition; but Christianity, in raising the prospect of emancipation from sin, offers a philosophy of wonder, laughter and joy, the joy that comes from experiencing a sense of meaning and purpose in the universe. Chesterton had no time for theologians who questioned the doctrine of original sin.

Free Will and Determinism

Chesterton's position on free will – a key creed of Christianity, but under attack from determinist philosophers – was that it was best understood as "a sacred mystery". Christianity allowed for "apparent contradictions" like free will, leaving it as a sacred mystery, whereas determinism "makes the theory of causation quite clear" but left the determinist unable rationally to say "please pass the mustard" to his predetermined neighbour at the table.[8]

This reference to the folly of determinism harks back to Chesterton's celebrated controversy with the socialist Robert Blatchford in 1903-1904. Blatchford had written a series of anti-Christian articles for the *Clarion*. Chesterton replied and the debate raged on for almost two years, Blatchford defending evolutionary science and determinism, Chesterton religion and free will. Chesterton described Christianity as mystical yet eminently practical, more complex and paradoxical than religions like Islam, which in the end made it more resilient and adaptable. Blatchford had held that the doctrine of free will was contradictory because (as Ker summarises Chesterton):

> … if man is created by God then man can only act as God created him to act; but then so is determinism, which denies free will in theory and yet assumes it exists in practice. The difference is that, unlike the determinist, the Christian "puts the contradiction into his philosophy". And yet paradoxically the "mystery by its darkness enlightens all things". On the other hand, the determinist "makes the matter of the will logical and lucid: and in the light of that lucidity all things are darkened". Chesterton insists that it is not a choice between "mysticism and rationality" but between "mysticism and madness. For mysticism, and mysticism alone, has kept men sane from the beginning of the world. All the straight roads of logic lead to some Bedlam...". Christianity as a religion of mystery "accepts the contradictions" of this world and can therefore "laugh and walk easily through the world".[9]

Chesterton was sharply critical of intellectuals who used (and thus abused) their intellectual freedom to set up theories that fatalistically portrayed humans as bound by iron laws of necessity. Historians, for example, proclaimed iron laws of causation that left little or no room for free will. They were certain that "history has been simply and solely a chain of causation", which led to "a complete fatalism", the opposite of a "liberating force": "It is absurd to say that you are especially advancing freedom when you only use free thought to destroy free will".[10]

In *A Miscellany of Men* (1912) Chesterton contrasted the medieval period with later eras. Medieval Catholicism (he said) believed in free will, whereas seventeenth-century Calvinism and nineteenth-century science (he had Darwinism in mind) "darkened this liberty with a sense of doom". The result was that modern society had "lost the idea of repentance" and criminals were now seen as "a separate and incurable kind of people". By contrast the church sought not to avenge or punish, but to forgive criminals and sinners. It was "the only institution that ever attempted to create a machinery of pardon". Medieval Catholics believed that "Man was free, not because there was no God, but because it needed a God to set him free. By authority he was free.... The mediaeval Christian insisted that God gave man a charter".[11]

Chesterton admired Aquinas, writing a brilliant book on him in 1933. It was an appropriate year, for the rise of Hitler signalled a victory for the forces of irrationalism, whereas Aquinas was a famous defender of reason, as also was Chesterton. Unfortunately – in Chesterton's view – the enlightened tradition of St Thomas had been fatally undermined by

Luther and the Reformation. Luther had been an Augustinian monk in Germany "who may be said to have had a single and special talent for emphasis; for emphasis and nothing except emphasis; for emphasis with the quality of earthquake". That emphasis was the Augustinian emphasis on:

> ... the impotence of man before God, the omniscience of God about the destiny of man, the need for holy fear and the humiliation of intellectual pride, more than the opposite and corresponding truths of free will or human dignity or good works.[12]

Luther called for an emotional and elemental religion and the destruction of scholastic philosophies:

> Man could say nothing to God, nothing from God, nothing about God, except an almost inarticulate cry for mercy and for the supernatural help of Christ, in a world where all natural things were useless. Reason was useless. Man could not move himself an inch any more than a stone. Man could not trust what was in his head any more than a turnip.[13]

Chesterton decried Luther as "one of those great elemental barbarians, to whom it is indeed given to change the world". One of those changes was a terminal threat to the doctrine of free will, and thus to the whole idea of human liberty.[14]

Sense of Wonder

Chesterton gave great importance to the sense of wonder as an essential ingredient in Christian faith. The ideas of wonder, mystery, humour and the grotesque permeate his writings. They are his antidote to prevailing materialism and misguided idealism.

He put his idea of wonder in the mouth of the protagonist of his short story of 1929 *The Poet and the Lunatics*. This poet, as Ker says, "stands out as a figure of Chestertonian sanity in a mad world". The poet is just himself, accepting his limitations (contrasting with the ideas of illimitable liberty that then flourished), celebrating the small, real things of life, the practicalities of life, over and against the grandiose visions of the age. He has a sense of wonder, wonder about the very existence of things in this world, wonder about life itself, God's gift. In this sense of wonder "the main object of a man's life was to see a thing as if he had never seen it before". This was the way to happiness, seeing life as "a gift or present", a surprise, implying that "a thing came from outside ourselves; and gratitude that it comes from someone other than ourselves". For the poet, "everything has a halo... which makes it sacred".[15] Elsewhere, Chesterton related this sense to "the dream of all democracy, the seeing of all things as wonderful".[16]

In his *Autobiography*, Chesterton tells us that his earliest childhood memories were of a pervasive sense of wonder. To him as a child (and children generally) "anything in [life] was a wonder. It was not merely a world full of miracles; it was a miraculous world".[17] Later, during the 1890s, while he was studying art at the Slade School, part of University College, London University, Chesterton suffered a psychological crisis, brought on, he always said, by the prevailing culture of Decadence and Pessimism.[18] As he says in his *Autobiography*, after suffering:

> … the darkest depths of the contemporary pessimism, he had "a strong inward impulse to revolt; to dislodge this incubus or throw off this nightmare... With little help from philosophy and no real help from religion [I invented] a rudimentary and makeshift mystical theory of my own... [that]even mere existence...was extraordinary enough to be exciting. Anything was magnificent compared to nothing... no man knows how much he is an optimist, even when he calls himself a pessimist, because he has not really measured the depths of his debt to whatever created him and enabled him to call himself anything.[19]

Religion and art were meant "to dig for this submerged sunrise of wonder; so that a man sitting in a chair might suddenly understand that he was actually alive, and be happy".[20] Ker suggests that Chesterton was to some extent indebted for such ideas to Walt Whitman, Robert Browning and Robert Louis Stevenson, writers he imbibed avidly. He particularly admired Browning's *The Ring and the Book*, "the great epic of the enormous importance of small things", which exhorted readers to look at the world with new eyes. Browning was "passionately interested in and in love with existence".[21]

In an article collected in his book *The Defendant* (1901), Chesterton again championed the sense of wonder, the sense that ordinary people had (or supposedly had in Chesterton's romanticised vision) as against the fashionable anomie of the intellectual elite of the time: "The great sin of mankind, the sin typified by the fall of Adam, is the tendency, not towards pride, but towards this weird and horrible humility [of] tending to undervalue their environment, to undervalue their happiness, to undervalue themselves". Again he invoked a "simple sense of wonder at the shapes of things, and at their exuberant independence of our intellectual standards and our trivial definitions".[22] In *Heretics* (1905), he again championed the ordinary person's sense of wonder:

> To the humble man, and to the humble man alone, the sun is really a sun; to the humble man, and to the humble man alone, the sea is really a sea. When he looks at all the faces in the street, he does not only realize that men are alive, he realizes with a dramatic pleasure that they are not dead.[23]

It was Dickens's genius that he had this sense of the infinite variety, strangeness and wonder of life. So also was it with William Blake, another of Chesterton's heroes.

Chesterton had a great love for the Irish. He thought them not only unjustly exploited by the English (part of his anti-imperial creed), but they exemplified his ideal of the small scale peasant proprietor; and, going with this, they had preserved a sense of wonder and faith. In his *Irish Impressions* (1919) he fastened on to this sense of wonder, even if it was to do with a front door:

> Even one's own front door, released by one's own latchkey, should not only open inward on things familiar, but outward on things unknown. Even one's own domestic fireside should be wild as well as domesticated... all the most dramatic things happen at home, from being born to being dead.[24]

Chesterton was aware that a philosophy of wonder standing on its own was not only inadequate, but could lead into senseless mysticism (he certainly had a mystic tendency). After his conversion, he wrote in an article for a Catholic periodical (1923) that the optimism of wonder was only a half-truth that needed to be taken into "the culture of the Catholic Church" where it could be "balanced by other truths". Otherwise it could become "an orgy of anarchy or a stagnation of slavery";[25] or as he said in his autobiography, turn into solipsism and "political Quietism".[26]

Limitation

Closely related to wonder is Chesterton's central theme of limitation. Humans needed limitations in order to appreciate the beauty and wonder of life. It was necessary in art as well as religion. As he said in *Tremendous Trifles* (1909), to "love anything is to love its boundaries [since] boundaries are the most beautiful things in the world";[27] or as he said in 1920, limitations were "the frame that creates the picture".[28]

Again, in *What's Wrong with the World* (1910), he argued that while the joy of God was unlimited creation,

> … the special joy of man is limited creation, the combination of creation with limits. Man's pleasure, therefore, is to possess conditions, but also to be partly possessed by them; to be half-controlled by the flute he plays or by the field he digs. The excitement is to get the utmost out of given conditions; the conditions will stretch, but not indefinitely.[29]

He gave an example from sexual love. A ferocious opponent of sexual freedom and doctrines of free love that floated around at the time, he insisted on the need for sex to be limited, the need for marital fidelity, because of "the earthquake consequences that Nature has attached to sex". He was referring to the importance of family life and unity; but also to the need for all pleasures to be constrained, since "in anything worth having... there is a point of pain or tedium that must be survived, so that the pleasure may revive or endure".[30]

In *The Uses of Diversity* (1920) he declared limitations to be vital to humanity. He compared the God of Pantheism to the Christian God. Our God was limited by comparison, but by being limited the Christian God was set free. For Christians, "God is not bound down and limited by being merely everything; He is also at liberty to be something".[31]

Chesterton linked limitation to definition and dogma, both essential to clear thought. He criticised contemporary thought as being far too vague and limitless. Definitions helped to clarify and test ideas: "If the idea does not seek to be the word, the chances are that it is an evil idea. If the word is not made flesh it is a bad word". He had no time for the critics of the day, the modernists who had jettisoned more rigorous traditional criticism. He ridiculed critics who were unable:

> … to translate beauty into words [saying] it is untranslatable – that is, unutterable, indefinable, indescribable, impalpable, ineffable, and all the rest of it.... They can explain nothing because they have found nothing, and they have found nothing because there is nothing to be found.[32]

Dogma

Chesterton's emphasis upon limitation and respect for detail led him to defend dogma as essential to the Christian religion. He lived in an age when dogma was dismissed as a blockage in the religious system. "Dogmatic" had become a term of abuse. Chesterton, in his usual contradictory way, set out to reverse this, to rehabilitate a term – dogma - that had once been respected.

In an article of 1909, he attacked what he saw as the tendency of movements such as Catholic Modernism to abandon rigour in theology for a wishy washy "liberalism". (One can imagine the indignant response to this of the Catholic Modernist George Tyrrell.) Chesterton wrote: "The dogma of the Church limits thought about as much as the dogma of the solar system limits physical science. It is not an arrest of thought, but a fertile basis and constant provocation of thought".[33] In his writings he constantly defended dogma, as he did limitation and definition, as liberating not constraining thought, by setting what he called "creative limits", as against formlessness or chaos.[34]

He once said:

> Man can be defined as an animal that makes dogmas. As he piles doctrine on doctrine and conclusion on conclusion in the formation of some tremendous scheme of philosophy and religion, he is, in the only legitimate sense of which the expression is capable, becoming more and more human.[35]

After his conversion he predictably defended what many attacked in Catholicism, its complexity of doctrine, defined elaborately over more than a thousand years. Chesterton here was reacting against those who wanted Christianity to be "simplified" into belief in God's love for the world, and little else. This was a doctrine that would simply fade into futility in the face of the real challenges of a complex and increasingly secular world. This was a prescient prediction.

In *The Everlasting Man* (1925) Chesterton insisted that the purity of the Christian creed was "preserved by dogmatic definitions and exclusions. It could not possibly have been preserved by anything else".[36] Rigour went with liberation, something that the theological liberals couldn't understand. Free will, for example, encouraged personal freedom. "If dogma is incredible," he wrote, "it is because it is incredibly liberal. If it is irrational, it can only be in giving us more assurance of freedom than is justified by reason".[37]

In *The Resurrection of Rome* (1930) he said that the great councils of the church, "those vast and yet subtle collaborations for thrashing out a thousand thoughts to find the true thought of the Church" were founded on fine distinctions. He went on:

> It is the fact that many a man would be dead today, if his doctors had not debated fine shades about doctoring. It is also a fact that European civilization would be dead today,

> if its doctors of divinity had not debated fine points about doctrine.[38]

Ritual

In early life GK had been drawn to Anglo-Catholicism, then a powerful force within the Church of England. He felt this way partly because it was ritualistic, arguing for and largely succeeding in obtaining in many parishes a return to traditional, pre-Reformation ritual and ceremony, with its colour and pageantry and emotional impact, a contrast to the austerity and simplicity of most Protestant worship. Anglo-Catholics tended to regard themselves as martyrs in this cause as they had been branded Papists and persecuted in the heated "ritualist" controversies in the second half of the nineteenth century.[39] Chesterton was definitely on their side.

He agreed with Yeats that ceremony went with innocence, but there was more to it than that. Ceremony and ritual took people out of themselves. He put this into his usual paradox. The essence of ritual was:

> … the concealment of the personality combined with the exaggeration of the person. The man performing a rite seeks to be at once invisible and conspicuous. It is part of that divine madness which all creatures wonder at in Man, that he alone parades this pomp of obliteration and anonymity... it is the noble conception of making Man something other than and more than himself when he stands at the limit of human beings.[40]

Elsewhere he declared that ritual was not something artificial (as critics claimed) but perfectly natural and normal:

> The old ceremonial gestures of the human body are necessary to the health of the human soul... a man actually can think with his muscles; he can pray with his muscles; he can love with his muscles and lament with his muscles. All religion that is without that gesture, all Puritan or purely Intellectualist religion that rages at ritual, is raging at human nature.[41]

Ritual could go beyond words, especially when worshippers in the face of "sacred riddles" felt at a loss for words: "in the presence of... sacred riddles about which we can say nothing it is often more decent merely to do something".[42]

Mysticism

Given that the world is itself mystical, Chesterton saw no problem in accepting mysticism. In fact mysticism, he said in a striking phrase in *Orthodoxy*, keeps people sane:

> As long as you have mystery you have health; when you destroy mystery you create morbidity... [one] can understand everything by the help of what [one] does not understand.... The morbid logician seeks to make everything lucid, and succeeds in making everything mysterious. The mystic allows one thing to be mysterious, and everything else becomes lucid.[43]

(This is unfortunately typical of his style, especially in works such as *Orthodoxy* – insight struggles against opaqueness).

In an essay on the mystic William Blake written in 1910, Chesterton said that far from being vague the mystic like Blake "does not bring doubts or riddles: the doubt and riddles exist already... the 'mystery' of life [was] the plainest part of it".[44] Blake, the mystic, brought "the brightness of colour and clearness of shape" with his incomparable drawings: "the highest dogma of the spiritual is to affirm the material". Blake saw God, not as "vague and diaphanous" but solid, a person and a fact, not the "impersonal God of the Pantheists". The ideal was more actual than the real. Imagination did not mean for Blake "something shadowy or fantastic, but rather something clear-cut, definite, and unalterable... images; the eternal images of things".[45]

Secularisation

There has been much historical debate about the timing of the onset of secularisation and the decline of traditional religion in Britain. Older histories took this decline back as far as the Reformation or the Enlightenment. More recent histories focus on the twentieth century, recognising – to varying extents, and with varying timings – much inbuilt resilience of the churches. As an example, the revisionist Calum Brown dates the eclipse of religion essentially from the "swinging sixties".[46] The distinguished Oxford historian Simon Green argues that the "agonised abandonment of a long-domesticated protestant, Christian tradition" took place between 1920 and 1960.[47]

On Chesterton, one is struck by how early he was making statements about the decay of Christianity in Britain. He sees a progressive decline across his life. Although he always has some optimism that things can be reversed, he warns constantly about the power of factors such as aggressive nationalism, and new ideologies based upon power and greed, to replace religion in people's lives. Of course all this is embedded within his idiosyncratic religious framework. Especially after his conversion to the Catholic faith in 1922, his basic themes are that Catholicism, despite its failings historically, is old but vibrant, reflecting essential truths about God and the human condition; whilst Protestantism, even from its birth-time, was flawed and rigid.

We find him at the onset of the Boer War (1899) – a war he vigorously opposed, along with a group of young Liberals writing in the radical weekly *The Speaker* – referring to a general lack of morals and belief. As he wrote in his *Autobiography*: "... for most men about this time Imperialism, or at least patriotism, was a substitute for religion. Men believed in the British Empire precisely because they had nothing else to believe in".[48] In *Heretics* (1905), he again complained of a general lack of opinions, and argued that it was "a fundamental point of view, a philosophy or religion which is needed.... We need a right view of the human lot, a right view of the human society". For this we needed a "clear idealism... a definite image of good". It was those without opinions who were the most bigoted, the most fanatical. Bigotry "may be roughly defined as the anger of men who have no opinions... the appalling frenzy of the indifferent". Chesterton went on to observe that in fact everyone had some general view of existence "whether we like it or not; it alters, or, to speak more accurately, it creates and involves everything we say or do.... [In that sense] religion is exactly the thing which cannot be left out – because it includes everything".[49] Instead people were turning to all sorts of alternatives. They professed no beliefs, but in fact their "alternatives" – ranging from scepticism and scientism to vegetarianism and nature worship – were dogmas. The "modern world is filled with men who hold dogmas so strongly that they do not even know that they are dogmas".[50]

In 1911, during one of his verbal duels with the socialist and playwright Bernard Shaw, he learnt that Shaw had been criticised for being blasphemous. Chesterton replied that one could only be blasphemous in a Christian country, which England was not.[51] By 1925, in *The Everlasting Man*, he was speaking of living in a post-Christian age, one in fact that had turned against religion in "an atmosphere of negation and hostility". Post-Christians, he said, "still live in the shadow of the faith and have lost the light of the faith.... They cannot be Christians and they cannot leave off being Anti-Christians". They were not:

> ... far enough away not to hate [Christianity, nor] near enough to love it... while the best judge of Christianity is a Christian, the next best judge would be something more like

> a Confucian... the worst judge of all is a man now most ready with his judgments; the ill-educated Christian turning gradually into the ill-tempered agnostic.[52]

In his *Autobiography* he recalls how he had early in life turned away from his Unitarian background, feeling that even the many people of goodwill who were involved in good causes seemed to lack "a fundamental principle of morals and metaphysics". He "began to piece together the fragments of the old religious scheme; mainly by the various gaps that denoted its disappearance". He sought an explanation for the malaise of the time, the erosion of traditional belief, in the current culture of pessimism and power-worship, and also in Darwinian slogans of "survival of the fittest". (He failed to note that many religious thinkers, Benjamin Kidd being only one, sought to reinforce Christianity from Darwinian ideas, or at least to try to reconcile science and religion.) Chesterton says:

> Men who believed ardently in altruism were yet troubled by the necessity of believing with even more religious reverence in Darwinism, and even in the deductions from Darwinism about a ruthless struggle as the rule of life. Men who naturally accepted the moral equality of mankind yet did so, in a manner, shrinkingly, under the gigantic shadow of the Superman of Nietzsche and Shaw. Their hearts were in the right place; but their heads were emphatically in the wrong place, being generally poked or plunged into vast volumes of materialism and scepticism, crabbed, barren, servile and without any light of liberty or of hope.[53]

At other times, he blamed paganism, with its natural fleshly temptations. Nationalism, as we have seen, he regarded as a substitute for religion, and later, in the 1930s Nazism and Communism. Such ideas were to become almost clichés in intellectual circles. Chesterton was an early opponent of Hitlerism, with its racism and eugenics. He began talking, after Hitler's rise to power in 1933, of a phenomenon he labelled Prussianism. It had arisen with the decay of German Protestantism, which had:

> … long been dissolving in the acids of... scepticism; in the laboratories of the Prussian professors.... And the more they evaporated and left a void, the more the void was filled up with new and boiling elements; with tribalism, with

> militarism, with imperialism and (in short) with that very type of patriotism that we call Prussianism.[54]

All this "new and naked nationalism had come to many men as a substitute for their dead religion".[55]

Chesterton however retained a persistent optimism that Christianity at its core – which he located in the Catholic Church – was alive and kicking. Historically, despite persecution and indifference, it had survived. He spoke of the Catholic Church as an old religion that refused to grow old.[56] In *The Everlasting Man* he said: "The Faith is always converting the age, not as an old religion but as a new religion". There had been attempts in the nineteenth century – as with the Oxford Movement or the French Catholic Revival – to reform, or in GK's view "dilute", Christian doctrine, but "again and again there has followed on that dilution, coming as out of the darkness in a crimson cataract, the strength of the red original wine". Christianity "has survived its own weakness and even its own surrender... the Church grows younger as the world grows old", refusing to go along with "the tide of apparent progress" because it is alive: "A dead thing can go with the stream, but only a living thing can go against it".[57]

GK's historical view of Protestantism is interesting if predictably negative; and it went against much contemporary comment that saw Protestantism – especially in the United States (Pentecostalism, etc) – as the only vital religious force around. Chesterton rather saw the Protestant churches as "fossils", with no inner life. In *The Well and the Shadows* (1935), he observed that those churches - the churches of the Reformation – were clearly dying: "but in a much deeper sense, they have long been dead... [they had] really died almost as soon as they were born". In spite of all that was "deservedly unpopular" about the Catholic church, the "incredible clumsiness of the Reformers" had resulted in their miserable failure. He was thinking of Luther and Calvin, on whom he had written commentaries:

> They waged an insane war against everything in the old faith that is most normal and sympathetic to human nature; such as prayers for the dead or the gracious image of a Mother of Men. They hardened and fixed themselves upon fads which anybody could see would pass like fashions.... Calvin was logical, but used his logic for a scheme which humanity manifestly would not long find endurable.[58]

Kerr remarks:

> Unkindly, Chesterton suggests that perhaps "the most successful" of the Reformers were the founders of the Church of England, "who really had no ideas to offer at all". "They at least did not exasperate human nature; but even they showed the same blindness, in binding themselves instantly to the Divine Right of Kings, which was almost immediately to break down".[59]

At the beginning of his revolt against Rome (Chesterton argued), Henry VIII was "a Catholic in everything except that he was not a Catholic.... And in that instant of refusal, his religion became a different religion.... In that instant it began to change; and it has not stopped changing yet".[60] Chesterton had as a young man been attracted to Anglo-Catholicism (although he was not an Anglican). As he says in *The Well and the Shadows*, and elsewhere, it was when the Anglican Church, from the late twenties onwards, lost out in a battle with the state over issues such as Prayer Book reform, and then began to approve or consider social policies such as divorce, contraception, even eugenics, that he rose up in open revolt. (One of his targets was Dean Inge, who championed eugenics.) The problem for Chesterton was the fact that the Anglican Church had become a state church at the time of the Reformation, a state church in which, illogically, "God holds his authority from Caesar, instead of Caesar holding it from God".[61] A number of devoted Anglican divines, it can be said, had expressed similar concerns to these of Chesterton, seeing church establishment as a weakening force within the church. Some of these divines even advocated disestablishment.

Secular Issues: Capitalism, Socialism and Eugenics

Chesterton was well known for his searching critiques of capitalism, socialism and eugenics. He did this from a populist basis, championing popular culture against the sneers of the elites with their contempt for (or was it fear of?) the masses, while contending against cultural currents of the time such as Nietschean pessimism and Supermanism. One of his perennial foes in such matters was Bernard Shaw (also paradoxically a lifelong personal friend, if a polar opposite – the obese enjoyer of English beef and beer against the skinny, abstemious vegetarian).

Chesterton made a typical attack upon capitalism and English intellectuals in his 1917 book of essays *Utopia of Usurers*. The intellectuals of the day, including exponents of current ideologies such as capitalism and socialism, failed to realise that society was the sum of a multitude of individuals (even English liberalism was forgetting this). They "find it easy to realise an individual, but very hard to realise that the great masses consist of individuals". Every serious religion or philosophy of life must have "some trace of the doctrine of the equality of men" but capitalism "really depends on some religion of inequality". The modern state was tending towards the "Servile State" (a phrase he borrowed from his good friend Hilaire Belloc whose book *The Servile State* came out in 1912). Capitalist control over the proletariat was achieved in many ways, ranging from the payment of slave wages (only slowly being redressed by social reform, which capitalists and their capitalist press blocked at every chance) to eugenics (breeding of the more useful and elimination of the weaker), and to imprisonment laws that targeted the poor or rebellious.

History had also been rewritten to demonise the ordinary people (when they were allowed into the picture). Many decades before historians such as Christopher Hill, E. P. Thompson or Eric Hobsbawm, with their "history from below", Chesterton called for a Working-Man's History of England. This would demolish the current Whig version, which held that England:

> … had emerged slowly from a semi-barbarism in which all power and wealth were in the hands of Kings and a few nobles; that the King's power was broken first and then in due time that of the nobles, that this piece-meal waking improvement was brought about by one class after another waking up to a sense of citizenship… until we practically became a democracy... there is not one word of truth in it from beginning to end.[62]

He argued that power and wealth had in fact been more popularly distributed in the Middle Ages, a model for his own programme of "distributism", a cause to which he devoted many years of his life (without success, it goes without saying). He went on to argue that the extension of the franchise was really the result of a power deal between the aristocracy and the emerging middle classes: "The Great Reform Bill [1832] was passed in order to seal an alliance between the landed aristocrats and the rich manufacturers of the north" as well as "to prevent the English populace getting any political power in the general excitement after the French Revolution". Further extensions to the vote were also the result of political manoeuvrings, while "the solid and real thing that was going on was the steady despoiling of the poor of all power or wealth, until they find themselves to-day upon the threshold of slavery".[63]

Anti-capitalist sentiments are threaded throughout Chesterton's writings. A passage in *The Well and the Shallows* (1935) encapsulates much of this. Capitalism had destroyed the family:

> … broken up households, and encourages divorces, and treated the old domestic virtues with more open contempt... forced a moral feud and a commercial competition between the sexes... destroyed the influence of the parent in favour of the influence of the employer... driven men from their homes to look for jobs... forced them to live near their factories or their firms instead of near their families... [and had] encouraged for commercial reasons, a parade of publicity and garish novelty, which is in its nature the death of all that was called dignity and modesty by our mothers and fathers.[64]

Communism did exactly the same, but as Ker says: "Chesterton thought that if he had to choose between the two he would choose Communism: 'Better Bolshevist battles and the Brave New World than the ancient house of man rotted away silently by such worms of secret sensuality and individual appetite'".[65] This view was to cut less ice in later generations, when more details of Stalinist repression emerged, as people became more conditioned to commercial advertising, and as less restrictive attitudes developed about sex, marriage and traditional moral codes.

Capitalism and socialism were inextricably tangled together in Chesterton's analyses. Both, he thought, involved indefensible interventions and control over ordinary peoples' lives. Both aimed to place the ordinary wage-earner under the same kind of "centralised, impersonal, and monotonous... unification and regimentation".[66] Early in life he had been attracted to socialism, as were many intellectuals and others, when charismatic activists flourished such as William Morris and Bernard Shaw. As Ker points out, GK was drawn to socialism during the 1890s, when he encountered young socialists in his debating circles. As he wrote to one of them: "those early Christians were the only true socialists... for democracy is an essentially spiritual idea, a contradiction of the modern materialism which would encourage the brute-tendency to an aristocracy of the physically 'fittest'".[67] In 1893 he was struck by the themes in the best-selling *Merrie England*, written by the socialist editor of the *Clarion* Robert Blatchford (the man with whom he was later to have a protracted feud). As Ker notes, Blatchford was influenced by William Morris, who had been inspired by "idealised pre-industrial societies in which workers could be artists and craftsmen": "It is quite possible that the book influenced Chesterton's own later idealization of the Middle Ages. Be that as it may, it certainly confirmed Chesterton in his Socialism".[68] However Chesterton's was essentially a Christian Socialism, and his enthusiasm for it soon waned.

Within two years he was warning that contemporary socialism had little in common with Christ's teachings. Whereas Christ taught humility, socialists like Shaw were arrogant, and seemed to know almost by osmosis what people at large wanted, without actually consulting them. They were also joyless, well-intentioned but joyless, whereas Christianity – in Chesterton's philosophy – was based upon joy, joy at salvation, a sense of the wonder of God's universe. Socialism by contrast was mechanistic and authoritarian, a matter of social engineering. Fabians like Sydney and Beatrice Webb sprang to mind. In 1908 Chesterton wrote an article called "Why I am not a Socialist". He was fully aware of the injustices of the present system that was the target of the socialists: "To say that I do not like the present state of wealth and poverty is merely to say I am not a devil in human form. No one but Satan or Beelzebub could like the present state of wealth and poverty".[69] What Chesterton objected to in the socialist utopia was, as we have seen, its mechanistic approach. We would have state ownership of property replacing capitalist ownership. There would be no real democracy because the socialists did not have his strong belief in "the mass of the common people":

> Caught in the trap of a terrible industrial machinery, harried by a shameful economic cruelty, surrounded with an ugliness and desolation never endured before among men, stunted by a stupid and provincial irreligion, the poor are still by far the sanest, jolliest, and most reliable part of the community... [they despised] the whole smell and sentiment and general ideal of Socialism.[70]

What they were attached to was "the privacy of homes, the control of one's own children, the minding of one's own business... [the] opposite to the tone of most Socialists". In a swipe at his favourite foes, Chesterton declared that ordinary people had no time for the type of socialism preached by "a handful of decorative artists and Oxford dons and journalists and Countesses on the Spree".[71] GK's bucolic love of ordinary English folk was to be echoed by George Orwell. Despite their political and religious differences, GK and Orwell had much in common.[72]

Eugenics

Chesterton was a noted opponent of eugenics, which began flourishing from the late nineteenth century under the aegis of the statistician Francis Galton, with his analysis of "hereditary genius", and the rise of the "new biology" of that time, which seemed to give a new genetic basis for the controlled breeding of humans.[73] Bodies such as the English Eugenics Society, and many geneticists, favoured punitive measures against the "feebleminded" – a very loosely defined concept. These punitive measures included sterilisation and segregation. I have covered such issues in an essay focussing on eugenic, medical and practitioner discourse, and will quote some introductory remarks here:

> During the 1920s in Britain there was a robust debate between sterilisationists and segregationists, between those who favoured sweeping sexual sterilisation of the mentally deficient and those who advocated their comprehensive sexual segregation in custodial institutions. Although the debate often widened to include the congenitally "unfit" generally, sweeping up the insane, mentally disordered and anti-social "misfits", the main focus was upon the intellectually disadvantaged. They were viewed, in the hereditarian/geneticist language of the day, to be the product of defective germ plasm, genetically flawed, and were widely believed to be "swarming" in numbers, posing a threat to the racial health of western societies. Terms such as "vermin" were used. Pest control seemed in order.[74]

Believing as he did in the essential soundness of ordinary folk, including the unfortunates, Chesterton passionately opposed such attitudes and policies. His hard-hitting tract *Eugenics and other Evils* (1922) became a classic. In it he attacked such champions of eugenics as Nietzsche, Yeats, W. R. Inge ("The Dismal Dean"), and of course Bernard Shaw. These were a sample of intellectuals with contempt for the masses of humanity. They were not only judging people before they were born, but even wanting to prevent them being born. They believed, as Nietzsche frankly said, in the breeding of a higher race and the annihilation of life's "failures".

Chesterton was in essence asking for Christian charity towards all. God's love was directed towards the poor and afflicted, those in need of care and sympathy, as well as towards the "normal" or the well off – in fact the Bible was harsher towards the rich and powerful. Chesterton asked on what supposedly scientific grounds people were relegated to categories such as the "imbeciles" or "morons" of the IQ tests of the day, or the mentally ill, rightly hitting on the flaws that underlay many such tests or categorisations. He said, for instance, of the Mental Deficiency Act of 1913: "It is, and quite simply and literally, a Bill for incarcerating as madmen those whom no doctor will consent to call mad. It is enough if some doctor or other may happen to call them weak-minded". It was "to prevent any persons whom those propagandists do not happen to think intelligent from having any wife or children. Every tramp who is sulky, every labourer who is shy, every rustic who is eccentric, can quite easily be brought under such conditions as were designed for homicidal maniacs".[75]

He saw all this as part of the authoritarian tendencies of the "scientism" of the age, an age which no longer burnt witches, but was increasingly punitive towards the poor, expanding the whole concept of criminality (even to include the right to strike, or household negligence) and cracking down on the pleasures of the people such as drinking and smoking (what would he say of today's laws on smoking and workplace health and safety regulations?). He saw capitalism as in league with eugenics. The great goal was to produce a plentiful supply of suitable workers, and the smallest number of unwanted humans who were nothing but a source of wastage within the system.

He made a very modern point in highlighting the impersonal and jargonesque language used by eugenists and other social engineers. Such language emptied out the emotional dimension of the issues being discussed or proposed. Here he foreshadowed Orwell's attack on "Newspeak" in *Nineteen Eighty Four*. Eugenists, Chesterton said, were "as passive in their statements as they are active in their experiments". Instead of saying it was necessary to kill off the old (for example), they spoke of "euthanasia" or of remedying "the burden of longevity". They wanted to eliminate the "disabled", even when they were highly intelligent, because of the cost to the state. They would have prevented consumptives from coming into the world, thus weeding out geniuses such as Keats and others: "they have discovered how to combine the hardening of the heart with a sympathetic softening of the head".[76]

This was the new religion, the religion of science: "that creed is the great but disputed system of thought which began with Evolution and has ended in Eugenics. Materialism is really our established Church; for the Government will really help it to persecute its heretics".[77] Chesterton had been pursuing this theme for many years. We find an attack upon eugenics in his 1910 book *What's Wrong with the World*. We also find there his ultimate source of optimism about the world, but only if humans have the will to tackle their challenges. They needed to embrace the ideals of democracy and Christianity, both being dreams that were unfulfilled. As he said of the Christian ideal, it had "not been tried and found wanting. It has been found difficult and left untried".[78]

Concluding Comment

It is clear that Chesterton offered many original insights across a range of topics, including those discussed above. Whether he is, as Ian

Ker claims, a worthy successor to the great Victorian sages Newman, Carlyle, Arnold and Ruskin is problematic. I personally doubt it. He never gives us a completely thought out, tightly and coherently argued body of ideas, such as Newman does, for example. (He is perhaps closer to the prophetic Carlyle, whose works are also unsystematic.) Chesterton's major works such as *Orthodoxy* or *The Everlasting Man* are flawed, in my opinion, by his relentless use of paradox. Although he defended paradox elaborately, humorously and often, it ultimately seems to hinder rather than clarify his arguments. One constantly wonders, just how justified is this strange juxtaposition of concepts? Would it really stand up to rigorous scrutiny? T. S. Eliot complained that GK's style was "exasperating to the last point of endurance." I frequently feel the same when reading him.

Having said that, his big books inspired a religious readership world-wide. Even today, when he is no longer a household name, he has a large band of followers, especially among Catholic Americans (his ideas are frequently discussed on Catholic TV channels in the United States). He gave fresh insights into the nature of faith, Christ and the Gospels. His studies of figures such as Aquinas and Luther were penetrating and original. Especially after he converted to Catholicism in 1922, he overturned conventional views on Catholicism, Anglicanism and Protestantism. As he himself suggested, his upbringing in an atmosphere of Unitarianism/pantheism may have made him less susceptible to the usual English prejudices on these subjects.

Many of his campaigns, most notably that for "distributism", or more equal distribution of property, were failures. At the same time he memorably championed popular culture against the disdainful cultural elitists of the day, and also protested strongly against the ideologies of pessimism and power- worship that flourished in his time, culminating in the totalitarianism and total warfare of the twentieth century. He had his blind-spots, which were shared, it should be said, by many at the time: women, Jews, Buddhism, Islam and Italian Fascism.[79] These were areas where his deeply embedded values seem to blinker him from genuine historical understanding. Despite his massive reading, he was not deeply informed in some of these discourses. In reality he was a lazy researcher, relying on his prodigious memory. (This sometimes let him down, notoriously in his study of Dickens. Critics were quick to detect misquotes from the works. It did not worry Chesterton in the least, as he professed to have no regard for his own prowess or his legacy.)

As a personality he was lovable but strange, probably partly autistic, and certainly in many ways unworldly (he took cabs everywhere, to his wife Frances's dismay as their income was not high, and would leave his taxi with the meter running all afternoon outside his office).

When cogitating some issue or other, he was known to stand still in the middle of Fleet Street traffic until he had arranged his thoughts. He was notoriously forgetful. He tells the classic story in his autobiography of an occasion when he was scheduled to give a talk. He telegraphed his wife in London: "Am in Market Harborough. Where ought I to be?"[80] Some versions of this story add "why am I here?"

Despite these flaws (if they are flaws), he emerges from Ian Ker's massive and meticulously researched biography as a remarkable Renaissance figure. He was also impressively brave. As I wrote in a recent review of Ker's book: "He was a truly heroic figure, warring against the modernist currents of his age, including aestheticism, art-for-art's sake and decadence. When many Christians were timid, he doughtily championed his faith, pugnaciously taking the fight to the secular enemy". He predictably admired Don Quixote, but where Quixote tilted at windmills with his lance, Chesterton used his famous umbrella.

---

[1] Ian Ker, *G. K. Chesterton: A Biography* (Oxford, Oxford University Press, 2012).
[2] *Ibid*, p. 151.
[3] *Ibid,* p. 165 (quoted from *Charles Dickens*).
[4] *Ibid*, p. 223.
[5] *Ibid.*
[6] *Ibid.*
[7] *Ibid,* p. 228.
[8] *Ibid*, p. 215 (quoted from *Orthodoxy*).
[9] *Ibid*, p. 119(quoted from *Daily News*, etc).
[10] *Ibid,* p. 214 (quoted from *Orthodoxy*).
[11] *Ibid*, p. 304. Chesterton throughout his work uses the term "man", as was the common usage of the day, to mean humanity at large, male and female.
[12] *Ibid,* p. 689 (quoted from *Aquinas*).
[13] *Ibid.*
[14] *Ibid*, p. 690.
[15] *Ibid,* p. 597.
[16] *Ibid*, p. 331.
[17] *Ibid*, p. 9.
[18] The prevailing milieu at Slade has been well captured by Pat Barker in her novel *Life Class* (London, Hamish Hamilton, 2007). Chesterton was taught by the renowned Henry Tonks, a perfectionist and hard taskmaster, who features in Barker's novel.
[19] Ker, *G. K. Chesterton*, p. 34.
[20] *Ibid*, p. 35.
[21] *Ibid,* p. 114.
[22] *Ibid,* p. 84.
[23] *Ibid,* p. 151.
[24] *Ibid*, pp. 402-403.

[25] *Ibid*, p. 484.
[26] *Ibid*, p. 482.
[27] *Ibid*, p. 253.
[28] *Ibid*, p. 426.
[29] *Ibid*, p. 267.
[30] *Ibid*, p. 268.
[31] *Ibid*, p. 426.
[32] *Ibid*, p. 306 (quoted from *A Miscellany of Men*).
[33] *Ibid*, p. 239.
[34] *Ibid*, p. 418.
[35] *Ibid*, p.149 (quoted from *Heretics*).
[36] *Ibid*, p. 526.
[37] *Ibid*, p. 527.
[38] *Ibid*, p. 658.
[39] For a readable account of these controversies, see Alec Vidler, *The Church in an Age of Revolution* (Harmondsworth, Penguin, 1961), chapter 4. Among the outward and visible manifestations of ritualism Vidler lists such things as altar lights, vestments, wafer bread in communion, making the sign of the cross, incense, genuflections, surpliced choirs, much singing and chanting, use of holy water, confession to priests; and more broadly, churches adorned in the medieval style (linked to the Gothic Revival in architecture), and the revival of religious communities (including women communities, we might add). Vidler comments: "It must be emphasized that Ritualism was not merely a matter of external rites and ceremonies. It was felt to symbolize and safeguard deep doctrinal convictions, especially the presence of Christ in the eucharist. The strength of Ritualism lay in its devout sacramentalism and its encouragement of a disciplined and winning spirituality that seemed to be lacking in ordinary, conventional Anglicanism" (Vidler, *The Church in an Age of Revolution*, p. 160). On the other hand, as he points out, it ran counter to deep Protestant conservatism in church attitudes in England, and deep-seated fears of "popery" and the spread of Catholicism in Britain (not unconnected with the influx of Irish immigrants).
[40] Ker, *G. K. Chesterton,* p. 304 (quoted from *A Miscellany of Man*).
[41] *Ibid*, p. 665 (quoted from *All is Grist*).
[42] *Ibid*, p. 253.
[43] *Ibid*, p. 215.
[44] *Ibid*, p. 275.
[45] *Ibid*, p. 276.
[46] Calum Brown, *The Death of Christian Britain* (London, Taylor and Francis, 2001), and other works.
[47] S. J. D. Green, *The Passing of Protestant England: Secularisation and Social Change, c.1920-1960* (Cambridge, Cambridge University Press, 2011). See Green generally on this subject.
[48] Ker, *G. K. Chesterton,* p. 61.
[49] *Ibid*, p. 147.
[50] *Ibid*, p. 148.

[51] *Ibid*, p. 295.
[52] *Ibid*, p. 516.
[53] *Ibid*, p. 211.
[54] *Ibid*, p. 698.
[55] *Ibid.*
[56] *Ibid*, p. 483.
[57] *Ibid*, p. 529.
[58] *Ibid*, p. 707.
[59] *Ibid.*
[60] *Ibid*, p. 708.
[61] *Ibid*, p. 709.
[62] *Ibid*, p. 383-384.
[63] *Ibid*, p. 385.
[64] *Ibid*, p. 713.
[65] *Ibid.*
[66] *Ibid*, p. 559.
[67] *Ibid*, p. 23.
[68] *Ibid*, p. 24.
[69] *Ibid*, p. 234.
[70] *Ibid*, p. 235.
[71] *Ibid.*
[72] See Bernard Crick, *George Orwell: A Life* (London, Secker and Warburg, 1980). Orwell's first English publication appeared in *G. K.'s Weekly* in December 1928. Crick speaks of Orwell as a "Tory anarchist" as well as a socialist (p. 21).
[73] For a discussion of eugenics see essays 15-17 in my book *Darwin's Coat-Tails* (New York, Peter Lang, 2007); also Edwin Black, *War Against the Weak* (New York, London, Four Walls Eight Windows, 2003).
[74] Crook, *Darwin's Coat-Tails*, p. 269.
[75] Ker, *G. K. Chesterton*, p. 462.
[76] *Ibid,* p. 464.
[77] *Ibid*, p. 465.
[78] *Ibid*, p. 267.
[79] The iconoclastic, and lately lamented, Christopher Hitchens labelled Chesterton a "reactionary" who embraced "bucolic conservatism": "Chesterton became part of a forgettable rear-guard operation against the age of uncertainty, which has now definitely become our age": *The Atlantic* (March 2012), pp. 79, 81. (Hitchens wrote this article on his death-bed in hospital).
[80] Ker, *G. K. Chesterton*, p. 139.

4. Lionel Curtis: The Commonwealth of God

Lionel Curtis spent much of his life arguing for world government as the solution to humanity's abiding problems such as war and violence. We can find in his writings a foundation for such supranational government in religious values. In this he was applying values that he had inherited from his background.

Brief Life

Lionel Curtis (1872-1955) was an influential British public servant, a "mandarin" in the colonial service, associated with attempts to set up Imperial Federation, and he was the founder of the international affairs group and journal *Round Table*. He was born in Derby, England. We might note that he came from a strongly evangelical Christian family. His father was rector of Coddington Church, Ledbury, and his mother was a clergyman's daughter. As the *Oxford Dictionary of National Biography* says, he came to question the literal Biblical beliefs of his parents, but he inherited their evangelical fervour and conviction that distinctions between religion and politics were false.[1] Curtis argued this in his many writings. It underlay his faith in the possibility of a greater British empire, and his later espousal of ideas that seem to foreshadow the United Nations, the European Union, and H. G. Wells's world government.

Curtis was educated at Haileybury College (something of a training ground for colonial administrators) and then New College, Oxford, where he had an undistinguished career, a third in classics. You would not have put money on him having a glittering career. Like quite a few intellectuals and upper middle class people in the late nineteenth century, he took an interest in the plight of the poor. (It became almost a fashion for upper class people to take a tour of destitute slums such as those of London's East End at this time. Bernard Shaw lampooned such patrician philanthropy.) Curtis read the Christian philosopher F. D. Maurice and even spent two vacations from Oxford on walking trips dressed as a tramp. (George Orwell was to do much the same thing for his 1937 book *The Road to Wigan Pier*). Curtis was influenced in this respect by the social reformers Octavia Hill and Canon Barnett.

Curtis became a barrister in Inner Temple, London (1902), then private secretary to Lord Welby, vice-chairman of the London County Council. Thus he built up contacts, and especially from his days in Oxford, which, after a stint as a volunteer in the Boer War in South

Africa, gave him excellent credentials to become one of "Milner's Kindergarten", young Oxford men recruited by Lord Milner to work with him as administrators. Milner was a famous "pro-consul", a very high grade English colonial administrator. He took a leading part in helping to reconstruct the South African colonies after the Boer War. Curtis became Milner's assistant imperial secretary. He was given broad responsibilities at a young age. As the *Oxford Dictionary of National Biography* comments, despite an abrasive personality (he was cockily self-confident, strong willed and used to getting his own way), his efficiency and hard work won him many admirers. He became assistant colonial secretary for the Transvaal. There his "White South Africa" policy brought him into conflict with the young Mahatma Gandhi (this was the beginning of Gandhi's career). Curtis's later plans almost always had the key controlling role going to the white British, the white dominions and the Americans, although he generously permitted other "advanced" states such as Holland, Belgium or Sweden in Europe, even the Indians after they had demonstrated their capacity for independence, into the charmed circle when it suited him.

Curtis was prominent in the drive to unify South Africa into one colonial state, becoming a member of the Transvaal Upper House, editing journals, helping to set up and then have approved by London a South African constitution. The South African Union was proclaimed in 1910.

Milner and Curtis organised a group called the Round Table (the core being Milner's Kindergarten, including people like Leo Amery and Lord Robert Cecil) which aimed basically at Imperial Federation, where the British Empire would become a sort of self-governing federation. The self-governing colonies would cede most of their powers to a controlling Parliament based in London and including the United Kingdom, with elected representatives from each country responsible for overall governing, including foreign policy. It never really got off the ground because the dominions were never ready to cede their powers to a body based in London, but the aims were in many respects idealistic. Such a body would supposedly prevent the break-up of the empire and would provide security for hundreds of millions of diverse peoples. This, it was hoped, would set such an example to the world, that it would almost ensure world peace, the federation acting as one of the largest power blocs in the world in its own right and thus able to exert crucial pressure on warlike nations (like Germany) not to make war.

To cut the story short, Curtis spent much of the rest of his life fighting for this ideal, or something similar. He relentlessly agitated, proselytised and recruited colonial politicians, did a lot of back-room politicking, set up committees and think tanks and visited numerous countries for the cause. His Round Table groups made an impact (not least encouraging the study of international affairs in universities in places like Australia), but increasingly they became split about Curtis's projects and controlling personality.[2] Should the imperial government have the power of direct taxation? Should India and other "dependencies" (not yet self-governing) be ruled by the dominions as well as Britain? Such issues were divisive. Curtis planned and wrote (slowly) great volumes on the imperial problem, which of course came up sharply at the end of the First World War. He argued that imperial federation would probably have prevented the Great War (a controversial view).

Much of his energy from 1916 was devoted to the problem of Indian independence. Campaigns for independence were already strong, with leaders like Gandhi and Nehru. Curtis contributed the idea of "diarchy", whereby responsibility for certain areas could be gradually transferred from British-controlled provincial administration to a parallel, Indian-controlled one (implemented in the *Government of India Act 1919*). He also argued for a system of trusteeships or mandates set up by the League of Nations (he was on the United Kingdom delegation at the Paris peace conference). He helped set up the Royal Institute of International Affairs in 1919, and persuaded a sponsor to buy its famous centre Chatham House in St James Square for the Institute. From a fellowship at Oxford he subsequently involved himself in Commonwealth relations, issues in the Far East and Africa. In works such as *Civitas Dei* (3 volumes, 1934-1938) he promoted his ideas on commonwealth from the Greeks onwards with much attention to Christian history. As the *Oxford Dictionary of National Biography* says: "His assertion that he saw the hand of God in the British empire was derided by more sceptical colleagues... but it was well received, especially in liberal Anglican circles". As time went on, he broadened his vision to include the idea of a union of western democracies and their empires. Let's remember that such ideas were not new, having been espoused by writers such as Rudyard Kipling and H. G. Wells. After the Second World War, Curtis advocated union between the British Commonwealth, western democracies and the United States. In order to put his religious ideas into the context of his world government ideas, let us look briefly at some of the concepts he put forward in his 1938 volume of the *Civitas Dei.*

The Commonwealth of God

This was the title of his 1938 volume.[3] His historical argument was that two things had led the followers of Christ to adopt what was basically an unrealistic view of life. These things were: (1) the expectation of Christ's imminent return and the creation of God's perfect kingdom; and (2) the expectation of an impending Apocalypse which would destroy this world. Such expectations discouraged realistic thinking about the future governance of the world.

As Curtis saw it, Christ had lived in a violent age, during a clash of civilisations. The Jews prophesied that the Messiah would vanquish the hated Romans and set up a Jewish kingdom. Jesus wanted to divert their attention from this violent and visionary project "to realities as he saw them". To him the final reality "was the spirit of goodness personified – God, conceived as a Father possessed with desire to perfect the children he had made in his likeness and not as a despot absorbed in the thought of his own glory and power". He wanted a society based on morality, on goodness, on a creative instinct that was incarnate (imperfectly) in humanity. This should be the principle of Christian life, the Christian society, something capable of growth and adaptation. Humans should serve each other, not themselves:

> To develop the best in themselves they must strive to create a system based on realities, a divine polity, as the work of their own hands. [Christ's] view of life was the outcome of faith that the ultimate reality was mind, not matter; that mind was eternal. So also was its work of creation in which men could share in communion with God.[4]

However, the idea that Jesus would soon return to earth clothed with the power of God had the unfortunate effect of causing a sense of unreality in Christian thought. In Curtis's words, it produced in the course of ages a "pantheon of idols" which dominated civilisation:

> The notion of church and state, of two authorities competing for sovereignty, is among them and has led us to seclude religion and politics in separate compartments of our minds. In the teaching of Jesus there is no such distinction. To his mind religion and politics were merely two aspects of life, a sphere viewed from two different angles. He believed that men could grow to perfection in so far as they based their relations on the infinite duty of each to all. This supreme conception could only be realised by gradual developments such as we, in our language, would describe as political.[5]

The other problem was that for more than eighteen centuries,

> Christendom held the belief, crystallised in the writings of St. Augustine, that the life men live on this earth is destined to end in a sudden cataclysm which may be expected at any moment. A belief held for a period like this creates unconscious habits of mind which determine the conduct of generations which no longer accept it. To this can be traced a political outlook which is short in its range and narrow in scope, which envisages little beyond the immediate interests of national groups. It explains why Christendom has failed to realise its supernational aspirations. No society can learn to think of itself as a whole which does not believe in its own future. Still less can it realise its own capacity for improvement and the structure it ought to attain, and so work on a plan. The growing confusion of the world is due to this failure and will only be ended by those who face the question where it is going or ought to go.[6]

Curtis cast himself in the role of the enlightened statesman who faced up to such questions and had a plan. His intense activities in his various causes can thus be traced back, at one level anyway, to his evangelical upbringing and to his theological analysis of Christian history, however amateur and problematic.

Science, according to Curtis, provided compelling evidence that the earth had an enormously long future ahead of it.[7] Christians should thus junk their old concepts of Christ's immediate return and the Apocalypse. They should plan scientifically and realistically for world government and world peace. Once accept that a world commonwealth is the goal of human endeavour, "we shall find our minds are equipped with a standard which helps us to judge what ought to be done in the politics of a village no less than in the politics of the greater world". The world commonwealth ideal should be the test by which measures are judged: "In so far as that test is satisfied, economic and political problems will begin to find unexpected answers". On the crucial issue of avoidance of war – a very ominous issue as Curtis was writing only a year or so before the outbreak of the Second World War – he attacked those who merely advocated the minimalist and negative policy of war-avoidance. Using Christ's example, he said: don't have codes of "thou shalt not" but positive and life-asserting codes of "thou shalt". It would not suffice for nations to abstain from coercing each other by force:

> They must learn to think how by steps slow but patient and persistent, they can bring into being an order of society based on the duty of each to all, irrespective of national

> limits.... Man can attain peace, but only by learning to aim at an end which is greater than peace.[8]

Even if it could not be proved, spiritual values were the ultimate reality for Curtis:

> In the search for truth the limits of human knowledge must be recognised. Belief, in the true sense of the word, is not an assertion of knowledge, or dogma, but courage to act on the best hypothesis we are able to conceive. Unbelievers are those too timid or idle to guess at the truth and act on the guess.[9]

Inevitably nations did not come to act according to Curtis's ideals, and he came to think of himself as a prophet crying out in the wilderness, unregarded. Yet one could argue that some of his ideas have come to be implemented, however imperfectly, in broad bodies such as the United Nations and the European Union.

---

[1] I have relied on the *Oxford Dictionary of National Biography* for details of Curtis's life (entry by Alex May).

[2] During his year as lecturer in colonial history at Oxford in 1912-1913 the professor there complained that in Curtis's presence he felt like a country rector with the prophet Isaiah as his curate: *Ibid.*

[3] Lionel Curtis, *Civitas Dei: The Commonwealth of God* (London, Macmillan, 1938).

[4] Curtis, *Civitas Dei*, volume 3, pp. 281-282.

[5] *Ibid.*

[6] *Ibid,* pp. 283-284.

[7] "... our race has before it in this planet aeons of time; perhaps as long as those that covered the whole development of life in the past – that is to say, millions of years.... I feel joyfully sure that men will achieve a government of the world responsible to themselves before the first of those millions is passed, within centuries fewer than those since man became man. The human race is still in its early youth". *Ibid*, p. 931.

[8] *Ibid,* p. 285.

[9] *Ibid*, p. 288.

5. Middleton Murry: On the State of English Christianity

Life

John Middleton Murry (1889-1957) was a writer and literary critic, who (for better or worse) is best known these days as the husband of New Zealand born writer Katherine Mansfield, and controversial curator of her papers after her death in 1923. However, in his day Murry was a prominent commentator on a range of contemporary issues, most especially the state of religion and English Christianity. He was on the Anglican fringe, his doctrinal views verging on the unorthodox. As his friend the leading Anglican historian and divine Alec Vidler said of him:

> … he was one of that numerous and uncoordinated class that finds it impossible honestly to accept the official claims made by the Christian Church and for Christian dogma, but nonetheless retains… the conviction that in the spiritual experience of Jesus and in the spiritual movement that stems from him there lies the clue to what human history and human experience ought to be.[1]

Murry was born in Peckham, London, the son of a clerk in Inland Revenue, a man who was a great advocate of education, being a self-taught man himself. Murry studied hard and eventually won a scholarship to study classics at Oxford, getting second class honours in 1912. He went on to found and to edit modernist journals, being passionately interested in literature and cultural movements. This was a very exciting cultural time in Europe and Britain, of course, with such movements as Impressionism in painting, and avant-garde philosophy, poetry, novels, Marxist and Freudian theory, and religious ideas such as Catholic and Anglican Modernism. The Bloomsbury Group were active in England, and Murry became close friends with D. H. Lawrence for a time.

Murry encouraged innovative writers, such as Aldous Huxley, T. S. Eliot (great poet and apostle of religious symbolism and myth[2]), and Virginia Woolf. Murry went on to write over forty books and pamphlets. They include a biography of Dostoevsky (1916) and a popular text on

English style (1922). Murry had an established English reputation by the early 1920s, even though he is now largely forgotten:

> His controversial, often mystical, criticism and journalism returned obsessively to the ideas of the sanctity of art and the need for a new order of pseudo-religious brotherhood, although the forms these ideas took changed through his life. He designed his journal, *The Adelphi*, which he edited from 1923 to 1948, specifically to promote his often fluctuating, but always passionately held principles.[3]

He went on to write books on Keats and Shakespeare, Blake, Swift and Lawrence, and an acclaimed autobiography *Between Two Worlds*.[4] During the 1930s he became an advocate of socialist and pacifist causes. In the 1940s he started a Christian commune on a farm in Norfolk. As Alec Vidler observed, he was strongly committed to this ideal of spiritual rural living. He always believed that rural living was more conducive to a genuine religious spirit than the hectic and ugly life of cities (the "evil" of cities was an enduring theme in much English commentary from the 1890s on). But the commune idea also fitted into the broader context of Murry's philosophy. As Vidler acutely explained, Murry was a seeker after a way of life that would enable people to find the deepest experience of which they were capable. He thus engaged with every available social philosophy. Vidler sees three aims in Murry's quest: (1) to achieve a free society that could assimilate new economic, political and technological developments "and triumph over the natural drift of the modern State to a power-driven collectivism"; (2) as a corollary, there needed to be "a greatly heightened consciousness of personal responsibility throughout the body politic, in local communities as well as centres of power"; and (3) he saw that he himself must show the way by drawing together:

> … a small community of persons who shared his ideals and would try them out in a common enterprise… farming. He reckoned that this thoroughly down-to-earth way of testing their social beliefs would teach them a great deal of living and working together and about the roots of democracy. The members of the community were, to begin with, pacifists, but the experiment continued after Murry ceased to be a pacifist.[5]

The community was not professedly Christian, but for Murry himself it was "an attempt to discover what Christianity really means today in terms of individual and corporate experience". Vidler often visited the farm. Murry would give "lay sermons" to those assembled for worship on Sunday evenings. In these sessions, and in other retreats that they both attended over more than ten years, discussing the fundamental questions of human existence, Vidler "was always deeply moved by Murry's contributions to our discussions, above all by his profound sensitivity and sincerity and integrity".[6] He later collected Murry's farm addresses as *Not as the Scribes: Lay Sermons* (1959). The commune eventually folded, but as the *Oxford Dictionary of National Biography* wryly comments: "the farm was a success, and Murry ended his life as a well-off gentleman farmer, [and] a Conservative voter". You may or may not think this a good thing.

His Ideas

Put briefly, Murry was constantly grappling with the issue of making religion relevant to the troubled world, warlike and secular, that he lived in. Although he was pessimistic that secularism could be reversed, he fervently believed that core and essential Christian beliefs could be the salvation of the planet.

Like many others at the time, he thought that the churches were in decline and he sheeted much of the blame for this on the churches themselves for not engaging enough in contemporary issues, international and social problems. The churches were not idealistic or visionary enough for him. They didn't do enough, he complained, to put Christianity into real practice. These themes reoccur throughout his writings.

To give an example, take his *Pledge of Peace*, published in 1938, with the world on the brink of global war. He saw the church as the only solution: "No institution in the world is so committed by its own profession as the Christian Church to combat the world-sickness". The trouble was that those who ran the churches lacked courage to meet that commitment; they suffered a "fearful dumbness" in the face of the world peril. Murry thought that it was "the deep and inarticulate desire" of people for a brave church, braver than they themselves:

> The common man shrinks from the doctrine of losing his life to save it.... But to the Christian Church it should be easy, or if not easy, a doctrine for which it has always been prepared. "He that will lose his life for my sake and the Gospel's the same shall save it".... Now that the condition of the world really does demand the simple Christian heroism to which each Christian dedicates himself anew when they partake in Christian worship, to which each

> Christian priest is dedicated by profession, the Church fades away. Of the Fatherhood of God and the brotherhood of Man, it knows nothing when it comes to the pinch.[7]

As a dedicated pacifist, a leader of the Peace Pledge movement in Britain, Murry felt part of a beleaguered minority in the Anglican Church, although he must have been aware of the many activists within that church, and others, fighting for peace and also for issues such as social justice and an end to poverty. Many worked against the loathsome Nazi ideology, including bishops; they gave refuge to Jewish and other exiles from the Third Reich, including academics and scholars who were found posts in British universities and colleges. (Adrian Hastings's *A History of English Christianity* is good on this topic.)[8] All the same, Murry's denunciation seems like a cry of deep anguish at the ultimate ineffectiveness of such work.

The Paradox of Protestantism: *The Price of Leadership*

In this section I would like to look at the ideas expressed in Murry's book *The Price of Leadership*.[9] Some of these ideas were unusual for the time (although there are echoes in the historical writings of R. H. Tawney and E. P. Thompson). Murry had quite a lot of respect for the Protestant faiths, their enthusiasm, ethics and drive. However, he blamed them for inadvertently clearing the path towards a secular society, a society – and here is a paradox – that ultimately had no real ethics. Protestantism had done this in a number of ways. By being so strongly individualistic in nature, it had undermined the older Catholic Christian tradition of community and thus of a more universal system of communal morality and standards. In other words, it had had an atomising effect, also the result of the historical process by which the more feudalistically oriented aristocracy and gentry had been challenged by an emerging commercial and industrial middle class. An organic society was being replaced by an individualised, splintered and less cohesive society – one that was full of capitalist competition and class conflicts. (This idea was not all that new. G. K. Chesterton put forward similar views.)

Murry argued at some length that this process had also weakened English education. The older universities of Oxford and Cambridge, for example, had been closely allied to the old order, Anglican (excluding Dissenters) and mainly based upon the classics and humanities. The breaching of this order in the nineteenth century, a slow process involving the rise of new institutions more geared to science and technology, was a side product of the rise of the middle classes, and owed a lot to Protestantism. But what was the result? It "involved a reduction of Christian faith to an emotional experience and a separation of it from humane wisdom and learning".[10]

The Puritan/Evangelical approach had as its central point "a conviction of sin and conversion… [and this] dissociated it from the social texture of people's lives". The Protestants had rejected the older Christian tradition that emphasised the sacraments and age-old rituals. These tended to be dismissed as merely external and perfunctory (and Murry admitted that this was often the case). But the older tradition had "inexhaustible significance for the imagination" and maintained "the social implication of Christianity". Age-old rituals reminded people:

> that Christian profession was the condition of full membership of the secular society, which therefore could never be wholly secular. To be an Englishman was to acknowledge oneself a member of a Christian society. In such a society it was natural that the Christian Church should be "established"; that is, endowed by the nation, and that education should be under its control.[11]

This was, to say the least, an unpopular position for a reformer like Murry to take. But it was related to his inherent rural conservatism and dislike for urban modernism and capitalism.

In Murry's historical scenario, the zealous Puritans of the seventeenth century had powerfully contributed to the "lamentable secularization of the Church" in the eighteenth century. Influential thinkers began to drift outside the Church of England. Spiritual fervour became diffused into secular pursuits:

> Their business was religion, and their religion was business. The Church of England became a hollow shell, and its endowments and foundations a preserve of the landed interests…. Even the old universities ceased to perform any educational function. Thus Christian sentiment, finding no true expression in a cynical and perfunctory Church, secularized itself into a nascent movement of equalitarianism and political democracy. Christian energy was diffused into business enterprise, and Christian brotherhood into radicalism.[12]

The "Jacobin principle of personal rights" ran parallel with the Protestant principle of individual rights (the right to worship, to interpret the bible, and so on). It ran parallel even with the business principle of "laissez faire" or the right to follow one's economic interests wherever they led. The paradox here (we might add) was that business "freedom" often led to the gross exploitation of workers, and to the opposite of equality. But he had some awareness of this. The Protestant/Jacobin theory of democracy (Murry said) theoretically gave every individual the right to share in the political sovereignty of the nation, thus to become a member of the ruling class. What Murry seems to be suggesting here (he is annoyingly vague about the exact processes) is that the emerging business interests exploited this intellectual milieu by embracing "reform" of the parliamentary system to further their own claims to greater political power. (They in fact wanted only limited franchise reform, based on property, and certainly not full-blooded democracy for Burke's "swinish multitude", the illiterate and irresponsible proletariat.)

According to Murry, the pro-reform ethos around the late eighteenth and early nineteenth century "gave the opportunity for the pragmatic reconciliation of the democratic principle with the generically different principle of natural selection of a ruling-class by wealth-possession and wealth-accumulation".[13] So here we have some promising hypotheses, much that is problematic, but similar themes were to be taken up by leftist historians and made into much more workable interpretations.

Murry had been much influenced by Matthew Arnold's ideas on education, especially by Arnold's criticism of modern education for failing to have a moral centre. Murry took this up, arguing that the older religion was being supplanted by a new religion, a worship of nationalism. British education, he said, lacked a real theory of society. Religion had become politicised. Democracy and nationalism had sidelined religion, had pushed it out of education almost entirely and replaced it by the new gods of the nation state.

It was a great irony that political democracy had been achieved as "a kind of by-product of the struggle for religious toleration and religious equality",[14] but the end result of this historical process was that religion had been effectively divorced from education. Partly this was because the concept of religious equality, the idea that all religions are equally valid, meant finally that no religion should be centrally placed at the core of education.

Murry commented:

> Because in this country Protestant sect after Protestant sect came to the conclusion that religion was more important than anything, because one religious society after another was prepared to make heroic sacrifices rather than relinquish that worship of God which it felt to be the best – because, in a word, this country was exceptionally alive to

> the necessity of Christianity, it became a democracy. But so soon as it had become a democracy, the only kind of education it could allow itself to provide for its members was non-religious. A formidable paradox it is. A secular basis to democratic education is comprehensible enough in a country like France where the revolution into democracy was made against the Catholic Church; but in England, where democracy was mainly achieved by the religious passion of the Christian sects – the situation is very strange.[15]

Murry agreed with the poet William Blake that humans must, and will, have some religion. If it was not orthodox religion, it became substitute or fake religion. He argued that the very sick religion of the age was nationalism. Secular education was in fact nationalistic education: "that is education for chaos and death". The nation had become "the real God" whom people in fact adored and obeyed. Religion had become, for many, a pretend religion. People pretended to believe in a Christian God, but in fact, whether they went to church or were outside the church, they really believed in a God "who bids them do what the national state commands them to do". This applied not only in obviously totalitarian states such as Hitler's Germany or Mussolini's Italy, but also in supposedly liberal democratic Britain:

> … the unconscious religion of our world, which is nationalism, comes to consciousness with a sense of shame and dismay. When it utters itself, in Germany and Italy, we are horrified, and desperately persuade ourselves that it has nothing to do with us. But it has. Nationalism is our religion, no less than that of Germany. We can gloze over it a little longer; we can still pretend. But not for long now. The real conflict that is preparing in the world is not the conflict between Communism and Fascism (as the Fascists and Communists say) nor is it the conflict between Christianity and Communism (as General Franco says). Those are both unreal conflicts, behind which the real adversary hides. The real conflict that is preparing is the conflict between Christianity and anti-Christian nationalism; and as that conflict develops, Christianity will be divided into the false and the true.[16]

Why had the church lost out to the forces of nationalism and capitalism (working together in an iron embrace)? Murry suggested a number of answers. The old Christian church had once had the power and moral authority to curb the excesses of economic forces, but it had thrown away that chance to curb because it had itself become immensely wealthy and then corrupt. There was no inevitability about the rise of capitalism, or the Reformation. They came about because of the Catholic church's loss of moral authority. Usury was a case in point. The traditional church condemned the excessive taking of interest, thus effectively controlling the growth of capitalism and nationalism. This "curbing" could well have continued into later ages. But the church lost its moral authority and thus the power to enforce its control. The forces of capitalism and nationalism were unleashed.

Murry was at odds on this with most economic historians of his day (and today – take Niall Ferguson as an example). Almost to a man they ridiculed usury as backward and anti-business. But for Murry it was an example of ethical control over economics: "That morality and religion can govern economic forces is a truth which must be asserted again and again".[17] We today – after the Global Financial Crisis – could say amen to that. This whole debate is raging once again.

And, for Murry, it all went back to the moral failure of the old Christian church, which once held the western world in its hand. (Murry was inclined to romanticise the overarching moral authority of the great Christian Roman Empire that ruled the western world in the post-Constantine age.) For Murry it was a great lost opportunity:

> Had the Church been less corruptible, its authority would less easily have been compromised. True, it would be inhuman to demand that the Church should have been absolutely incorruptible; but it is not inhuman to demand that it should have been a great deal less corrupt than it was, or that its effort should have been towards far greater austerity and simplicity. Had this been so, there might have been a profound difference in the economic basis of European history.[18]

He saw this also as a betrayal of the simple agrarian system, of the simple human being, personified by the simple villager. Once the backbone of the agrarian life, the church had battened on to agrarian profits, through tithes, benefices and neglect at the higher levels:

> If the Church had become the protector of the poor, as a landlord setting the pattern of justice, as the spiritual power within every village using her strength to compel the lay-

> lords to follow her example, I do not believe her authority could have been shaken.[19]

As said before, Murry had an aversion to cities, and an idealised vision of the medieval British village. He saw the ugliness, overcrowding and human suffering in city slums as the end-products of industrial capitalism. They were contrasted with the cohesive sense of community of pre-industrial village life, in which the church played a central role. Murry painted a glowing picture of the village-community as a real commune, the parish church the focus of life, a place of worship and safe-keeping, a meeting-house, the parson "the mind and soul, the consciousness and the conscience", the bond between parson and villagers "natural and organic". By his "priestly ministrations of the Sacraments, their dependence upon the powers of Nature was translated into imaginative terms, and reflected back to them as the knowledge of their dependence upon God". Ceremonies such as the harvest-festival brought people together, and underlined the "natural piety" of the village. This sort of parish was a natural creation, not like the artificial creations of city parishes, "where the parish church is merely a rival religious building amid a bunch of coeval competitors".[20]

Such views were common in literature at the time. We see it in Hardy's Wessex novels, in D. H. Lawrence, and certainly in Chesterton's Father Brown detective stories. Both Murry and Chesterton took to living in the country. Murry tells us how it was the Great War which led him to feel alienated in London. Life there became "utterly intolerable" and he had an "unreasoned and instinctive" desire to escape:

> To me, the city and the War were unanalysably one single thing. The great city remained the symbol of that mass-hysteria and mass-degradation of which it had been the forcing house – the hysteria and degradation which had horrified me in modern war,[21] and which had thrust me into a condition of isolation, at once intolerable and unescapable. Very gradually, in the country a sense of community returned to me. I now had real neighbours. And slowly my religious faith, which had been real, but private and ecstatic, passed out of my consciousness into my being.[22]

For Murry thereafter the rebirth of life meant a return to the simple sources of living.

Let us look briefly at Murry's attitude to Marxism. The key here is to remember that he was essentially a Christian Socialist. (There was a strong tradition of Christian Socialism in England, flourishing especially around the late 1840s.) Murry did not believe in ideas such as the dictatorship of the proletariat or the classless society, and he rejected the atheism of Marxism. But he did see great truths in the Marxist analysis. He did not think that you could simply dismiss the Marxian idea of historical necessity, the idea of humans being governed by the iron laws of economics and class struggle, by asserting a simple-minded Christian belief in individual free will, the unfettered freedom of the individual to do good or evil. This, at the simplest level, was "pious nonsense".

> What Marxism has to tell the individual member of a modern industrial society is that the ordinary man's conception of himself as a responsible, freely deciding person is almost entirely illusory. It tells him that nine-tenths, or even ninety-nine hundredths of him, is the passive and unconscious slave of an economic system which he does not understand, and which he makes no attempt to control.[23]

The Christian could not solve this problem by simply following the Ten Commandments or diligently going to church. What was needed was a greater commitment to thorough-going social and economic reform, to effective regulation of capitalism, on the part of the churches. The drastic criticism of the capitalist system made by the Marxists had to be taken to heart by serious Christians. Such criticism "comes to a genuinely Christian mind as a mighty corroboration of its own deepest insights, as a providential renovation of its most intimate spiritual disciplines".[24] The answer to the "barbarities of contemporary mechanical society" was not a Marxist revolution, but a moral conversion of society, led by a revived Christianity. Society was bringing upon itself universal degradation and catastrophe, led by militaristic nationalism (the impending war was weighing heavily upon Murry's mind). Secular humans lacked the moral will to avoid this catastrophe: "The 'natural man' cannot do it". Only Christian love could bring a better society into being. And for this the Christian church had to be created anew. Murry had little expectation of this, but he kept his hope alive.

Murry was pessimistic because he saw Britain as sinking into an amoral secularism, even betraying its democratic basis. His ideal was that of Thomas and Matthew Arnold – that the state in a new society "must be regarded as the representative of the higher self of its citizens, and that the primary function of the state is the education of its citizens",[25] an education into a Christian knowledge of their higher duty. Murry was sympathetic towards the Oxford Movement for the "beauty of holiness" with which it had re-endowed the Anglican church; but he chided the

Oxford Movement people for conceiving their message in ecclesiastical terms only. (This was probably a bit unfair, especially as the later Oxford priests devoted themselves to missions to the poor.) What was needed – what Murry fervently hoped for – was "acknowledgment of the national as the Christian society, ... [which was] the first necessary step towards the creation of a new catholic unity of Christendom".[26] He dreamed of a wonderful Christian unity, in which sectarianism would gradually die away, a sort of modern day recreation of the old Christian Roman Empire. It was an ecumenical vision, education being Christian, clerics being the real religious and civil servants of the new moral state:

> Then Christianity would be manifest in its true power, as the only source of a national unity that is neither enforced nor automatic; and as this reality of Christian unity worked through society, like the leaven of the parable, unity of Christian worship would be naturally sought.[27]

Sadly things were not going this way. Atomistic Protestantism, self-centred capitalism, and loud-mouthed patriotism had encouraged the forces of secularisation. England was failing to be true to itself as a Christian national society:

> For England is a Christian nation that has forgotten that it is one; it has lost the key to its own nature, and secularized its own principles, so that they have ceased to be dynamic. It has lost the power of moral initiative.[28]

Britain and other western nations were being challenged by anti-Christian nations, such as Soviet Russia and Nazi Germany. Murry blamed the victors in the First World War for undermining the real principles of democracy at Versailles: "The democratic governments of England and France behaved towards the defeated Germany with more ruthlessness and less sense of responsibility, than any absolutist or oligarchical government in a like situation before them".[29] Demagogy and herd-emotions had undermined real statesmanship, and enforced a draconic peace that had finally resulted in Hitler and his totalitarian regime. Christian ideas of forgiveness and generosity, even moderation, had been forgotten. This signalled the beginning of a serious moral decline in western democracies.

Democracy, Murry concluded, could not exist without Christianity: "Christianity created it, breathed into it the breath of life, and inspires it from day to day and year to year".[30] When democracy "spews the coal of fire out of its mouth", it becomes not only barbaric, "but something new in the history of the human race: something new, and therefore impossible to describe: a Christian society which has reverted, and bears the marks of its apostasy upon it".[31]

---

[1] Preface by A. Vidler to John Middleton Murry, *Not as the Scribes: Lay Sermons* (London, SCM, 1959), p. 8. Murry was a communicant of the Church of England, and later in life was elected a member of the parish church council where he lived.

[2] Eliot converted to Anglicanism in 1927, which horrified his Bloomsbury friends – typically agnostic. Virginia Woolf wrote: "I was shocked. A corpse would seem to me more credible than he is. I mean there's something obscene in a living person sitting by the fire and believing in God": Quoted in Adrian Hastings, *A History of English Christianity: 1920-2000* (London, SCM, 2001), p. 236.

[3] I have relied on the *Oxford Dictionary of National Biography* for details of Murry's life (entry by John Clute).

[4] John Middleton Murry, *Between Two Worlds: An Autobiography* (London, John Cape, 1935).

[5] Vidler's introduction to Murry, *Not as the Scribes*, pp. 7-8.

[6] *Ibid*, p. 9.

[7] John Middleton Murry, *The Pledge of Peace* (London, Herbert Joseph, 1938), pp. 75-76.

[8] Adrian Hastings, *A History of English Christianity.*

[9] John Middleton Murry, *The Price of Leadership* (London, SCM, 1939).

[10] *Ibid*, p. 37.

[11] *Ibid*, pp. 37-38.

[12] *Ibid*, p. 38.

[13] *Ibid*, pp. 38-39; see also pp. 120ff.

[14] *Ibid*, p. 63.

[15] *Ibid.*

[16] *Ibid*, pp. 78-79.

[17] *Ibid*, pp. 96-97.

[18] *Ibid*, p. 96.

[19] *Ibid*, pp. 98-99.

[20] *Ibid*, pp. 90-91.

[21] In fact Murry worked in the War Office during the First World War, doing intelligence work from 1916-1919.

[22] Murry, *The Price of Leadership*, p. 93.

[23] *Ibid*, p. 152.

[24] *Ibid*, p. 153.

[25] *Ibid*, p. 168.

[26] *Ibid*, p. 170.

[27] *Ibid.*

[28] *Ibid*, p. 172.

[29] *Ibid*, p. 175.

[30] *Ibid*, p. 180.
[31] *Ibid*, p. 181.

6. "Jolly Jack" Priestley: Jottings on Life, Death and Time

John Boynton Priestley (1894-1984) was a very well-known figure in Britain during his lifetime: novelist, playwright, essayist, broadcaster and much else, a public intellectual one might even say, although he would have detested that description. His most popular novel was *The Good Companions* (1929); his most successful play probably *An Inspector Calls* (1946). Typically, he was better regarded by the populace at large than by what he called the elitist critics of London and academia. He always griped that he was put down because of his regional background: he was born in Bradford in Yorkshire, the son of a schoolmaster. But his Yorkshire accent became enormously popular during the early years of World War 2 when he made a series of broadcasts for the BBC. The BBC finally dropped him after political pressure from the Churchill government, mainly because he was calling for a better post-war deal for the working classes than they had got after the Great War of 1914-1918. As the *Oxford Dictionary of National Biography* says:

> In later life Priestley was continually referred to as Jolly Jack Priestley, the somewhat rotund, bluff, pipe-smoking, archetypal Yorkshireman, but he was far more complex than that, and the roots of the dark side of his character go back to his service on the western front in the First World War.

He wrote widely on social and political issues, and much on what he saw as the ills of modern civilization. Although he was no fan of organised religion, some of his comments reflect his concern for the loss of traditional values that was happening in a modern world where religion was in decline. Like C. S. Lewis, he had a yearning for something beyond the meaninglessness and banal materialism of modern life, a yearning for a "deeper and richer reality".

*   *   *

Here I would like merely to give some extracts from Priestley's book *Over the Long High Wall*, in the hope that they might be of interest.[1]

Our Western society, with America setting the pace, has clearly been increasingly dominated by the masculine principle. This can be discovered in its general aggressiveness, its desire to "conquer" everything, its ruthless industrialism, its lack of concern for personal relationships and the state of our inner private world, its curious rootlessness and want of feeling for earth itself, its blind devotion to scientific and technological experiment at all costs. Now there may be plenty of individual women who accept and even admire all this, but it is still safe to say that Woman herself, represented by the feminine principle, is deeply concerned with an entirely different set of values. What I have listed above seems to her either idiotic or menacing. Existing in such a society Woman has suffered a defeat and lives in an occupied country. She has been bribed to keep quiet by being given washing machines, racks of bright cheap dresses, more skin foods and lotions. Our society may pet her but does not really share itself with her. So she feels discontented. (Yes, yes, yes, of course there are exceptions!) As if there had been some evil enchantment – this is not her world.[2]

Indeed, it isn't. How are fundamental feminine values honoured in our society? It demands she should be rootless when in the depths of her being she asks to be rooted. It puts miles of concrete and cement between her and the longed-for earth and all that grows and blossoms there. Personal relationships and the state of her inner private world are more important to her than the combined decisions of all the boards of directors in the country. At heart she doesn't give a damn for all this "conquering", or for all this bigger and bigger and more and more, or the monstrous elaborations of technology. Half the time she feels she is living among crazy overgrown boys.[3]

More harm than good has been done, I feel, by the sentimental religiosity that describes a universe with love laid on without stint, suns blazing with it, galaxies glowing with it. The idea of this treacly cosmos hinders rather than helps us to achieve the real thing, which is unwavering conscious love. I happen to believe there are levels of being in this universe far higher than ours, which at its best is probably near the bottom of all lists. I can imagine, if only vaguely, that highly conscious love may exist on such levels of being in blazing magnificence. But only after aeons of conscious effort. So we might do better to ignore this easy sweet talk of a starry agapemone [free love community] and imagine ourselves among indifferent stars and terrible dark spaces, so many helpless little creatures – but still capable, if we choose and try hard, of creating unwavering, unshakeable conscious love. To create it and sustain it, against heavy odds, may be what this universe is all about, may fit some secret pattern behind the illimitable dazzle of its particles.[4]

The mass of men now live in a society that dismisses all talk of our inner world as pseudo-mystical poppycock. Even the people sitting in churches and chapels every Sunday don't believe that the Kingdom of Heaven is within them. Our world has been busy for years now disinheriting itself. It is trying – as men have rarely attempted to do before – to achieve a non-symbolical way of life, opaque and never translucent, never suggesting a deeper and richer reality, content to starve the imagination and shrivel the spirit. We are trying to live short of a dimension or two, like solid creatures hoping to enjoy Flatland.... Not that contemporary science – except among its camp followers – menaces any attempt to enrich our lives. The real enemy is a thick body of opinion, based on late Victorian science, on dogmatic materialism now at street level, that can be found in mediocre books, newspapers, clubs, superior saloon bars. It would argue us out of belief in our own experience, if such experience reversed any consensus judgement, surprised us by sudden joy, lifted the grey veil for a moment.[5]

Perhaps so many people now have an intense desire to feel secure, on the level of pensions, endowment insurances, property investments and the like, because they are sharply reacting against a deep-seated feeling that our whole civilization is desperately insecure. It is not only that a nuclear Doomsday may be waiting for us. The city, town, or even countryside we live in begins to seem unreliable, brittle, no longer reasonably civilized, as if the barbarians, ready for vandalism, robbery with violence, rape and murder, are no longer outside the walls but are arriving every night from some underworld at the Town Centre or the market square.[6]

In our Church of England and in all but the most reckless nonconformist sects, there is today a wary vagueness about what happens after death. Being immortal our souls will still be there, possibly facing an immediate and rather perfunctory trial, like a magistrate's court, or sleepily awaiting the grand assize, that Day of Judgment which still terrifies us in the requiems of the master composers. (Great music always makes me feel it is expressing the hopes and fears, the joys and sorrows, of much larger and grander beings than we are.)[7]

[For millions] the thought of the inevitable end, the "big sleep", has helped to take the savour out of living. They are trapped in a vicious circle: they are ready to die because the one great thing they know is that they have to die. They feel it is all meaningless. We are here by accident. Any idea of purpose, of supernal design, has vanished. They know better than that, they tell one another – can't be landed with that old load of rubbish. But nothing worth bothering about takes the place of that load of rubbish: they face a blank there. It is this state of mind that creates the legions of the apathetic, unresponsive to any reasonable appeal, only roused to action by the screams and commands of madmen. (We have already watched it happen.)[8]

Nations behave badly because ruthlessly ambitious men impose their will on mindless mobs. Our whole civilization behaves badly because its real values, as distinct from those it professes on special occasions, are shoddy and contemptible. What I have called its "consensus opinion", while it may be very different from the views and outlook of distinguished minds, has invaded our streets and created the atmosphere in which so many millions have grown up to lead their bewildered lives. It has offered us psychologies that deny consciousness and philosophies that abolish the mind. It has produced technologists whose computers, they tell us, will soon compose better music than Beethoven.... It is making us seem smaller and smaller as its machines get bigger and bigger. It is impoverishing life by narrowing horizons, curtailing dimensions, scaling down human personality. It is trying to keep awkward truths under close arrest.[9]

The monster has come out of abstracts and extrapolations, new extensions of analysis and scientific method, advanced technology and computerism, heavy bias and arrogance. Its secret dream is of a world in which groups of brilliant scientists and technologists enjoy supreme power, controlling countless numbers of robots, creatures that are half-humans, half-robots, and men and women who are no longer persons. This reads like science fiction, but that is where the monster exists when it is taking its ease.[10]

Then let us have done too with the self-hypnotizing notion that anything that can't be tested in a lab may be ignored, its very existence denied. (The worst offenders are not the physicists nor even the biologists but the fringe men like the experimental psychologists and sociologists who want to prove they are as scientific as the scientists.) I am not myself "anti-scientific" – though this is what I was accused of being in Russia – and have long enjoyed the friendliest relations with scientists of very considerable distinction. We should be respectful, admiring, grateful to science when it is minding its own business. But as soon as it tries to turn itself into a dogmatic ersatz-religion, it is not minding its own business. And inevitably it behaves badly; though here I would acquit almost all the upper ranks of scientists; it is the lower ranks and all the philosophical and psychological camp followers who so often are at once arrogant and stupid.[11]

Among the very greatest names of the last hundred years, those of men whose influence can hardly be over-estimated are Marx, Darwin and Freud. And with all due respect for their personal qualities, I say that all three of them, working in their very different fields, have been Life-shrinkers. If, as I declared at the very beginning, most of us now live in a society we detest – and indeed in a society that dislikes itself - these three, powerful and original thinkers but dangerously one-sided, must share a large part of the responsibility. They used the "nothing but" hatchet on a gigantic scale. They began to fence us in and then trim us down. They left

> mankind half the size they found it, and not even half as hopeful.[12]

> The Ice Age of the spirit is arriving.... Even the Stone Age men, like the Australian Aborigines, had their "Dreamtime" shining above the passage of the years. The East had its incarnations and avatars and aeons upon aeons blown like bubbles by the gods. Ancient Greeks and the earlier Romans, before the long sad twilight of the Empire, could believe that Time, wheeling with the stars, brought everything back again. Then through century after century – an extraordinary record – the Christian churches offered immortality, the end of this bad world and the chance of celestial bliss – and do in places to this day if they are not entangled in ultra-liberal theology and bright services with pop bands. But now so many people know better, don't they? Unfortunately, what they know better seems to make machines more and more important and men and women less important. Previously, struggling but hopeful common people could believe they played a part, however small, in some divine plan, some gigantic purpose that kept the stars alight in the sky. Now they mustn't believe any such fairy-tale. It seems that Man, in our existential age, must fend for himself, having accidentally acquired intelligence in a mindless universe.[13]

> That is the world lying in the shadow of the long high wall, the passing-time wall, which we have imagined into existence as our beliefs have shrunk and hardened, denying God, the Creator, The Absolute, emptying the universe of higher levels of being and all far-flung adventures of the spirit, and refusing to accept the one magical gift we possess – our consciousness.[14]

---

[1] J. B. Priestley, *Over the Long High Wall: Some Reflections and Speculations on Life, Death and Time* (London, Heinemann, 1972).
[2] *Ibid*, p. 7.
[3] *Ibid.*
[4] *Ibid*, p. 32.
[5] *Ibid*, p. 35.
[6] *Ibid*, p. 39.
[7] *Ibid*, p. 47.
[8] *Ibid*, p. 55.

[9] *Ibid*, p. 63.
[10] *Ibid*, p. 64.
[11] *Ibid*, p. 66.
[12] *Ibid*, p. 136.
[13] *Ibid*, p. 138.
[14] *Ibid*, p. 142.

7. Arnold Toynbee: On History and Religion

Arnold Joseph Toynbee (1889-1975) was a world famous, if controversial, twentieth century historian. Toynbee's views on religion were conditioned by his world historical theories, as expressed in his monumental *A Study of History.*[1] This memorably compared the great civilisations of the past, trying to deduce from them the underlying laws and meaning of human history. His religious faith intensified in later life after some traumatic life events (most notably the loss of a son through suicide and divorce from his first wife Rosalind); and also after personal mystical experiences. The later volumes of his *A Study of History* and other works from the 1950s were frankly more mystical than his earlier works. His opinions also became steadily more ecumenical in tone, ultimately embracing all major religions.[2]

This can be illustrated from an examination of two works from the 1950s: *An Historian's Approach to Religion* (1956)[3] and *Christianity Among the Religions of the World* (1958).[4] The first, short book was based on the Gifford lectures he gave at the University of Edinburgh in 1952 and 1953. Toynbee was an inveterate giver of public lectures, as well as an incredibly productive (some think over-productive) writer. This dated from his more impecunious early days, and an enduring memory he had of his father's financial difficulties. Toynbee himself achieved his brilliant university career (he was at Balliol College, Oxford, under the famous Benjamin Jowett) only by winning scholarships. He never afterwards missed an opportunity to earn money by giving public speeches and lectures (he toured the US many times basically to make some money), and by writing for newspapers and magazines. He never became financially secure until the brilliant success of D. C. Somervell's abridgment of the first six volumes of *A Study of History* in 1946, and he was never really secure in his mind about his financial safety. He had an almost visceral anxiety about being poor. (This was a constant source of friction with his wife Rosalind, who was an aristocrat, the daughter of the celebrated scholar of Greece, Gilbert Murray and Lady Mary Carlisle. The family seat was Castle Howard in Yorkshire. Rosalind was – at least in her husband's eyes – far too spendthrift.)

Although the Gifford lectures were supposed to be about philosophy, Toynbee centred his on religion (he changed the original topic to suit his purpose). "An Historian's Approach" forecast that the future would see, eventually, after the present world's discontents, that wars and divisions had somehow been overcome, that humanity had achieved a more "oecumenical" political regime. Unluckily for liberals, this regime would use the powers of science and technology to restrict freedom in the spheres of politics, economic and even domestic life. He detected signs of this beginning even in the 1950s. (He didn't say so, but the evolving European common market must have seemed such a sign.) Toynbee had of course imbibed ideas such as H. G. Wells's world government during the 1930s, when he was deeply involved in international efforts to avert another world war. His basic reasoning was that humankind would ultimately accept an "oecumenical" regime as a security against war, against accidents and against want. Totalitarianism was always a danger, but Toynbee didn't go down George Orwell's path in predicting the horrors of *Nineteen Eighty Four.* He seemed willing, in the final analysis, to accept greater regimentation, hopefully a sort of benevolent despotism, because alongside it he believed would emerge an "oecumenical" religion, and higher human spirituality. This was because great empires historically had done better when they had tolerated religion. So would this new world regime:

> ... it might be forecast that, in the next chapter of the World's history, Mankind would seek compensation for the loss of much of its political, economic, and perhaps even domestic freedom by putting more of its treasure into its spiritual freedom, and that the public authorities would tolerate this inclination among their subjects in an age in which Religion had come to seem as harmless as Technology had seemed 300 years back.[5]

This seems a strange prophecy. Toynbee by the 1950s was already living in an age of growing secularism. That modern indifference to religion could somehow facilitate a general revival of spirituality may have seemed implausible to many of his readers. However he believed he had historical backing for that view. Religion, he argued, had been the sphere of activity in which subjects of past ecumenical empires had been allowed by their rulers to seek and find compensation for their loss of freedom in other areas. They dare not be too "totalitarian" (a concept not then invented). People who were oppressed in every area of life would feel a sense of intolerable claustrophobia and were likely to revolt (ancient rulers had not learnt the art of total brain-washing, although they of course used some of the techniques). Religious toleration was a sort of "vent" for freedom, an insurance policy against rebellion. Thus a number of empires allowed themselves to be used as mission-fields by "higher religions": The Achaemenian empire was a mission-field for

Zoroastrianism and Judaism; the Maurya empire for Hinayana Buddhism; the Han empire for Mahayana Buddhism; the Roman empire for Isis-worship, Cybele-worship, Mithraism and Christianity; the Gupta empire for post-Buddhistic Hinduism; and the Arab caliphate for Islam. Even repressive regimes, as most of these were, when surveyed synoptically showed comparative forbearance towards alien, non-official religions.

This was, in hindsight, a wise policy. Toynbee pointed to the disastrous consequences that often followed from the opposite policy. The Mughal Muslim raj in India (he argued) was wrecked

> … by Awrangzib's departure from a policy of tolerating Hinduism that had been taken over by the Mughal dynasty from previous Muslim rulers in India. The Roman Empire, after Constantine's adoption of Catholic Christianity as the imperial government's official religion, brought crippling eventual losses upon itself when Theodosius I abandoned Constantine's prudent policy of toleration for all faiths and replaced this by a militant policy of persecuting all varieties of religion except the now officially established one.[6]

Constantine had in fact been faithful to the spirit of pre-Christian Roman regimes. Theodosius's ban on paganism, like Diocletian's ban on Christianity, was an aberration that led to calamity.

There were lessons here for the modern western world. State tolerance was useful to religions if they wanted to survive. But of course, more was required. The realm of the spirit was freedom's citadel. But spiritual freedom must also be alive in the hearts of people themselves:

> … true spiritual freedom is attained when each member of Society has learnt to reconcile a sincere conviction of the truth of his own religious beliefs and the rightness of his own religious practices with a voluntary toleration of the different beliefs and practices of his neighbours.[7]

The motives for toleration historically had varied. Negative motives ranged from prudential policies against rebellion, fears that religious conflict was a public nuisance that could easily become a public danger, to the "lowest negative motive" for toleration, which was that it was of no practical importance, or was an illusion that could be disregarded.

Toynbee interpreted the age of the Enlightenment, when science and materialism were embraced in the west, as predominantly motivated by an essentially negative reaction against the seventeenth century

Catholic-Protestant "wars of religion". (He tended to accept uncritically this prevailing labelling of those wars, ignoring research that revealed the political and nationalistic factors at work.) Such Enlightenment toleration was precarious, as had been shown by the rise of nationalism, Fascism and Communism in the twentieth century. At this point Toynbee departed from strictly historical analysis (if he ever had been exclusively engaged in it). He gave as his belief that religious conflict was not just a nuisance, but was a sin. It was a sin "because it arouses the wild beast in Human Nature". (This was something of a throwback to end-of-the-century thinking, when wild beast theories flourished, Dr Jekyll and Mr Hyde being only one manifestation. Toynbee after all was born in 1889.) Religious persecution was sinful because "no one has a right to stand between another human soul and God".[8]

Toynbee believed that the west, after it had gone through its phase of disillusionment with religion – a phase still in full swing as he wrote – would ultimately have to face up to its discarded religious heritage. It would have to come face to face again with its ancestral Christianity. At the same time the churches were changing and needed to change. The fact was that the world's religions were coming closer together as science and technology achieved "the annihilation of distance" (a phrase that Toynbee repeated endlessly). As a scholar of the "higher religions", he knew the substantial differences that separated them in terms of doctrine, liturgies and practices. The great challenge was to overcome these differences in order to make an overarching ecumenical religion. The task for our society (or the next) was to winnow the chaff from the grain in mankind's religious heritage. The task was to retain the essential counsels and truths of the higher religions – he believed that at their core they held to the same essential spiritual truths – while getting rid of the "accretions" that had built up within and around those religions as a product of historical accident or necessity. Toynbee spent much time elaborating on the circumstances in which such accretions had arisen.

In his perspective, the innermost religious impulse, the intimations of a spiritual presence accompanying humans on their life pilgrimage, had been coeval with humankind. It had been with us from the evolution of early humans:

> In this presence, Man is confronted by something spiritually greater than himself which, in contrast to Human Nature and to all other phenomena, is Absolute Reality. And this Absolute Reality of which Man is aware is also an Absolute Good for which he is athirst.[9]

No matter how this spiritual light reached mankind, whether by discovery, intuition, or revelation, it was indisputable that it shone in all the great religions. And it was the cause of their success and longevity.[10]

However those religions all became institutions and had to adapt to the historical environment in which they lived in order to survive and flourish. This meant accommodating themselves to existing beliefs and customs, earlier religions and cults and cultural forces generally. Inessential and alien practices became attached to the churches:

> These historical accretions are the price that the permanently and universally valid essence of a higher religion has to pay for communicating its message to the members of a particular society in a particular stage of this society's history.[11]

This adaptation may have been necessary at the time, but it had perils. Such accretions could prove extremely difficult to eradicate, became ossified within church traditions, and threatened disaster when more modern circumstances required the development and reform of doctrine and customs:

> ... if a higher religion is unable or unwilling to change its tune when it is carried by the current of History to new theatres of social life in other times and places, its undiscarded adaptation to a past social milieu will put it even more out of tune with the present social milieu than if it had presented itself without any accretions at all.[12]

One major problem was that the people who ran churches were prone to make an idol of their institution. Toynbee here sounded very like Alec Vidler when criticising the flaws in church institutions. To administrators and devotees, the church was often seen as more important than the beliefs it enshrined, although the church ought in truth be merely an agency for the radiation of essential spiritual truths and counsels. Power and wealth corrupted churchmen just as it did ordinary mortals. But even the most righteous of churchmen feared change and tended to insist that their religious heritage must be treated as an indivisible whole. There were psychological and prudential reasons for this also. Priests were afraid of alienating the weaker brethren, afraid that small changes might lead to wholesale ones:

> … they are afraid that, if once they admit that any element in the heritage is local and temporary and therefore

> discardable, they may find themselves unable to draw a line or make a stand anywhere, till the very essence of the religion will have been surrendered.[13]

Toynbee had surely put his finger on a vital point here. But he strongly believed such obduracy was wrong: both bad psychology and bad statesmanship. Essentially it was an admission that their central faith, the innermost truths of their religion, was inadequate. It was a failure of faith. And modern people sensed this as hypocrisy.

How to separate the chaff from the wheat? Toynbee admitted that this was a hazardous task. No wonder ecclesiastical authorities flinched from their duty of undertaking it. Any religious heritage was made up of a complex compound of essential elements and accidental accretions. It was a delicate and difficult job to dissect this composite body so accurately that it would distinguish accretions from essence. The surgeons themselves were products of their own time. In trying to correct mistranslations of the past, they risked making mistranslations of their own time. Accretions could also be in the eye of the beholder: for one eye, a blinker shutting out the light, for another a lens letting in the light. He compared the theological critic's task with that of an expert cleaning a painting. One could go on cleaning the painting, stripping off successive coats of varnish and paint until – horror of horrors – one was left with only the bare canvas. The best restorer went only so far, until the masterpiece was revealed under the dirt, but no further.

Despite these warnings, Toynbee then proposed the most draconian of reforms to the major religions. Among the "accretions" he proposed to abolish were: holy places, rituals, taboos (such as fasting in Lent), celibacy, myths (which he saw as mere poetics) and theology. Hopefully believers would be left with enough of the essential truths to form the basis of a newly synthesised religion. Lovers of places like Jerusalem, Lourdes, Mecca and Varanasi, devotees of the Passover, Christian and Buddhist liturgies, even theologians at Oxford and Cambridge, were hardly likely to embrace this prospect with much enthusiasm.

His likely support might come from those involved in the ecumenical movement, those who were disquieted by modern materialism and scientific scepticism, and those who were opponents of nuclear warfare. Toynbee was no fundamentalist-style opponent of science. As an enlightened man of his age, he accepted the great achievements of science and saw no problems with issues such as evolution. Science had certainly been spectacularly successful in widening the human understanding of the universe. Science (he argued) occupied one sphere of knowledge about nature, religion another. It was as reasonable to explore the universe in terms of one as of the other:

> Human Nature will not account for the aspect of the Universe that mathematics and physics reveal; but then these will not account for the aspect that is revealed in Human Nature. There is no ground except caprice or prejudice for treating the mathematico-physical aspect of the Universe as being real in any fuller measure than the spiritual aspect is.[14]

Even the supposedly objective physical reading of the universe was in fact no more objective than our reading of ourselves. (He may have been aware of the implications of theories of relativity and quantum physics for this issue.) His point about the hubris of science, and of scientists who contemptuously dismissed things spiritual and religious, would have touched a nerve in the age of looming atomic warfare.

The book concluded on a note of generous ecumenism. Every great religion aimed to help its adherents, indeed humans generally, to overcome the central human sin, "Man's Original Sin", of self-centredness. Every effort in that direction deserved respect. It ill behoved those of one religion to dismiss out of hand the attempts of other religions to divine man's inner truths and the vision of absolute reality. No one religion had a monopoly on truth. Religious intolerance and hatreds had caused immense suffering in human history. As Symmachus had declared in ancient times (when his ancestral religion was being persecuted by the Christians), the heart of God's mystery could never be reached by following one road only.[15]

Toynbee looked forward to a time when the local heritages of different nations, civilisations and religions would have coalesced into a common heritage of the whole human family: "We are perhaps within sight of this possibility, but we are certainly not within reach of it yet".[16] Indeed not. As he warned, the present age was undergoing a searching practical test:

> The practical test of a religion, always and everywhere, is its success or failure in helping human souls to respond to the challenges of Suffering and Sin. In the chapter of the World's history on which we are now entering, it looks as if the continuing progress of Technology were going to make our sufferings more acute than ever before, and our sins more devastating in their practical consequences. This is

going to be a testing-time, and, if we are wise, we shall await its verdict.[17]

In *Christianity Among the Religions of the World*, Toynbee examined the rise of secularism more closely, expanding on some of his theses. He saw the unrest in Europe and the western church from the thirteenth century as essentially the product of a number of factors. One was the growing materialism of the church, an almost inevitable side-product of it becoming a large and wealthy institution. This not only weakened clerical spirituality, but the church itself. Its glittering places of worship and its flourishing monasteries became the target of covetous monarchs and others, one motivation behind the Reformation.

More important to Toynbee was the vein of fanaticism and intolerance that he believed was embedded in Judaism, Christianity and Islam (Buddhism and Hinduism were admirable contrasts to this). This spirit led those churches to try to impose their doctrines by persecution and force, when persuasion and genuine conversion were the true paths. Such fanaticism (he said, problematically) was not a feature of "primitive, pre-Christian" forms of paganism. It was inherited from two incompatible concepts of God: God the merciful and compassionate versus God the jealous God. This produced an inner contradiction within the common tradition of Christianity, Judaism and Islam. Duality of vision was accompanied by duality of conduct: "The jealous god's chosen people easily fall into becoming intolerant persecutors".[18]

From the thirteenth century on, for over four hundred years, Western Christendom was rent by wars, hatred and strife. There were struggles between the Papacy and the Holy Roman Empire, domination of the Papacy by the secular power of the French monarchy, the Babylonian Captivity at Avignon, the Great Schism, conflicts over the Consiliar movement, and ultimately the Reformation, followed by the "wars of religion". The eventual consequence of this long series of scandals in the church was a progressive reaction in the west "first against the Papacy, then against the Catholic Church, and then against Christianity itself".[19]

As he had argued in previous works, Toynbee saw the eighteenth century as witnessing "a deliberate transfer of spiritual treasure from religious controversy to the promotion of science and to its application for use in technology".[20] Initially this was not an anti-religious reaction, far from it. Most of the originators of the movement (such as the founding fathers of the Royal Society in England) wanted, not to kill religion, "but to salvage religion by liberating it from the fanaticism that had rightly brought it into discredit".[21] Science seemed a useful and harmless field, "a field in which it was possible to ascertain facts, a field in which there were no political or theological parties, a field in which agreement could be reached on the basis of demonstration and experiment, and, above all, a field in which no ill feelings would be aroused". It was calculated that, by diverting public interest from theology to technology, "the temper of the Western World might perhaps cool down to a degree at which it would become possible once again to be religious-minded without being intolerant".[22]

Unfortunately, this calculation proved erroneous. The attack against religious fanaticism ultimately turned into an attack against religion itself. In the disastrous twentieth century, a century of world wars and totalitarian ideologies, spirituality was weakened, perhaps fatally. But fanaticism increased. The utopian hopes of the eighteenth and nineteenth centuries were dashed. The new ideologies were merely variations on a very old religion, "the religion of man-worship, the worship of collective human power, which is an older religion than Christianity and was, in fact, in the Roman Empire, Christianity's earliest adversary":

> Communism is a worship of collective human power on a world-wide scale, and in this respect it is a modern counterpart of the worship of the goddess Rome and the god Caesar. Nationalism is a worship of collective human power within local limits, and in this respect it is a modern counterpart of the worship of Athens and Sparta and the other city-states of the Graeco-Roman World before the foundation of the Roman Empire. Man worship proved to be evil and destructive in its pre-Christian manifestation, but in its present revival its capacity for evil is evidently greater, because it is now armed with new and terrible weapons.[23]

These fearsome new weapons, of course, were the product of technology. We had for two hundred years devoted ourselves to technology instead of religion. This world catastrophe was the result. And it was the result, not of a technology that was evil in itself, but of a technology that had been employed by humans for evil purposes. The old Original Sin had re-emerged.

The higher religions thus found themselves facing a common enemy: the old religion of man-worship in the form of a Communist-Nationalist ideology, ultimately stemming from Jewish-Christian-Muslim fanaticism. That enemy held an enormously important negative article of faith. That was denial of "the conviction that Man is not the greatest spiritual presence in the Universe, but that there is a greater presence –

God or absolute reality – and that the true end of Man is to place himself in harmony with this".[24]

In these grave circumstances, Toynbee urged the need for religions to subordinate their historic differences and stand together against the common adversary. He looked forward to a day when peace and social justice should reign. But, as he warned fellow Christians, their urgent task was to overcome their ancient tribal conviction that Christianity was unique. "Exclusive-mindedness" was a sinful state of mind, the sin of pride. If Christians continued to embrace the same Christian arrogance that had led to widespread rejection of religion, there was no hope for the future. What contrite Christians should do was to embrace the central truths in all religions. As Toynbee exhorted:

> I think it is possible for us, while holding that our own convictions are true and right, to recognize that, in some measure, all the higher religions are also revelations of what is true and right. They also come from God and each present some facet of God's truth.[25]

---

[1] Arthur Toynbee, *A Study of History* (Oxford, Oxford University Press, 1934-61), 12 vols.

[2] For details of his life see the excellent biography by William H. McNeill, *Arnold J. Toynbee: A Life* (Oxford, New York, Oxford University Press, 1989); also the entry in *Oxford Dictionary of National Biography* by Fergus Millar. Apart from his historical writings, Toynbee was perhaps best known as the director of the Royal Institute of International Affairs (appointed 1926), and the driving force behind its celebrated *Survey of International Affairs.*

[3] Arnold Toynbee, *An Historian's Approach to Religion* (London, New York, Oxford University Press, 1956).

[4] Arnold Toynbee, *Christianity Among the Religions of the World* (Oxford, Oxford University Press, 1958).

[5] Toynbee, *An Historian's Approach to Religion*, p. 244.

[6] *Ibid*, pp. 246-247.

[7] *Ibid*, p. 249.

[8] *Ibid*, p. 250.

[9] *Ibid*, p. 263.

[10] Toynbee's perceptions of ultimate mysteries and absolute reality, human nature as a union of opposites (reason and passions, greatness and wretchedness), the need for tolerance and charity were influenced by his knowledge of the Bible and classical texts, and on these issues especially Symmachus, Pascal and Thomas Browne.

[11] Toynbee, *An Historian's Approach to Religion*, p. 264.

[12] *Ibid.*

[13] *Ibid,* p. 267.

[14] *Ibid*, p. 288.
[15] *Ibid*, pp. 296-297.
[16] *Ibid*, p. 296.
[17] *Ibid.*
[18] Toynbee, *Christianity Among the Religions of the World*, p. 19.
[19] *Ibid*, p. 75.
[20] *Ibid*, p. 76.
[21] *Ibid*, p. 77.
[22] *Ibid*, pp. 78-79.
[23] *Ibid*, p. 79.
[24] *Ibid*, p. 81.
[25] *Ibid*, pp. 99-100.

8. R. H. Tawney: Christian Idealism and Social Reform

Richard Henry Tawney (1880-1962) is widely regarded as the great champion of ethical socialism and British Labour's greatest theorist. He is remembered for those twentieth-century classics *The Acquisitive Society*, *Religion and the Rise of Capitalism*, and *Equality*.[1] His biographers, and most serious students of his thought, agree that his socialist and social reform ideas were founded upon a Christian moral basis. Recently, however, there have been some revisionist attempts to qualify this and to give a more secular, or humanistic, reading of him, especially in his later writings. I will here give some context that may be of use to those interested in this debate.

Tawney's Life

Tawney was born in Calcutta, his father a Sanskrit scholar and senior educationist in the Indian civil service during the high point of British imperial power there. If he imbibed a sense of benign paternalism there, "Harry" was never an imperialist. As a boy he was educated at the elite Rugby School, still under the influence of its great master and ethicist Thomas Arnold, and then Balliol College, Oxford, where he mixed with Benjamin Jowett's reform-minded intellectuals and liberals. Again he imbibed a sense of moral mission and gentlemanly obligation to encourage working-class education and tackle such problems as slums and poverty. He took influences from across the spectrum: from the Oxford Movement followers, inspired by J. H. Newman's moral mission; mainstream Anglicans such as his life-long Balliol friend William Temple, later Archbishop of Canterbury; Idealist philosophers such as T. H. Green and particularly his tutor, the reformist philosopher Edward Caird; "New Liberals" such as Leonard Hobhouse and J. A. Hobson wanting to give individualistic liberalism a more humane face through moderate welfare measures; the nineteenth century Christian Socialists and John Ruskin; and the Labourite William Beveridge (another Balliol man) who was to become the architect of the post-1945 National Health system (Tawney married William's sister Jeanette in 1909).

Tawney and Beveridge became involved in the Oxford-sponsored Christian activist centre at Toynbee Hall, whose mission under Canon Samuel Barnett was to bring education and culture to the slum-dwellers of London's East End. Tawney was eventually to repudiate the paternalism of bodies such as Toynbee Hall and Octavia Hill's Charity

Organization Society. He embraced worker self-help and self-education through agencies such as the Workers' Education Association (WEA), with which he formed a crucially important life-time association. At the end of his life he considered that his major and noblest achievement was his work with the WEA. Quite vital was his lifetime work in consolidating the adult education system in Britain. He taught adult tutorial classes in Lancashire and Staffordshire from 1908 to 1914, learning about working class life at the coalface so to say. He enlisted as a humble private in his local Manchester regiment in 1914 and was badly wounded in the Somme offensive in 1916. After the war he was immensely active in the cause of educational reform, writing influential pamphlets and serving on numerous committees, the net outcome being the important Education Acts of 1918 and 1944. The latter was based on Charles Trevelyan's 1926 report, hugely influenced by Tawney, recommending universal primary and secondary education. Tawney was maddened that politicians took so long to implement it.

Tawney had shifted from Manchester to London in 1913, and in 1919 was appointed lecturer at the London School of Economics (LSE) under the headship of the socialist thinker and activist Harold Laski. Tawney had done a stint at LSE before the war directing the Rata Tata Foundation, studying the causes of poverty. Tawney stayed at LSE for the rest of his working life, appointed professor of economic history in 1931 and retiring in 1949, by which date he saw the implementation by the Atlee Labour government of much of the welfarist reform he and Beveridge had so strenuously striven for in the inter-war years. Tawney has been widely regarded as the leading theoretician of the British Labour movement at this time, as well as being a key publicist and adviser in the cause. He produced a plenitude of policy reports and pamphlets. *Labour and the Nation* (1928) and *For Socialism and Peace* (1934) are two examples. His scholarly reputation was built on his widely influential books *The Acquisitive Society* attacking capitalist greed; *Religion and the Rise of Capitalism* studying the nexus between new economic forces and religious social thought in the sixteenth and seventeenth centuries; *Equality*, which proposed solving the inequalities of capitalism through such measures as progressive taxation, public ownership and a welfare safety net for the poor; and less well known later works such as *The Attack* and *The Radical Tradition*.[2]

Tawney visited China in 1931-1932 and in the later thirties became alarmed at the threat of Japanese expansionism. A consistent critic of both Fascist and Soviet totalitarianism, he never joined the leftist pacifist movements that sprang up at the time. He was at heart both a realistic pragmatist and a patriot.[3] He was dismayed by the factionalism within the Labour party and movement during the thirties, but his personal influence upon younger leaders would bear fruit in the post-war period. He staunchly supported the war effort against Hitler, recognising that the war was also an opportunity to inspire a widespread campaign for a far-reaching programme of social and economic reform. It was a chance to achieve greater social justice for all. He witnessed many of his ideas expressed in the historic Beveridge Report of 1942, the basis of the welfare state. Tawney's later years were filled with activities and honours. His last book was a study of the Jacobean trader Lionel Cranfield, earl of Middlesex.[4] He was buried in Highgate cemetery, an uneasy neighbour of Karl Marx.

In his splendid recent biography of Tawney, Lawrence Goldman uses new materials and with fine discrimination analyses aspects of his thought and life.[5] He emphasises Tawney's faith in a morally-based, communalist, voluntarist and free socialism; his belief in grass-roots democracy; and his faith in the essential virtues and capacity for self-improvement of ordinary people, if they were given the proper opportunities through education and a just social system. He was not as romantic about this as writers like G. K. Chesterton, partly because of his experience of fellow Tommies at the Somme.

Goldman, unlike some Tawney admirers, recognises the failings in Tawney, the thinker and the man. He lacked philosophical rigour, avoided definitions, was selective in subject matter, impatient of alternative perspectives, while his economics was vulnerable to attack as narrow on class differentiation, ignored consumption and was flawed on human psychology. He was weak on women's rights and race. A workaholic, he found it difficult to give out warmth and love. This resulted in an unfulfilling (and possibly sexless) marriage to his loyal supporter and wife Jeanette (a woman herself not without flaws, such as a spending propensity). Many however attested to Tawney's essential nobility of character: "The best man I have ever known," said Hugh Gaitskell at his funeral.[6]

Tawney's Ideas

There seems pretty general agreement that Tawney was greatly influenced by the Christian ethics he absorbed growing up, including 1850s Christian Socialism and Charles Gore's social Christianity; and also by other currents of thought that flourished in the late nineteenth and early twentieth century. They included Ruskin's ethical economics (in one sense he was merely elaborating Ruskin's dictum that "there is no wealth but life", redefining rather than redistributing wealth). Another key force upon him was British Idealism (a philosophy that he encountered directly from his Oxford teacher Edward Caird). Goldman vividly describes the "quasi-religious" milieu that spawned the organised

Labour movement from the 1880s. Tawney was a product of this milieu. He was to become something of a lone wolf in continuing this tradition well into the next century. Goldman recognises the undoctrinaire religious foundation of Tawney's thought (a fact commented upon by his friends and contemporaries. Beatrice Webb found it very puzzling[7]). Goldman himself is revisionist on one key theme: he shows how Tawney's early idealistic and radical personal socialism evolved into a more instrumentalist, less original, variety – consistent with the twentieth century Labour policy of state socialism. However, Goldman feels, with reason, that the "authentic" Tawney – who kept re-appearing to the end – was the Christian egalitarian rather than the secular state socialist. Christian ethics continued to be fundamental to him, even though he was more cautious in publicly espousing it in an increasingly secular age.[8]

Tawney quite early on justified his social democratic ideals on absolutist Christian values, rejecting ethical philosophies based on relativistic, cultural or utilitarian grounds. In an early diary not published until 1972, ten years after his death, under the title *Commonplace Book*, we can find key guides to his mainstream thought. He saw the issue of reform of society as a moral issue, not some expedient or politically practical solution to grievances and problems within society. For example:

> The industrial problem is a moral problem, a problem of learning as a community to reprobate certain courses of conduct and to approve others.... The rule is clear, no convenience can justify any oppression.... One may not do evil that good should come.... The essence of all morality is this: to believe that every human being is of infinite importance, and therefore that no consideration of expediency can justify the oppression of one by another. But to believe this it is necessary to believe in God.... The social order is judged and condemned by a power transcending it.[9]

As Alistair Duff remarks, from a basis of Christian socialism, and under the influence of people such as Charles Gore and the Anglican prelate and his lifetime friend William Temple, "Tawney diligently extracted a reformist politics comprising a potent blend of the core left-wing values of freedom, equality and fraternity".[10] Tawney attacked the amoral profiteering basis of classical capitalism in his iconic books *The Acquisitive Society*, *Religion and the Rise of Capitalism* and *Equality*. He put forward an older alternative of communal service, a morally-based voluntarist and free socialism, which, in Goldman's words, called for a reform of the economy to meet collective needs and for a re-ordering of human values that would make economic activity a means to life rather than an end in itself. There are echoes here of Ruskin of course, and other thinkers – such as G. K. Chesterton – agreed, sharing a touch of romantic nostalgia for a lost medieval past.

Tawney's egalitarianism was frankly based, as seen above, on the model of early Christianity, on Christ's teaching of the essential equality of all humans. As Goldman indicates, as late as 1953 (in *The Attack*) and 1954 (*Christian Politics*), Tawney reiterated his youthful faith that human equality derived from the divine:

> Here he returned to the argument of the Commonplace Book that man's humanity is God-given and shared with the deity, and that compared with this, all social, national and racial differences are simply trivial and by their nature "anti-Christian" because they are a denial of God's intent and purpose.[11]

Tawney wrote:

> The necessary corollary, therefore, of the Christian conception of man is a strong sense of equality. Equality does not mean that all men are equally clever or equally virtuous, any more than they are equally tall or equally fat. It means that all men, because they are men, are of equal value.... The essential point – the essence of equality – is that such diversities must be based, not on accidents of class, income, sex, colour or nationality, but on the real requirements of the different members of the human family.[12]

His educational reforms were based on the same assumptions. Equality:

> ... denoted neither equality of opportunity nor equality of outcome but an equality of status and respect. Since we are all equal in the sight of God, argued Tawney, we should be equal in each other's valuations and behaviour. All should be treated justly, all respected equally and have their needs met; but because we differ, our needs must be met in different ways.... Arguably this is the authentic Tawney, the Christian egalitarian rather than the secular state socialist.[13]

You could argue that Tawney's critique of capitalism was essentially ethical rather than – or, better, as well as – structuralist. The Marxist critique was of course basically structuralist. Although the Marxists used ethical language to deplore the injustices and exploitation of capitalism, they ultimately saw moral systems as cultural superstructures built upon the fundamental reality of the class structure of society. Remove class distinctions through the revolution, they believed, and an ethical society would automatically emerge. Tawney disagreed. He embraced much of the Marxist criticism of capitalism, but he wanted first and foremost a spiritual or moral regeneration, from which would follow fairer social outcomes. His deepest outrage about the existing industrialist society was that it was "a moral labyrinth", a new version of slavery, treating human beings as property, as cogs in a colossal machine "which grinds wealth out of immortal spirits".[14] As Duff aptly says:

> For Tawney… even Marxists were "not revolutionary enough", since all they seemed to want was a volte-face in the class distribution of resources, the restoration of the booty, rather than a spiritual emancipation from enslavement to physical wealth… This moralist was seeking not just a community of freedom and equality but also a new overall social consciousness, a post-materialist society.[15]

Duff goes on to admit the serious weaknesses in Tawney's brand of guild socialism - which was popular at the time and a reaction against the more mechanistic brands of socialism around - but a return to handcraft industries and small scale local economies was hardly a practical option in an increasingly globalised system. Tawney also tended to demonise private enterprise, markets and the profit motive. However the important dimension to his thought was the pre-eminence of the ethical category:

> Tawney was always clear that public ownership or control was only a means to an end, only half the story of social justice. The other half was egalitarianism…. In this latter regard, Tawney represents the high watermark of Christian socialism, perhaps even the "crowning figure" of ethical socialism generally…. At one level, Tawney articulated equality as a logical extension of political democracy…. However, egalitarianism for Tawney went far beyond legal or democratic categories, to express a "spiritual relation" [to strengthen the common humanity that united people rather

> than the class difference that divided them]. When viewed in such a searing light, class divisions are anathema, shallow man-made appearances militating against a divinely instituted order of things. This is egalitarianism not only as economic justice, nor merely as ethical idealism, but as metaphysics.... This Christian-inspired vision of brotherhood is at the heart of Tawney's position: it is indeed "socialism as fellowship".[16]

Tawney's biographers show his religious belief changing from youthful interest in theology to a more generalised, non-doctrinaire, socially-oriented stance. Ross Terrill says this in his penetrating life and times of 1973:

> During the 1920s he was a discriminating satellite in the outer orbit of the Church of England. When he wrote on religion his topic was the church and the social order, no longer doctrine, religious feelings, and the ultimate grounds of Christianity, as in his pre-war diary [the *Commonplace Book*]. The basic issues were for him already settled.... His beliefs were uncomplicated.... From 1917, he and Temple were active in the "Life and Liberty Movement", a campaign to revitalize the church for new social tasks. At the end of the war, he drafted, with Bishop E. S. Talbot and others, the report on "Christianity & Industrial Problems" of the fifth of the archbishops of Canterbury's committees of inquiry.... In 1924 he took part, also with vigour and some impact, in the important Conferences on Politics, Economics and Citizenship (COPEC). Tawney was a religious man and a social moralist more than he was a churchman, even at this time. His intimacy with Temple no doubt kept him nearer to the organized church than he would otherwise have been. Both of them figures in the WEA , both concerned with the church and the social order, they often talked to each other about things that mattered most to them.... [Temple would sometimes talk the night away at Tawney's house at Mecklenburg Square.] Thus the informality of the tie between these two quite different Rugby old boys. The mutual influence was great. Intellectually, perhaps Tawney was an even greater influence upon Temple than Temple upon him, partly because Temple was more eager and able to rummage in Tawney's

> field of social questions than Tawney was to tackle Temple's discipline of theology.[17]

Some Anglican historians have described Tawney's behind-the-scenes influence, in conjunction with the powerful William Temple, as a major force and dynamic in Anglican developments at this time. He continued to be active for a long time in committee and conference work in English Christian affairs. In 1937, for example, he took part in the Oxford Conference on Church and Society. More research needs to be done on the Tawney-Temple collaboration. Hopefully the opening of new archives will shine light on all this.

Although his Christian values saturated his social analysis, Tawney could be vitriolic about the actual failure of the church in Britain (and elsewhere) to do anything significant about social reform. The churchmen talked, but at the highest level they did little. The revitalisation he and Temple worked for did not eventuate. That was his judgment. As Terrill says, works such as his *Religion and the Rise of Capitalism* attacked capitalism historically, and deplored its undermining of Christian ethics by its emphasis on profiteering,

> … and it dared the churches to recover the proper concern of Christianity with the whole range of social and economic life. The challenge to historians produced rich fruit; that to the churches came to little. Tawney's religious themes made more impact on his secular readers than his economic views did on his religious readers.[18]

Many socialist and reformist readers simply accepted his historical reading. They read *Religion and the Rise of Capitalism* as a call to arms against the industrial system, but ignored his call for a present day religious or spiritual revival. Terrill also makes the point that many of his historical critics missed the point that Tawney was as much an enemy of communism, certainly of the totalitarian Soviet Union, as of capitalism. He attacked the "servile cult of the inevitable", historical determinism, and championed individual freedom – especially that of grass-roots democracy emancipated from the shackles and materialism of global capitalism. Meanwhile the church did little.[19] Beatrice Webb noted in her diary that Tawney "profoundly dislikes and denounces the worldliness of the Anglican church and its toleration of capitalist exploitation".[20]

Tawney wrote relatively little during the 1930s, no major book for twenty years after *Land and Labour in China* in 1932:

> It is a curiosity of Tawney's career that he faded somewhat from the scene during the 1930s, the decade supposed to constitute a peak of influence for socialist intellectuals.... Tawney was depressed, and intellectually a bit paralyzed, by the intensifying concentration of irresponsible governmental power and the rise of totalitarian ideologies all over Europe.[21]

As a parallel we might notice that Aldous Huxley, the novelist and environmentalist, felt much the same, as he too favoured small government and localised democracy, and warned against the power of monoliths of the right and left.[22]

Why had totalitarianism arisen? One historical reason, according to Tawney, was the moral vacuum left by the decline of religion in the west: "The alternative to religion is rarely irreligion; it is a counter-religion". Fascism and Soviet Communism were such counter-religions; and so also was the materialist greed of capitalism:

> The apostasies waiting to succeed [religion] are legion; but the most popular claimants to the political throne have commonly been two. They are the worship of riches, and the worship of power.[23]

Keynes said famously that capitalism was absolutely irreligious. Tawney had put a similar, if more restrained, thesis with great originality in *Religion and the Rise of Capitalism.*

As Terrill concludes, Tawney from his Christian point of view saw capitalism as ungodly, both for "its irreverence toward nature" and because it was a counter-religion: "Instead of encouraging in man a creaturely attitude to the divine creation, capitalism puts a premium on a Promethean lust for limitless, almost blasphemous, exploitation of nature and dominance over nature". But Tawney did not see capitalism as the determined fate of humankind. He shared the common conviction of thirties intellectuals that it could well be displaced by other systems:

> History had no more granted to it the blessing of permanence than to feudalism before it. Its continuance was no more inevitable than its coming. In demonstrating the historical mortality of capitalism, Tawney strengthened the resolve of those who did not like capitalism but had no conviction of the possibility of replacing it.[24]
>
> In Terrill's opinion:

> Tawney hovered between affection and despair for the church, and for much of the latter part of his life (except in the very last years) he had little hope that the church could serve what he thought of as a Christian social purpose.... The church could not reclaim its former authority over English life. Christianity could now expect only the attention that the intrinsic merits of its ideas may command. Tawney's significance was that amidst the decay of the faith and authority of the church he formulated the most influential case from the socialist side for an expression of Christianity in political terms.[25]

This essentially was through his gospel of fellowship. Terrill categorises Tawney as an ethical idealist, "a democratic socialist with philosophic roots in Christian humanism".[26]

The Revisionist Debate

In an article of 2010, the Newcastle-Upon-Tyne political scientists Gary Armstrong and Tim Gray challenged three positions they believe had been taken by main commentators and biographers of Tawney (especially Ross Terrill, W. H. Greenleaf and Anthony Wright). To keep it brief, these "orthodoxies" were: (1) that Tawney's work never changed substantially over his life; (2) that Tawney's politics was largely derivative of his religion (or, as someone else put it more sympathetically, was continually informed by and articulated a deep Christian sensitivity); and (3) that the early *Commonplace Book* set the seal on his subsequent political thought, which was essentially consistent throughout.[27] These claims are backed by close analysis of Tawney's works.

Armstrong and Gray challenge the received assumptions

> ... by demonstrating that Tawney's political thought is not consistent but changes significantly over the course of his long writing career; that one important change is that he dilutes his early attachment to Christianity as the foundation stone of his political thought and that the diaries [the *Commonplace Book*] are not the key to an understanding of Tawney's political thought.[28]

They track through Tawney's writings chronologically to show evolution of his thought,

> … concentrating on the key concepts of equal worth and the political realm to demonstrate that his ideas underwent considerable change from a Christian exclusivity, which held that core values were conceptually dependent on a belief in the existence of God, to a predominantly secular position that core values were based largely on rational analysis.[29]

They speak of the gradual secularisation of his concepts. They argue that Tawney came to focus upon socialism and the Labour Party as the main architects of the Good Society rather than Christianity and the church. They agree that the young Tawney embedded his concept of equality and equal worth in a Christian ethical framework, but claim that "this restrictive conception is confined to Tawney's early work, and he adopts a humanist conception, which acknowledges the legitimacy of a secular appropriation, in his masterpiece *Equality*". They reject the suggestion that Tawney tactically adopted a secular idiom to appeal to non-religious readers: "The change in Tawney's thought is not merely tactical, but philosophical: an inclusive secular formulation of equality cannot but undermine an exclusive Christian core".[30] He initially suspected politics as morally bankrupt, but came to accept the state as a necessary agency to implement a new ethical society based upon social service. (This is perhaps compatible with Goldman's theme that Tawney abandoned his early Christian radicalism for an instrumental state socialism, but note Goldman's belief that the "authentic" early Tawney still stayed there at his core and re-emerged at the end.)

Armstrong and Gray analyse *The Acquisitive Society* as "a predominantly secular work", barring some "sparse biblical allusions" and "a dramatic reversion to the hyper-religiosity of the Commonplace Book" in the final chapter.[31] The later Tawney, they seem to be saying, accepted that political ideologies such as socialism, or even more pragmatic Labourism, could make meaningful moral appeals, without needing transcendental foundations. (Whether that rules out Tawney using both religious and secular justifications is not made clear.) They end: "Simplistic assertions of consistency, dependence and derivation fail to capture the complex and varied nature of the relationship between Tawney's political thought and his Christianity".[32]

The complexities of Tawney are certainly brought out in Lawrence Goldman's biography (and I imagine would hardly have been denied by his earlier biographers). Goldman barely bothers with the Armstrong/Gray thesis. In a single reference he mentions that they had drawn attention to the changes and inconsistencies in Tawney ideas, "though Tawney himself would have been the first to admit that he was not a systematic social thinker and that the construction of a philosophical system was never his aim".[33]

One of the more interesting responses to Armstrong and Gray came from the American scholar Adam Seligman, a Tawney admirer. In a review labelled "Tendentious Debunking" he recalls: "I first encountered Tawney's writing in public high school in Brooklyn in the 1960s and it made perfect sense in those times of social protest, activism, and visions of a better world".[34] While welcoming this addition to Tawney scholarship, and hoping that it might increase familiarity with his important writings, Seligman has his reservations:

> At times they seem to overstate their case and, in making their argument, seem to impose distinctions and divisions in the trajectory of Tawney's thought that feel foreign to the felt experience of reading Tawney's prose. At times such reading borders on the tendentious. Thus Tawney's book *The Attack* (1953), which was published less than ten years before he died, did indeed contain earlier essays from the 1920s and is discussed in this context by our authors. They, however, totally disregard the strong religious or spiritual elements to be found in this work – most especially the importance of Christian fellowship as the basis of equality and ethical action.... Doubtless most people's thought grows and changes over time and the circumstances of life, but equally, some threads and concerns remain constant, if with changing hues and emphases.[35]

Asking why the authors protest so much about the religiosity of Tawney, Seligman makes a telling point:

> One almost feels it reflects current political concerns and conflicts much more than those of the first half of the twentieth century. We are today caught in a world where the religious and secular roots of action, morality, and understanding are thought to be antithetical, as ultimate contradictions. This was not always so. It certainly was not so of the world inhabited by the likes of Tawney, Hugh Gaitskell (leader of the Labour Party), and Archbishop Temple.[36]

In the above I have tried to give at least some context and to present differing views on the revisionist debate, and much else. If you are interested in these issues, you can obtain much more detail from the sources cited. Goldman lists over nine pages of books and articles by and about Tawney, so good hunting!

---

[1] R. H. Tawney, *The Acquisitive Society* (London, G. Bell & Sons Ltd., 1922); *Religion and the Rise of Capitalism* (New York, Harcourt Brace & Co., 1926); *Equality* (London, Unwin Books, 1931).

[2] R. H. Tawney, *The Attack and Other Papers* (London, Books for Libraries Press, 1953). The paper originally called *The Attack*, which recounts Tawney's experiences at the Somme was first published in the *Westminster Gazette* (London), August 1916; *The Radical Tradition: Twelve Essays on Politics, Education and Literature* (New York, Pantheon Books, 1964).

[3] "He could admire but not agree with the principled pacifist who was realistically prepared to accept all the consequences of his pacifism – not to use violence even if England were attacked, not to use violence even though loved ones were directly threatened with or subjected to humiliation, torture or death, not to use violence even though pacifism did not lead to peace.... But he could not join those who based their pacifism on the, to him, erroneous belief that there was no significant risk that an aggressor would take advantage of a pacifist country, or the equally erroneous belief that foreign invasion was to be preferred to war...": Norman Dennis and A. H. Halsey, *English Ethical Socialism* (Oxford, Oxford University Press, 1988), p. 167. Chapter 7, "Socialism as Fellowship: R. H. Tawney" gives a brief but sensitive account of Tawney's life and ideas.

[4] R. H. Tawney, *Business and Politics Under James I: Lionel Cranfield as Merchant and Minister* (Cambridge, Cambridge University Press, 1958).

[5] Lawrence Goldman, *The Life of R. H. Tawney: Socialism and History* (London, New York, Bloomsbury, 2014). See also Ross Terrill, *R.H. Tawney and His Times: Socialism as Fellowship* (Cambridge MA, Harvard University Press, 1973) and Anthony Wright, *R. H. Tawney* (Manchester, Manchester University Press, 1987). Goldman has written the entry on Tawney in the *Oxford Dictionary of National Biography*.

[6] Entry on Tawney in the *Oxford Dictionary of National Biography*.

[7] In her diary of 8 December 1935 Beatrice wrote: "In his religious opinions, he remains a mystery to his free-thinking friends" and another time wondered if Tawney was "a convinced Christian or a religious-minded agnostic": typescript in LSE Digital Library, quoted Goldman, *Life of Tawney*, p. 179; and generally on Tawney's Christianity, pp. 179-184.

[8] Tawney's *Commonplace Book* is a good guide to his early thought: *R. H. Tawney's Commonplace Book*, ed. J. M. Winter and D. M. Joslin (Cambridge, Cambridge University Press, 1972). For an excellent discussion of this and other Tawney sources, and his thought, see Alastair Duff, "The Sickness of an Information Society: R. H. Tawney and the Post-Industrial Condition", *Information, Communication and Society*, 7, 3 (2004), pp. 403-422. I have paraphrased some of Duff's readings in what follows. He argues that Tawney is still relevant in giving critical perspectives on the technocratic social structure and new modes of information and communication: "Tawney delineates a moral order against

which all political actions and institutions must be benchmarked, a theory of right for those steering a course amid the tempting, teleological currents of modern politics.... Tawney had affirmed the non-negotiable priority of the right over the good in the political order" (pp. 405-406).

[9] Tawney's *Commonplace Book*, diary for years 1912-1914, pp. 12, 65-68.

[10] Duff, *An Information Society*, p. 406.

[11] Goldman, *Life of Tawney*, p. 195.

[12] R. H. Tawney, *Christian Politics*, (London, Socialist Christian League, 1954), p. 13.

[13] Goldman, *Life of Tawney*, p. 196.

[14] R. H. Tawney, "An Experiment in Democractic Education", *The Political Quarterly* (2 May 1914), pp. 62-84.

[15] Duff, *An Information Society*, p. 407.

[16] *Ibid*, p. 410.

[17] Terrill, *Tawney and His Times*, pp. 57-59.

[18] *Ibid*, p. 60.

[19] S. J. D. Green gives an excellent account of the slow change in church attitudes in his *The Passing of Protestant England: Secularisation and Social Change c.1920-1960* (Cambridge, Cambridge University Press, 2011).

[20] Beatrice Webb's Diary, 1937.

[21] Terrill, *Tawney and His Times*, p. 139.

[22] See R. S. Deese, *We Are Amphibians: Julian and Aldous Huxley on the Future of Our Species* (Oakland, California, University of California Press, 2015).

[23] Tawney, Burge Lecture: "The Western Political Tradition". He spoke also of "the monstrous doctrine of national sovereignty".

[24] Terrill, *Tawney and His Times*, pp. 252-253.

[25] *Ibid*, pp. 265-266.

[26] *Ibid*, p. 269.

[27] Gary Armstrong and Tim Gray, "Three Fallacies in the Essentialist Interpretation of the Political Thought of R. H. Tawney", *Journal of Political Ideologies* 15, 2 (2010), pp. 161-174. They expanded this into a book: *The Authentic Tawney: A New Interpretation of the Political Thought of* R. H. *Tawney* (Exeter, Wiley, 2011).

[28] Armstrong and Gray, "Three Fallacies", p. 162.

[29] *Ibid.*

[30] *Ibid*, pp. 167-168.

[31] *Ibid*, p. 169.

[32] *Ibid*, p. 172.

[33] Goldman, *Life of Tawney*, p. 8.

[34] Adam Seligman, "Tendentious Debunking", *The Review of Politics* 73, 4 (2011), pp. 665-667. This is a review of Armstrong and Gray's book *The Authentic Tawney*.

[35] *Ibid.*

[36] *Ibid.*

9. Malcolm Muggeridge: Pundit to Pilgrim

Today's generation, I suppose, has largely forgotten Malcolm Muggeridge (1903-1990). However not entirely. It should be said that there is a journal, *The Gargoyle*, dedicated to him, that a Muggeridge Society exists and that his religious writings flourish, especially in the United States. I remember him vividly as a TV pundit of the 1970s and 80s. His TV presence was compelling. He was pungent, scathing, mordant, sarcastic, sceptical, iconoclastic, curmudgeonly, but also capable of being totally charming, witty and cuttingly intelligent. His gnomic appearance – great domed head, bulbous nose, wide mouth – had a slightly clownish aspect. His voice was unmistakeable but how to describe it? Resonating, close to gravelly, absolutely clear enunciation, the voice of an orator or debater, and he endlessly orated and debated, as well as producing, in his own words, a torrent of words for publication. As obituarists remarked, he had an unerring capacity to puncture pomposity; and he spent his life ridiculing authority. He was a rabid critic of modern western civilisation, of capitalism, materialism and moral vacuity, as also of all totalitarian regimes and ideologies, Fascist, Marxist, whatever. He is sometimes cited as a pungent social critic, but there is something missing. It is thoroughgoing social analysis. His judgments are often absurdly sweeping, paradoxical and inconsistent. Take his book *The Thirties*, finished, appropriately enough, in an army training camp as the world readied for World War Two. It is a fascinating, readable and amusing book, with wonderful pen portraits of the politicians and public figures of the age. But almost everything and everyone is reduced finally to the absurd. As history (for which he professed contempt) it is highly problematical, to say the least.

When in 1978 Muggeridge's youthful novel *In a Valley of this Restless Mind* was re-issued, he wrote an introduction to it that rightly redressed the common assessment of him as a lifelong sensualist and sceptic, until he "got religion" late in life:

> It is generally assumed, by those who know me only through the media, especially television, that for the greater part of my life my attitudes were wholly hedonistic and my ways wholly worldly, until, in my sixties, I suddenly discovered God and became preoccupied with other-worldly considerations. The fact is that, unlike Demas, I

> have never cared much for this present world, and have found its pleasures and prizes, such as they are, little to my taste even in pursuing them.[1]

As the novel showed, he was even then searching for spiritual meaning in life, although characteristically not finding it. And also in the process he vindicated Evelyn Waugh's reading of him as a Puritan at heart, his attitudes to sex being "that of a surfeited and rather scared Calvinist", a verdict Muggeridge accepted.[2]

Even as a student at Cambridge, Muggeridge was drawn to Christianity. There he met Alec Vidler, who was studying to become an Anglican priest, and was to become a leading church historian:

> Muggeridge also considered this vocation. Vidler would remain a committed friend and life-long Christian influence on Malcolm. He noticed that Muggeridge [potentially] "had a kind of genius as a talker and writer and even as a seer".[3]

Muggeridge continued during most of his early and middle age to waver between aggressive unbelief and religious yearnings. This is abundantly clear to any reader of his diaries. Patrick Walsh observed:

> Muggeridge was always peering behind the drama of human existence for God. He would explain this way of seeing by quoting the English poet William Blake:
>
> We are led to believe a lie
> When we see not Thro' the Eye.
>
> To see with the eye goes only half way toward encompassing reality. Microscopes, telescopes, and all instruments of modern science fall short. To see through the eye includes the invisible spiritual dimension of reality to which modernity, in its preoccupation with material progress, is blind. Muggeridge in reporting on his century created a new literary genre, a kind of eschatological journalism as yet unappreciated.[4]

I've been reading his autobiography *Chronicles of Wasted Time.*[5] I find myself getting quite fond of old Malcolm, with his biting sarcasm and absurdist sense of the world. But what a weird mixture there is of insight and staggering insensitivity, for example, his callous dismissal of Hiroshima, no doubt shared by many at the time. He spoke of the "hysteria" that was worked up over the dropping of the atomic bombs:

> Somehow it seemed to me that just having an enormously more powerful weapon altered nothing; it was the will to destroy rather than the means which mattered, and if human destructiveness had reached the point that our very earth itself could be turned to dust, this danger would not be averted by agitating for nuclear disarmament.[6]

Even a trip to Hiroshima in 1946 did not make him noticeably more caring about the human carnage done there. In 1950, at the height of the Cold War, he proposed dropping an atomic bomb.[7] No doubt his overall attitude was conditioned by his long stint during the thirties with the League of Nations at Geneva, where he became totally disillusioned with efforts to ensure world disarmament and peace. The "Dawn Seekers" who persistently placed their faith in a utopian human future continued to be favourite targets of his ridicule (his great friend Hugh Kingsmill coined the phrase "Dawn Seekers").

Also, again despite the grain of truth, there was his dismissal of the achievements of the Attlee government and its welfare system, e.g. the National Health System – yet his father, a prominent Fabian socialist, had been a passionate advocate of a more caring world and more social justice for the poor and disadvantaged (but Malcolm did see the potential for "rorting the system"). Malcolm greeted the election of the Labour government in 1945 with mixed feelings. They included a large dollop of *schadenfreude*. Despite his father's lifetime dream of a Labour government, "here was I in the office of a Conservative newspaper [*The Daily Telegraph*], and taking no joy in the occasion beyond a certain satisfaction at the confusion of all the pundits and the overthrow of a government in office".[8] In a diary entry in 1949 (8-9 June), he ridiculed the Welfare State "which, in its efforts to produce everything for everyone, would inevitably result in producing nothing for anyone". At around this time he began voting Conservative, but not without guilt feelings.

He also saw the downside of the Allied victory in 1945, especially the rise of totalitarian USSR and Stalinism. Was this a victory of good over evil?

> The Red Army coming in from the East bringing freedom on its wings; the Allied forces coming in from the West with enlightenment on theirs?... Had Berlin, in being reduced to rubble, become a citadel of democracy? Or were there, as before, just victors and vanquished, with some uncertainty as to which was which, and justice once more a fugitive?[9]

In the late 1930s Muggeridge began having mystical experiences:

> The first intimation is, quite simply that time stops, or rather one escapes from time. Then all creation is seen in its oneness; with each part of it, from the tiniest insect or blade of grass, to the vastnesses of space, with the stars and comets riding through them, visibly related to every other part. One sublime harmony, with no place for the discordances of hatred and the ego's shrill demands; the death of death, since each note in the harmony exists harmoniously for ever. Peace that is no one else's strife, sufficiency that is no one else's famine, well-being that is no one else's sickness. Flesh still, mind still, leaving the soul free to experience the inconceivable joy of seeing beyond the Iron Gates, to where the Creator watches over his creation.[10]

One is reminded vividly of Aldous Huxley's similar descriptions of mystical experiences he had after taking mescalin in California in the 1950s, which he published in his *The Doors of Perception*, 1954. Muggeridge writes of three such experiences he had while living at Whatlington in the countryside of southern England (near Battle). One was with his close friend, the journalist and writer Hugh Kingsmill, while they were standing on the cliffs just outside Hastings. The sight of the Old Town below wreathed in evening mist, chimneys smoking, their smoke merging into the grey, gathering night made him feel suddenly spell bound "as though this was a vision of the Last Day, and the wreaths of smoke, souls, leaving their bodies to rise heavenwards and become part of eternity", while he felt a sense of common destiny with all his fellow human beings. Another time was when he gave a blood transfusion to his wife Kitty: "Never in all our life together, had I so completely and perfectly and joyously experienced love's fulfilment as on that moment".[11] A third occasion was at harvest time at Whatlington. It was about 11 at night, full moon, "the field's abundance filled the air, almost visibly, like a mist of fulfilment". Behind stood the small, ancient church and beyond a massive yew tree, with grave-stones all around in lush grass:

> I suppose for a thousand years and more past, anyone standing on that little hill would have surveyed the self-same scene. I felt myself being incorporated into it, until I no longer existed, except as a voice in a choir of innumerable voices, swelling chorus of gratitude for the gift of life, of sharing in its plenitude, of experiencing its joys and

> afflictions, and treading its ordained path, from the womb where I was shaped, to a grave under that yew tree where I hoped to lie. Some ancestral memory formed on my lips the words *Gloria in excelsis Deo.*[12]

Muggeridge had an epiphany during World War Two, when he was working for British Intelligence in Lourenco Marques in Mozambique. One night he felt deeply depressed:

> I lay on my bed full of stale liquor and despair; alone in the house, and, as it seemed, utterly alone... in the world. Alone in the universe, in eternity, with no glimmer of light in the prevailing blackness... no God to whom I could turn, or Saviour to take my hand.[13]

He decided to take his own life, drove to the coast road, and waded out to sea in order to drown himself. As he prepared to sleep on his watery mattress, he was aware of the distant lights of a cafe and the Costa da Sol. Without thinking or deciding, he started swimming back to shore again, his eyes fixed on those lights.

> They were the lights of the world; they were the lights of my home, my habitat, where I belonged. I must reach them. There followed an overwhelming joy such as I had never experienced before; an ecstasy. In some mysterious way it became clear to me that there was no darkness, only the possibility of losing sight of a light that shone eternally.[14]

He felt that our sufferings and afflictions were part of a drama:

> … endlessly revolving round the two great propositions of good and evil, of light and darkness. A brief interlude, an incarnation, reaching back into the beginning of time, and forward into an ultimate fulfilment in the universal spirit of love which informs, animates, illuminates all creation, from the tiniest particle of insentient matter to the radiance of God's very throne.[15]

Although he scarcely realised it at the time, this episode represented for him one of those deep changes that occur in life:

> … a kind of spiritual adolescence, whereby, thenceforth, all my values and pursuits and hopes were going to undergo a

> total transformation – from the carnal towards the spiritual; from the immediate, the now, towards the everlasting, the eternal. In a tiny dark dungeon of the ego, chained and manacled, I had glimpsed a glimmer of light coming in through a barred window high above me... it was the light of the world. The bars of the window, as I looked more closely, took on the form of a Cross.[16]

Certain themes can be discerned throughout Muggeridge's writings and life. They are a continuing onslaught against materialism, individualist egoism and carnality; and a corresponding search for spirituality and goodness. He looked around him and found a western civilisation that had become deeply secular, wealthy but spiritually and ethically desolate. Although a fierce critic of communism, he maintained a constant offensive against capitalism, its greed and vices, throughout his life. His diaries when in America reflected this, with him wavering between admiration and disgust for Americans and their way of life. On one occasion, 8 October 1960, he observed fellow passengers queuing for a plane at Newark airport, and thought of them as like animals, forsaking liberty for food and pleasure, "collecting their viands, and then passing through the wicker gate, where they paid. This is a freely constructed concentration camp".

He noted the steep decline in churchgoing during the 1930s and 1940s, and the futile attempts of "trendy" clergy to revivify and modernise church life. This profoundly depressed him. He wrote in 1949: "Church services are very empty, and yet at their worst they have a kind of sweetness. Faces humbly downcast are more tolerable than when they are clamorous". Even as an unbeliever he found beauty, and something beyond this, in church ritual – he always preferred traditional colour and ceremony to nonconformist plainness. The church service, he observed, was designed to still rather than inflame the will, "at least to settle the dust of living for a little while". Candles shone like truth "and the wonderful phrases of the psalms and hymns and prayers and scripture tranquillize".[17] Predictably he liked the virile King James Version of the Bible better than the "flat-footed and banal" modern translations.

So profound was modern materialism and sex-worship, and so obvious the flaws of the churches, that he stood amazed that anyone still worshipped. It was nothing short of miraculous: "As Hilaire Belloc once remarked of his church, it had obviously enjoyed God's special favour and protection; otherwise, in view of the inane and often mischievous hands controlling its destiny, it would long since have disappeared".[18] Throughout his life, and especially in his earlier years, Muggeridge was cynical about the abuses of church power, as he was about the use of power and those exercising power generally in history. This was so even after his conversion in 1982 to Catholicism. His attitude was that he embraced Catholicism as the mainstream Christian tradition, despite its faults, these being the faults of humanity at large. He wrote in 1983:

> For myself the great boon and blessing of the Church is that it enshrines not a panacea for contemporary ills, or the promise of future happiness, but a mystery – that all creation, its totality, is one; the manifestation of a loving creator whose reach is between the furthermost limits of the universe and the counted hairs of each individual head.... Faith tells me it is possible to establish with this loving creator a living and loving relationship which makes all things joyously comprehensible and acceptable.[19]

On sex, Muggeridge had an almost Manichean suspicion of the flesh and of women as temptresses. He quoted from Augustine and Blake to make the point. He went so far as to name volume 2 of his autobiography *The Infernal Grove*, with these lines from Blake headlining the title page:

> Till I turn from Female Love
> And root up the Infernal Grove
> I shall never worthy be
> To step into Eternity.

And from Augustine: "There's nothing so powerful in drawing the spirit of a man downwards as the caresses of a woman". In an essay on Augustine in *A Third Testament* (1976), Muggeridge portrays him as peculiarly susceptible and knowing about all this. We realise that:

> … to a temperament as sensual and imaginative as Augustine's, sexual indulgence makes the greatest appeal precisely because it offers a kind of fraudulent ecstasy – joys that expire when the neon lights go out.... He was speaking from experience and I, for what it's worth, endorse his opinion.[20]

Augustine had in his wild youth not been immune to the attractions of Roman games and theatre, wildly expensive spectacles of violence and eroticism, against which he later thundered. Muggeridge noted the parallel between the early Christian churches, finding it difficult to counteract "the prevailing atmosphere of luxury, violence and self-indulgence", and the present-day crisis of western religion:

> The similarity between his circumstances and ours is striking, not to say alarming. There is the same moral vacuity, leading to the same insensate passion for new sensations and experiences; the same fatuous credulity opening the way to every kind of charlatanry and quackery, from fortune telling to psychoanalysis; the same sinister combination of great wealth and pointless ostentation with appalling poverty and unheeded affliction.[21]

Muggeridge knew of course that these things had existed to some degree in all ages. But it seemed to him that they were much worse in the Roman era and ours.

In their search for fulfilment humans had turned to a bewildering array of alternatives, not only to egomania and erotomania, "the two sicknesses of the godless", but to utopianism and science. All were false gods. Muggeridge, like his hero William Blake, thought notions of human perfectibility to be among the most dangerous forces in history. They had arisen out of the Enlightenment, science and the Industrial Revolution, and had spawned the destruction of the French and Russian revolutions.. Blake had ferociously opposed William Godwin's vision of humanity perfecting itself through reason and technology (Godwin's daughter Mary Shelley got it more right in her prophetic novel *Frankenstein*). Blake rightly saw in Godwin's vision "all the dreadful potentialities of human arrogance and destructiveness whose fulfilment we have witnessed in our time". In the end Blake came to see "that the only true freedom is spiritual, achieved through the imagination, and that the notion of progress in the world of space and time is an illusion that beguiles mankind with false hopes."[22]

Christ and the Media (1977) printed three lectures Muggeridge had given in London in 1976, in a series focussing on Christian thinking about contemporary issues, with BBC and other media people present and asking some very relevant questions afterwards. As some of them noted, despite his penetrating critique of television and other media, Muggeridge seemed to fall into the trap of demonising technology in itself, especially "the camera" and TV, rather than taking the more defensible position that technology was not good or evil as such but that it was the human use of it that was the key issue at stake. His wholesale condemnation of modern education and practices such as birth control (he refused to countenance any dangers to humanity in over-population), and his social censoriousness also laid him open to charges of lack of balance, even extremism and bigotry. Nevertheless, Malcolm the Jeremiah had some piercingly acute observations to make about modern capitalist civilisation.

Evoking the famous scene in Dostoevsky's *The Brothers Karamazov* between the Grand Inquisitor and the returned Christ, Muggeridge saw modern humanity embracing rather than spurning the temptations held out by the Devil, embracing the kingdoms of the earth rather than of heaven:

> Have we not been shown in the most dramatic manner how economic miracles end in servitude to economics? How the glorification of Man leads infallibly to the servitude of men, and his liberation through power to one variety or another of Gulag Archipelago?[23]

What to make of a civilisation materially so rich and powerful, yet spiritually so impoverished and fear-ridden? We had made remarkable inroads into discovering the secrets of nature and unravelling the mysteries even of the universe, developed massive powers of production and consumption, able "to transmit swifter than light every thought, smile or word that could possibly entertain, instruct or delight us... opening up possibilities beyond envisaging", yet we were haunted by fears of global swarming and nuclear destruction, and were promoting conspicuous consumption by the affluent alongside ever-increasing hunger among the rest of humankind. With all of science and technology at our backs, and intent upon the pursuit of happiness – or at least pleasure – the west was taking the opposite course, "towards chaos, not order, towards breakdown, not stability, towards death, destruction and darkness, not life, creativity and light".[24] The west, he said more than once, with its rampant but ethically debased capitalism, its worship of pleasure and violence, its neuroses and false gurus, its vulgar culture and conformism, had embraced Freud's "death wish". There are significant parallels here with G. K. Chesterton's concept of "the servile state", and the criticisms of C. S. Lewis and George Orwell.[25]

Muggeridge brilliantly ridiculed the absurdities and banalities of things such as advertising and television, dominated by money and ratings, distorting reality. In the place of Christianity, a cult of consumption had been founded upon the mystical basis of sex, "the mysticism of materialism" as evidenced by "the superabundance of erotica" in books, newspapers, films, theatre and TV, "all impediments and restraints swept aside, no moral restrictions, no legal ones either. And then, with the coming of the birth pill, the crowning glory, the achievement of unprocreative procreation".[26] It has to be said that, in the end, Muggeridge, albeit grudgingly, thanked God for the media, with all its capacities for corrupting fantasy and deception. He thanked God indeed "for everything, since everything that has ever been, is or ever will be manifests his existence and is part of the totality of his love".[27] Even the terminal decline of the West had its ultimate compensation. In the breakdown of power, we could discern its true nature. Jesus was the prophet of the loser's, not the victor's, camp:

> and proclaimed that the first will be last, that the weak are the strong, and the fools, the wise. Let us then, as Christians rejoice that we see around us on every hand the decay of the institutions and instruments of power; intimations of empire falling to pieces, money in total disarray, dictators and parliamentarians alike nonplussed by the confusion and conflicts which encompass them. For it is precisely when every earthly hope has been explored and found wanting... it is then that Christ's hand reaches out, sure and firm, that Christ's words bring their inexpressible comfort, that his light shines brightest, abolishing the darkness for ever.[28]

Then humans could again be caught up in:

> … the wonder of God's love flooding the universe, made aware of the stupendous creativity which animates all life, of our own participation in it – every colour brighter, every meaning clearer, every shape more shapely, every note more musical, every word written and spoken more explicit: above all, every human face, all human companionship, all human encounters recognisably a family affair.[29]

Muggeridge was a depressive personality. This is abundantly evidenced in his autobiography, diaries and writings. Apart from momentary periods of happiness and peace, he was morbidly gloomy about the world and his personal life. He constantly talked of ending his life because of its worthlessness and insignificance. One could quote almost randomly from his diary to illustrate these melancholy themes. Take for example these entries for 1945-1946. In December of 1945 he spent two days (14-16) in the House of Commons to report on the debates. Predictably he was unimpressed (very little, one might say, ever impressed him, either fact or fiction). The debate, he said:

> … was extraordinarily unreal, even absurd, and shabby.... It struck me then, as so often, how in my life everything I

> have seen or been connected with has given me that feeling of something past its prime, running down, growing shabby and decrepit.

A week or so later (23 December), on his way by train to Battle for Christmas, he:

> … suddenly began to be alive again.... Even the landscape, which had seemed dead, recovers its life.... I kept thinking of all the lives I might have lived – a left-wing life, or a life of devotion to writing; all that I might have done, and understood that life was so insignificant that it didn't matter, or so significant that it didn't matter.

(He admired Turgenev's novel *Fathers and Sons*, and one suspects that he would have felt some affinity with the key character in it, the nihilist Bazarov.) By March of 1946, well advanced on his edition of Ciano's diary, he was convinced that Europe was about to be conquered by the Bolsheviks:

> Their triumph is coming, and is comprehensible, but still disagreeable for us and for England. Perhaps it is necessary.... I have always known that what I belonged to was doomed, going down hill. The smell of decay was abroad. Even so, I belong to what is decaying and I will go down hill with it, not despairing, because it doesn't matter. Everything decays and in its decay fertilizes new life (8 March).

He went to America in late March 1946 as the Washington correspondent for the *Daily Telegraph*, worrying whether he was happy with Kitty, whether he was doing the right thing. Again, on the boat, he felt a moment of joy:

> Every now and again all my life I'd had a sudden mood of happiness, a kind of humility, a release from all fear, an awareness of the mysteriousness of my own being in relation to the universe. In such moods I recite the Lord's Prayer to myself, finding great comfort and delight in its words.... "Terrible is earth" is a phrase Hughie Kingsmill quoted to me once – terrible because of passion, which means the same as suffering. The realization that it is so implies a promise of release – to be patiently awaited, like

> sleep, and not angrily sought. I cannot be interested in anything except this reality, and if I had the courage I should give myself wholly to its pursuit (30 March).

Although he liked Washington, "I cannot shake off deep undercurrent of melancholy; seldom, if ever, had less zest for life than these days" (27 April). In May he lunched with William Bullitt, a former American ambassador, who still believed that global problems could be sorted out through personal contacts and playing politics. This was an illusory belief Muggeridge felt:

> Always a failure because the world's troubles are a consequence, not of circumstances and individuals, but of the collapse of a moral synthesis, and of the authority and power this synthesis generated. This chaos must go on spreading; the breakdown, economic and social, must get worse. There is no reason why it shouldn't (11 May).

A few days later a conversation with Wilmott Lewis of *The Times* "made me realize that the appalling melancholia induced by this country is due to the fact that the light of the spirit is quite out, making a kingdom of darkness, and my own spirit was correspondingly lightened" (18 May). A psychiatrist would find rich pickings here (in fact Muggeridge consulted psychiatrists at various stages of his life but was not forthcoming about their analysis of him).

Had Muggeridge anything to say about the decline of religion in modern times? He certainly believed that he was living in an age of terminal collapse of religion. The erosion of Christianity was, in his opinion, the critical cause of the impending death of western civilisation, because its bedrock had been Christianity. To quote his biographer Ian Hunter, who observed that Muggeridge was obsessed by the idea of living in the twilight of a spent civilisation:

> A civilisation, like a dwelling, must have a stable foundation or it collapses. Christianity was the foundation on which laws, customs, and regulations – a whole civil order, as well as our art, music and literature, rested. In other words, it provided the moral imperatives from which civil authority derived; destroy that foundation and the whole edifice topples. Where there are neither religious values nor an accepted manner of behaviour to impose a moral pattern on life, all that is left is the pursuit of power as such.[30]

Christianity had admittedly often succumbed to the temptations of power. Its fatal flaw was that it had allied itself with the pagan forces of the world, had been swept up in the tsunami of secularism, and had turned to stunts and trendy reform issues. Nevertheless, Christianity expressed a higher truth altogether in its essential teachings, as had been taught by thinkers that Muggeridge admired such as the church fathers, Augustine and Pascal. Again quoting Hunter:

> Undermine Christianity, venerate humanism in its place, and a true, immutable foundation capable of withstanding the buffeting tides of history, has been replaced by a false, shifting one. Instead of life being understood as a pilgrimage and man as a wayfarer, seeing at best through a glass darkly and fitfully, yet with a sure guide and a certain hope - a sojourner in time whose true home is eternity, humanism proclaims that life is a contest for survival in which man, having proved the fittest, has come of age and is capable of charting his own course, master of his own destiny. On such a foundation, Muggeridge contends, nothing can be constructed except fantasy; and there is no power, whether derived from wealth or arms, which can for long sustain fantasy.[31]

This places Muggeridge squarely in the traditional historiographical school that explains religious decline as the product of historical factors such as the Renaissance, the rise of capitalism and industry, science and evolution, liberalism and socialism – factors that bred materialism, excessive individualism and secular hubris.[32] He spilt much ink attacking these targets, but we look in vain for any systematically sociological explanations of religious decline, such as those much favoured in more recent historiography. Muggeridge's insights were based on his own, very idiosyncratic, experiences and an imaginative feel for the current *Zeitgeist.*

---

[1] Malcolm Muggeridge, *In a Valley of this Restless Mind* (London, 1978; 1st edition 1938), introduction p. 13. Elsewhere he wrote: "there was no point in my life when I underwent any dramatic change. I would say that for me at any rate, the process has been not a sudden Damascus road experience, but more like the journeying of Bunyan's Pilgrim, who constantly lost his way, fell into sloughs, was locked up in Doubting Castle and terrified out of his wits in the Valley of the Shadow of Death, but still, through it all had a sense of moving towards light, moving out of time towards eternity": *Christ and the Media* (London, Hodder and Stoughton, 1977), p. 89.

[2] Muggeridge, *Restless Mind*, p. 10.
[3] Patrick J. Walsh, "Malcolm Muggeridge: A Modern Pilgrim", *Modern Age*, 42 (2005), p. 182. Vidler in his autobiography *Scenes from a Clerical Life* (London, Collins, 1977) wrote of Muggeridge: "When I first got to know him he was being prepared for confirmation.... I do not consider that in his autobiography he has adequately assessed the sincerity and depth of his initiation into Christian faith and practice at this time" (p.33). Walsh notes that when, after graduation, Muggeridge went to India as an English teacher, he wrote a letter to his socialist father in 1926, asserting "that the ability to say 'Dadda' to God is what people need more than the minimum wage" (p.182). Walsh says that Muggeridge "imbibed a combative spirit against the forces of materialism" from Thomas Carlyle (p. 183).
[4] Walsh, "Malcolm Muggeridge", p. 183.
[5] Malcolm Muggeridge, *Chronicles of Wasted Time:* Vol.2, *The Infernal Grove* (London, Collins, 1973).
[6] *Ibid, p. 264.*
[7] This was on a BBC programme *Any Questions?* See diary entry for 13 July, 1950 in John Bright-Homes, ed., *Like it Was: The Diaries of Malcolm Muggeridge* (London, Collins, 1981). He also later expressed sympathy for at least some of Senator Joseph McCarthy's viewpoints: *Diaries* 24 February, 1954.
[8] Muggeridge, *Diaries*, p. 261.
[9] Muggeridge, *Chronicles*, p. 256.
[10] *Ibid*, p. 68.
[11] *Ibid.*
[12] *Ibid*, p. 69.
[13] *Ibid*, p. 184.
[14] *Ibid.*
[15] *Ibid.*
[16] *Ibid*, p. 185. Earlier, in 1936, he had experienced an unexpected sense of happiness, a consequence of feeling himself in contact with God: "Suddenly, and for the first time, life has a significance for me other than just its horror, or bizarreness, or the sensations it offers. I see into the heart of it. I sense a purpose, and know that I am part of that purpose. I can measure what troubled or tormented me against this purpose, and it is nothing. The mystery of my own being is no longer oppressive or fantastic, but glorified, because belonging to the universal Mystery": Muggeridge, *Diaries*, 26 August 1936.
[17] Malcolm Muggeridge, "Dayspring From On High" (1949) in *Time and Eternity: Uncollected Writings 1933-1983* (New York, Orbis, 2010), pp. 98-99.
[18] Muggeridge, "The Gospel of Jesus Egalite" (1972) in *ibid*, p. 213.
[19] Muggeridge, "Finding Faith", (1983), *ibid*, pp. 226-227. A major attraction of the Catholic Church to him was its official opposition to legalised abortion "and other aspects of the appalling, ostensibly humane, holocaust which turns hospitals into abattoirs wherein unborn children and the ailing old are systematically murdered" (p. 226). He was a lifelong opponent of eugenics and euthanasia.
[20] Malcolm Muggeridge, *A Third Testament* (London, Collins, BBC, 1976), p. 37.

[21] *Ibid.*

[22] *Ibid*, pp. 80, 98, 100. In 1933 Muggeridge wrote: "People who go all out for the scientific outlook end by producing the greatest of all absurdities – mysticised science; the worship of something idiotic like the [Soviet] Five Year Plan. After all, it is more sensible and more dignified to worship God than a Five Year Plan": Muggeridge, *Diaries,* 6 January 1933.

[23] Malcolm Muggeridge, *Christ and the Media* (London, Hodder and Stoughton, 1977), p. 39.

[24] *Ibid,* p. 54.

[25] On this see Adam Schwartz, "Conceiving a Culture of Life in a Century of Bones: G .K .Chesterton and Malcolm Muggeridge as Social Critics", *Logos*, 11 (2008), pp. 50-76, especially pp. 59ff. Muggeridge was well aware of the ideas of Chesterton, Lewis and Orwell. Generally kind about Chesterton, he was capable of cruelly debunking the others. As Swartz points out, Muggeridge saw the welfare state as a manifestation of capitalist materialism's deadly cultural ramifications: "concentrating state power further to facilitate social security would exacerbate the self-enslavement already fostered by dependence on oligopolies for an everlasting stream of consumer goods and the financial wherewithal to purchase them, leaving Westerners 'sleepwalking into our own Gulag'... capitalism also spawned an inhuman homogenization and humourlessness, a utilitarian aesthetic inimical to genuine imaginative art, and an unjust distribution of wealth...." (p. 61).

[26] Muggeridge, *Christ and the Media*, p. 57.

[27] *Ibid*, p. 59.

[28] *Ibid,* p. 77.

[29] *Ibid,* p. 75.

[30] Ian Hunter, *Malcolm Muggeridge: A Life* (London, Collins, 1980), p. 155.

[31] *Ibid.*

[32] In 1961 he had a swipe at "Rationalism, ethical societies, all the various organizations which sprouted out of Darwinism, fertilizers of the decay of the Anglican Church": *Diaries*, 23 April 1961. He never analysed in any depth the impact of Darwinian theory on religion, despite the fact that his great friend Alec Vidler had done so in his various writings, noting the complexity of the relationship.

10. Alec Vidler: On Christian Faith and Secular Despair

Born in Rye, Sussex, son of a shipping businessman, Alec Vidler (1899-1991) was educated at Sutton Valence School, Kent. After a brief spell in the artillery in the closing phase of the Great War, he read theology at Selwyn College, Cambridge (B.A. 1921), then trained for the Anglican ministry at Wells Theological College. He disliked Wells and transferred to the Oratory of the Good Shepherd, Cambridge, an Anglo-Catholic community of celibates, and was ordained priest in 1923. He retained a life-long affection for the celibate monkish life, never marrying but having a wide range of friends, including Malcolm Muggeridge, who was at Selwyn with him. Muggeridge's father was a prominent Labourite and Alec imbibed leftist sympathies in that circle. Vidler's first curacy was in Newcastle, working in the slums. He soon came to love his work with working class parishioners and was reluctantly transferred to St Aidan's, Birmingham, where he became involved in a celebrated stoush with the bishop E. W. Barnes, himself a controversialist of note. Vidler's Anglo-Catholic approach to ritual clashed with Barnes's evangelicalism.

Alec began a prolific career of publication in the 1920s and 30s. In 1931 he joined friends like Wilfred Ward at the Oratory House in Cambridge, steeping himself in religious history and theology, including that of Reinhold Niebuhr and "liberal Catholicism". In 1939 Vidler became warden of St Deiniol's Library, Hawarden (founded by a legacy from the famous statesman William Gladstone). Alec was also editor of the leading Anglican journal *Theology*, which he ran until 1964, exerting considerable progressive influence across those years. He also facilitated a number of religious think-tanks in these, and later, years. In 1948 he was appointed canon of St George's Chapel, Windsor, where he set up "his own unofficial theological college, which comprised middle-aged ordination candidates known as 'the Doves', or, less charitably, 'Vidler's Vipers'".[1] In 1956 he was invited to become Dean of King's College, Cambridge. He lectured in divinity and plunged into college life, attempting to combat the increasingly aggressive secularity of the student body:

> The beard, the flashing eyes, the black shirt, the white tie, all bring Alec irresistibly to mind, striding along King's Parade.... In these last years he remained a doughty

> controversialist and one glimpsed the almost puckish spirit of someone who was never a respecter of persons.[2]

He retired to Rye in 1967, leading an active life (mayor of Rye for some years), his beard and long habit making him a conspicuous figure. He died in 1991.[3]

* * *

Alec Vidler was a distinguished church historian. Although he disclaimed being a theologian, he was deeply versed in religious knowledge, writing and preaching on Christian belief and doctrine as well as being an authority on Catholic Modernism. He disliked being labelled in any way. In his early church career he was often dubbed an Anglo-Catholic, and later a "liberal Catholic" or simply a "liberal Anglican", then (around 1940) an advocate of Neo-orthodoxy, and after that of Christian Radicalism. He was, as has been well said, never the slave of fashionable notions and never a party activist.[4] His overall position became, it could be argued, an advocate of a synthesised Anglicanism that embodied the more authentic elements of Catholic Modernism, including acceptance of genuinely scholarly biblical criticism and history, and reconciliation between religious experience and a broader philosophical account of life and the nature of things.

He felt that the latter point was too often ignored. In this respect he had much in common with the English modernist Baron Friedrich von Hügel (1852-1925). Vidler said of von Hügel :

> [He] placed himself in the vanguard of the modernist movement.... It was just in so far as it ignored or treated with indifference the ontological reality of the supernatural world and the objectivity and transcendence of God, that von Hügel became ill at ease.[5]

Vidler discussed the multifarious types of Christianity in his great book *The Church in an Age of Revolution: 1789 to the Present Day.*[6] From his writings and memoirs it appears that his own position was sturdily in the Anglican tradition, and at variance with other schools such as liberal Protestantism and extreme Catholic Modernism, about which he nevertheless wrote with insight and understanding. As an historian he accepted the usual view that the Church of England occupied a unique place among Christian denominations. When at the Reformation western Christendom broke into Catholic and Protestant parts, "the Church of England adopted a middle course and attempted to combine the two forces which elsewhere were regarded as incompatible". Amid the shifting fortunes of history, it had continued this course:

> Its historical formularies, as well as it subsequent and recent official pronouncements, are generally marked by a studied ambiguity, which is evidently interpreted in an inclusive sense.... The consequence of its singular history is that Catholicism and Protestantism have each maintained a position within the Church of England as living religions, and at the same time neither has officially and finally been bound up with a hard and narrow theological system. The latitude of Anglican theology has been wider than any other Christian Church, and room has been found for those who are broadly attached to Christianity but not to Catholicism or Protestantism in particular.[7]

For Vidler, modern Anglican theology and attitudes generally had been shaped by the nineteenth century "Catholic Revival" or Oxford Movement, intensely spiritual but at first content to revive traditional Catholic orthodoxy. It was, in Vidler's memorable phrase, "academic, clerical and conservative".[8] Then came the influential and pioneering Lux Mundi (light of the world), 1891, "the first considerable attempt to adapt Catholic teaching in its Anglican form to the requirements of modern knowledge".[9]

Vidler wrote much on the theology of F. D. Maurice, whose stream of liberal theology influenced not only the Lux Mundi High Church theologians, but also flowed into a kind of Broad Church theology that was not unlike Adolph Harnack's European liberal Protestantism. (Vidler's book on *The Theology of F.D. Maurice* was to come out in 1949, when he was warden of St Deiniol's.) Maurice was one of his heroes. As remarked by Neville Masterman:

> Like Maurice he has often championed a minority view which has afterwards become popular; and as a result he seems to have lost interest in it. His method, though, has been all his own. Thus Vidler has been regarded as obscurantist when Liberal modernism was in fashion, then a modernist among obscurantists, an establishmentarian among disestablishers and a disestablisher among establishmentarians.[10]

In this way Vidler parted company with Harnack's Liberal Protestantism when it advocated a return to the pure teachings of Christ and a jettisoning of subsequent dogma, liturgy, institutionalism, and all that "useless addendum" in Matthew Arnold's phrase. Vidler was more in sympathy with modernism's essential defence of Catholic tradition "as a legitimate development of the initial response made to the impact of Jesus upon the lives and spirits" of people, while agreeing with its reformist agenda.[11]

Vidler's book on *Catholic Modernism* (1934) dealt briefly with some modernist influence upon Anglican thought. This impact was mainly upon a small group of High Anglicans who sympathised with modernism's attempt to adapt received Catholic theology to modern science and biblical scholarship, for which of course modernism had received Papal condemnation and repression (most notably in the papal encyclical *Pascendi gregis*, 1907). There were two main directions, Vidler observed, in which modernist influence upon Anglicanism could be traced: "(i) in the claim that biblical criticism must be an autonomous science and that the Catholic critic must be allowed the same freedom as other critics; and (ii) in the development of the argument from experience to the truth of Catholic dogma".[12] Among those High Anglicans who followed the modernist movement with sympathetic interest were the now little known figures of G. C. Rawlinson, T. A. Lacey and Will Spens.

Vidler himself was obviously influenced by the movement that he spent so much time studying, but he also accepted that it was in its own way a product of its time and culture. This was both a positive and a negative. As thinkers of their time, the modernists took fresh approaches and emphasised the need to reconcile religion with contemporary thought and feelings. But they also shared the defects of fashionable vogues such as:

> … pragmatism, Bergsonianism, and philosophical anti-intellectualism.... Thus the modernists tended in general to emphasize out of due proportion the doctrine of divine immanence, the purely evolutionary aspects of religion, and the practical and empirical aspects of dogma.... If dogma is rightly to be regarded as in the first instance a rationalization of religious experience, theology must also show the reasonableness of believing in the ultimate reality of the object of this experience.[13]

Vidler approvingly quoted Spens's nuanced modernist approach. In his *Belief and Practice* (1915) Spens, according to Vidler, arrived at the view that some of George Tyrrell's methods could lead to conclusions that were less subversive of traditional orthodoxy. (Tyrrell was a controversial English Catholic Modernist.) Spens's apologetic:

> … is based not on any metaphysical structure, nor on an appeal to the New Testament as itself justifying a supernatural Christology, but to the whole stream of Christian experience as requiring the theology, which is its intellectual expression, as the most adequate means of explaining and co-ordinating that experience. Religious experience, not a body of information or a series of propositions which were once upon a time revealed *ab extra*, constitutes the data of theology".[14]

Like science, Christian theology must pass the test that it produce a "sound general outlook", or "must be compatible with a general philosophy of the universe".[15] Vidler would return to the issue of science and religion in later writings.

The onset of the Second World War provoked Vidler into anguished ruminations concerning the crisis in western civilisation and religion. In February 1941 he ran a mission to students at Liverpool University. His addresses were collected (at first against his inclinations) into a book, entitled *Secular Despair and Christian Faith*, one of his most spontaneous works, printed virtually as given. Although church people in Britain were often complacent, Vidler believed that religion had become too diffused and unfocused. He noted that only a small minority now went to church or were practising members of any Christian communion. The country had become in practice secular, as had the west generally. How had this come about?

He chose the era of the Renaissance and Reformation as the defining watershed. As an historian he was aware of the pitfalls in ignoring continuities, and the folly of romanticising the Middle Ages. Nevertheless, he believed that the onset of secularisation in the west could be traced to the breakdown of "the medieval synthesis". As he wrote of the medieval era:

> ... allow for all that was sordid and cruel and primitive, it is still the case that Europe was then a whole as it never has been since. It had an integral culture. It was bound together by a common social system, a common religion, language, art, architecture, philosophy, law, literature, common institutions of all kinds. It was a hierarchical society in the sense that it was like a great pyramid, and at the top was God transcendent over the world, man's maker and judge and redeemer.... This visible world was dependent on another – invisible – world; that was taken for granted. To deny it was blasphemy. And blasphemy as well as faith was

> a terrific reality. It is almost impossible for us, who live in a world where faith and blasphemy of this kind have become practically meaningless, to imagine what the medieval atmosphere was like. For when God has been banished or transformed into a very doubtful hypothesis, blasphemy, too, ceases to have any point except as an idiotic survival, and sin becomes paltry and loses its magnificence when it is no longer rebellion against the living God – and death is sentimentalized when it is no longer a fateful transition to an eternal destiny.[16]

Vidler was no backward-looking romantic. He accepted that historical change was inevitable. The Renaissance and Reformation were necessary, in many ways beneficent: "The medieval synthesis was rotting from within... it had served its turn, and it had to give way to a new experiment". But the underlying religious consciousness persisted for centuries. Integration did not sharply pass into disintegration. There were rather a series of fresh and partial integrations: the humanist culture of the Renaissance, the new religious formations arising out of the Reformation, the rationalistic culture of the Enlightenment, the romantic, revolutionary and liberal movements of the eighteenth and nineteenth century. But a fundamental disintegration was continuing beneath the surface. By the warring twentieth century,

> … it had become almost meaningless to speak about an integral European culture.... The arts and the sciences, having achieved their autonomy, had all gone their own way; there was no common philosophy or religion; the one Church of the Middle Ages had given way to a multiplicity of disintegrating sects, and faith in God, so far from being the keystone in any arch, was an optional ornament which some people still cared to adorn a thoroughly secularized existence.... We had arrived at a material bounty, or at least at the possibility of it, but spiritually and morally we had arrived at the wasteland.[17]

A sense of despair had seized people. They coped with it, very often, by the demonic integrations of totalitarian ideologies, mystic idolatry of the state and power. Tyranny or slavery was preferred to unbridled chaos. Even the British, with their pragmatic complacency and hopes for a welfare or leisure state, were being swept up into this whirlpool as the world was sucked into another world war.

What humans had to face up to was that, as a species, they were both susceptible to dreams of perfection, but fundamentally incapable of resolving the problem of their own destiny. (He borrowed the Greek term *Abraxas* to describe this law of contradiction.) Man's creative powers turned into flagrant self-destruction. The wonders of modern civilisation had been accompanied by monstrous wars and atrocities. Humans left to themselves become inhuman or worse. This was not a present phenomenon but a permanent predicament in history. This was in fact the real meaning of "original sin", a matter of human pride and vanity constantly undoing our best intentions. Vidler told his audience that despair about this predicament was the first essential step towards exiting the realm of fantasy into what was – despite the scepticism of the age – the realm of fact, " the first essential step towards getting beyond man's delusions to God's reality".[18] His emotional message was that humans must recognise the unpalatable fact that it was only by a basic act of despair, "of repentance and submission to the living God," that they could come to live from a new centre, one of compassion rather than egotism.[19] In this there were undeniable echoes of Karl Barth's theology of crisis.[20] Vidler in fact was instrumental in getting Barth to send an open letter to Christians in Britain in 1941 – the same year as these lectures – encouraging resistance to Nazism, while criticising shallow sentiments about the virtues of western civilisation.

In 1941 Vidler was not optimistic about Christianity's chances of survival. Theology had badly neglected important social issues. It had failed to develop a Christian sociology. Attempts were being made to rectify this. (He had written earlier about the social doctrines of some types of Catholic Modernism, and would continue this theme much later in his book *A Century of Social Catholicism, 1820-1920*, published in 1964.) He detected a "real fermentation" of thought going on in the churches of the west.[21] Issues such as social justice and a planned society needed to be addressed:

> All would agree that in the long run Christians must aim at the growth of a new Christendom – which does not mean the resuscitation of a medieval Christendom or of feudalism – but at a unified culture inspired by and based on the authority of the Christian tradition and adapted to the changed technical and economic conditions of a new society.[22]

However he detected no signs of a great Christian revival in Britain or Europe (he said little about America). The future was likely to be secularist: "you cannot reverse in the course of a year or two the process of European secularizations which has been going on for generations".[23] As the secularised society proceeded to its final and sterile disintegration, Christians could only hope for a Phoenix-like revival from the ashes.

Vidler often considered the relationship between science and religion. While he accepted that science was widely seen as a dissolving agent upon religious belief, he did not accept that this was a necessary or logical consequence of science. He had respect for science. As he said in a series of lectures given in Cambridge in 1949, and published as *Christian Belief*:

> You will not hear from me any of those crabbing and belittling observations which some, at any rate, of the camp-followers of theology... are wont to make about the magnificent achievements of the natural and human sciences.[24]

In fact theology had only itself to blame for not making comparable advance. This was because theologians had simply not done the same amount of hard work and research, or given the same "disinterested devotion" to their subject as had scientists on theirs.

Nevertheless science did not have all the answers. To exist as a human being was to be surrounded by mystery (as Albert Schweitzer had famously said). There was such a thing as incomprehensible reality. Vidler held:

> … that when account is taken of all that is known or that is scientifically knowable, there still remain mysterious depths in the whole universe and in human existence which mortal man has not fathomed and which there is no reason to suppose he is capable of completely fathoming.[25]

The essential function of Christian belief was to cast light on those mysterious depths; or rather to testify to "the shining of sufficient light" to draw people to go on seeking, to direct and keep people "in the way of finding". Vidler's whole approach was this "way of finding".[26] The important thing for religion was not a set of hard and fast rules or abstract creeds, but a flexible way of constantly searching out the truth, a ceaseless striving after renewal. He had come to this conclusion after deep study of a range of Continental theologians. As his life went on he became even less attached to "abstract creeds", or "rounded-off" systems of doctrines, and ever more flexible and ecumenical.

He was unimpressed by "proofs" of God's existence. No such "proofs" could completely satisfy the criteria of rigorous philosophical analysis. Vidler was a great believer in applying the highest intellectual standards to religion (and not, as many sects did, accepting the shallowest beliefs):

> No belief about the nature of the world, no interpretation of all the facts of existence, is intellectually compelling or demonstrative. There are difficulties and unresolved enigmas in every great creed.... Probability is the guide of life.[27]

Thus we come to the necessity for doubt. This was something that so many Christians failed to comprehend. It was through our God-given intellects that we were enabled to doubt, "and that is a high and human prerogative". All belief was founded on preliminary doubt (as the theologian Susan Stebbing remarked). Sound faith would only grow after facing doubt: "if in this or any other time there is to be a renewal of Christian belief, of faith in a Living God, it will be in part the outcome of searching and rigorous doubting".[28]

This doubt should be applied like a blowtorch to the many bewitching doctrines of so-called spiritualists and mystics. There had been a batch of such doctrines floating about from late-nineteenth century Britain, and the west generally, ranging from theosophy to Druidism. Vidler was ready to appreciate the spiritual truths in other religions and philosophies (such as Buddhism). But he deplored the uncritical acceptance of much that was around:

> Because the Holy Spirit is the Spirit of Christ there can be no excuse now for confusing him with *mana,* with weird impersonal manifestations of psychic energy, with ideological dynamism, or with vague mystical sentiments.[29]

As the Gospel said, test the spirits whether they are of God. "Inspiration" as such was not a criterion of truth: "Claims to inspiration must be tested by the character and teaching of Christ, by the ways of God's working which he has revealed, and by the witness of the apostolic testimony".[30] Individuals alone could hardly expect to overcome the many barriers to attaining the full health and harmony that was the gift of God. Higher truths were more likely to be achieved by a corporate process, the work of groups and communities overcoming the rival ambitions, impulses and desires that were the lot of humanity. This was part of Vidler's defence of organised religion as opposed to the wild individualism of some Protestant sects. But humans would never attain to a final harmony or completion, even the greatest saints:

> To live here is to move, to learn, to change. Both individuals and institutions, however, are always being tempted to settle down, to close their minds, to become petrified.... It is the work of the Holy Spirit to disturb a man or an institution that is becoming settled or stiff.... The Holy Spirit works like an acid on all complacency. He points and presses men onwards into the unknown.[31]

What had Vidler to say about the failings and apparent decline of religion? He freely admitted the historic flaws in the history of the Christian church. Some came about because of the necessary need of the church to organise itself, to move from the inspiring but chaotic groups of the early church into a more effective broader organisation. As he said, for the sake of making a clear impact on the mind of humanity, and in the interest of the church's universal mission, it had to be definitely organised, to have a "palpable structure and ethos". However with new possibilities of good also came new possibilities of evil. The new structures also released powers and ambitions that the church had not had to handle before:

> … the history of the church has been darkened by all sorts of collapses and corruptions. Worst of all, and the root of all, have been lack of trust in the Holy Spirit, the Lord and Life-giver of the church, and the dependence of churchmen on other forces, and their greater attachment to a past which is obsolete than to the eternal which is always renovating.[32]

Vidler here anticipated the famous remark made by his friend George Orwell in *The Road to Wigan Pier* (1937) that, as with the Christian religion, the worst advertisement for socialism was its adherents. Certainly Vidler often expressed similar criticisms of his church and churchmen: "I am bored with parsons", he was to remark in a 1962 BBC TV show.

With large scale organisation came the temptation for the church to forget its distinctive character and to conform to the manners and methods of political systems, to abandon persuasion for coercion. Forgetting that its living spirit was God as its guide and governor, "the church allowed those men who were entrusted with the responsibility of leadership and government under [God] to acquire and wield unchecked forms of power". They set themselves up as lords over the church:

> This corrosion was the more subtle in that the language of piety and the docile sentiments of the faithful could easily be exploited in the interests of the hierarchy's or the pope's will to power. Nor is it only popes and bishops who have lorded it over God's people, but priests and deacons and laymen, too.[33]

Petrification of doctrine and rituals also set in:

> Thus the Bible and the creeds can be treated as infallible oracles like the Koran, instead of as witnesses which the Holy Spirit will enable the church to interpret in a living way and in the light of fresh insights and discoveries.[34]

Rites could become mechanical and even instruments that divided sects, instead of witnesses to the universal scope of Christ's saving work "and to the unity of mankind in the body of which he is the Head". However Vidler also saw the opposite danger – that beliefs and rites could become so attuned to the changing culture and climate of the ages, so relativistic and trendy, that they became futile:

> The church knows that it is not just a fluctuating product of historical relativity, but is a witness to the finality of God and his Law and of God's work in Christ for the race and for all ages.... Therefore there must always be a note of exclusion as well as of inclusion in the church.[35]

There was in Vidler's work, as in much other writing of the time, a recognition of religious decline, but no really incisive or deep analysis of the sociology of this change. It was a question of passing on hints, and valuable insights, but nothing systematic. Getting the word out, interpreting the Christian message more accessibly to people who were no longer so exposed to it: that seemed the greater priority. In his work at St Deiniol's, Windsor and Cambridge, he tried to gather Christians together in constant dialogue and renewal; to facilitate "faith's courteous and sensitive encounter with unbelief", searching for a contemporary presentation of the everlasting Gospel.[36]

Vidler had spoken of a sense of crisis in the churches during the 1930s, and urged that theology must change as the turbulent age around it changed. As David Edwards observed:

> In *God's Judgement on Europe* [1940] Dr Vidler, like Mr [T. E.] Eliot, saw Christendom destroyed not only by the militantly

> hostile creeds of Hitler and Stalin, but also by the secular ethos of a western liberalism in decay. A typical reference was to "a society which is being thoroughly collectivized and depersonalized by its subservience to the power of the machine" - a doom for which political and economic planning was no real solution.... The Divine wrath was prophetically observed, as it tore down the rotten structures of a Europe which had abandoned the Faith. In his description of the inability of liberal humanism to cope with this Apocalypse, Dr Vidler came very close to Amos or Jeremiah.[37]

In his book of 1950 *Christian Belief*, Vidler agreed that there was a "public sense of grievance that the church is not what it might be or ought to be". It was said to be boring and stale, no longer meeting the needs of the time, divided and confused. People connected the church, "not with the disturbing and renewing encounter of a Holy God", but with unattractive services, tedious homilies, the smell of hymn-books, old memories of strict observance: "And there is worse than that. The church makes large and lofty claims which are neutralized and even made to look absurd by its own conditions and its feeble practice". It claimed to have received a divine commission and to possess the secret of community, "but in a period like this when immense social changes are taking place and immeasurable disasters threaten... no plain word is forthcoming, but only what sound like archaisms or platitudes". The churches could not reconcile themselves one with another, "let alone reconcile the world". So the grave question must be asked "whether the church is anything but an institution like gothic or gothic-revival architecture which still survives from a civilization that is rapidly passing away – an institution which has not yet been replaced but will be replaced", attractive only to those who had nostalgia for the past, "or are without the courage or imagination to adapt themselves to the present and the future".[38]

Here Vidler was making a call to arms to fellow believers to revivify their ideas and the church. Part of the problem was the church failings already alluded to. Churchmen had tried to make their church, and themselves, higher than the Trinity itself. Yet the bible had warned that the church should always be subordinate to, and dependent upon, the Holy Spirit. Vidler blamed the divisions within the church partly upon a failure to comprehend this problem: "different beliefs about the church are rooted in different beliefs or unbeliefs about the Holy Spirit". Vidler also put blame upon society itself. People had become more hedonistic and self-centred. They were no longer prepared to make the sacrifices that the church demanded:

> There is that in us which resents the uncanny assertion that there is present and active in the human conscience the Spirit of a Holy God, who is pressing upon us when we would be left to ourselves, who is pressing us towards a way of common life in which we shall everywhere be responsible [not to the State nor to the will of a majority but] to an authority above all human authorities, and everywhere too responsible for one another, when all we wanted was to mind our own business and to pursue our own noble or sordid or dreamy enterprises.[39]

Vidler saw signs that the churches were beginning to transform themselves. But these signs were not enough to make him confident that the transformation would be carried through on the scale and with the speed required.

In 1956 Vidler became Dean of King's College, Cambridge:

> … a post that put him at the centre of the Cambridge ecclesiastical scene, and exposed him daily to full-bloodedly intellectual unbelief, for which King's had a reputation. In January 1958 he launched the most important network of his career, a group of radical theologians in Cambridge. His own *Essays in Liberality* (1957) had given some hints of the radicalism to come. The Cambridge group had been suggested by Hugh Montefiore and Howard Root, and also included John Burnaby and Harry Williams. After several years of deliberation the group produced *Soundings: Essays in Christian Understanding* (1962), edited by Vidler, which declared that traditional Christian theology was faced by a range of seemingly insuperable difficulties, and offered suggestions as to how these difficulties might be overcome.[40]

By 1963 Vidler was referring to "the radical unbelief of the contemporary world". He had helped to organise a course of lectures under the auspices of the Divinity Faculty of Cambridge University but addressed to a wider audience. Their purpose was not to be Christian apologetics, but – one of Vidler's dearest goals – to plumb the depths of objections to Christianity, enabling people to seek greater understanding of the fundamental doubts to which religious faith was exposed in a secular age. Mature belief (he felt) must genuinely face the worst that could be made against it. The sceptical case must be made even more forcibly than its exponents could put it themselves. (Today we might say that Dawkins needed to be out-Dawkinned!) Vidler insisted that the issues must not just be evaded, as many Christians in fact evaded them: "If there is to be a profound recovery of Christian belief – or a profound rejection of it – it will surely come out of such an experience rather than out of an awareness of only one side of the question". The Cambridge lectures were published as *Objections to Christian Belief*, and Vidler did the chapter on "Historical Objections" (the other contributors were D. M. Mackinnon of Corpus Christi, H. A. Williams of Trinity and J. S. Bezzant of St. John's).[41] The topic of unbelief was much in the air at the time. About 1,500 people attended the lectures per week, up to 20% of the student body, and the book was reprinted three times in two weeks.[42] However the Cambridge clerics were soon eclipsed by Bishop John Robinson's controversial (but more superficial) book *Honest to God* (1963).

In *Objections* Vidler canvassed the whole issue whether Christian faith depended upon the historical veracity of Christ's life, crucifixion and resurrection, or whether it could be founded simply upon Christ's teachings of certain moral and spiritual truths, and was not inescapably bound up with the historical facts of the New Testament. This issue had been a vexed one for Christianity since at least the rise of biblical criticism in the nineteenth century. Vidler was well versed in biblical scholarship and well aware of the uncertain nature of much of the evidence then available:

> … if we look closely into the question, we have to acknowledge that no beliefs about matters of history can be proved to be certainly true: strictly speaking, they can never have more than a very high degree of probability. Do Christians then live and die for what they must allow to be not certainly, but only probably, the case?[43]

No believer in absolute dogmas or the claims of "infallible" popes, Vidler also admitted the subjectivities and biases that could, and did, affect historians. It was a worry to him that, unlike on the Continent, British scholars of Christian origins were almost universally clergy. As he was wont to say, the elucidation of Christian origins was mostly carried on within the sound of church bells (in his case, as Dean of King's College, Cambridge, the bells of Great St Mary's and the solitary bell of King's College Chapel).

Vidler's approach – the product of a lifetime of study and contemplation – was that Christ's life must be put in the whole context of the Old and New Testaments, together with the subsequent history of the Christian movement. Judgments about the origins of Christianity needed to be influenced by assessments of the total Christian phenomenon in history. This did not make life easy. Christian history had a brighter and a darker side. On the brighter side (as even the agnostic T. H. Huxley conceded) there were the ideals of strength and patience, justice and pity for human frailty, compassion and self-sacrifice, ethical purity and nobility, the faith of martyrs and millions of followers. On the darker side, there was:

> … the quarrelsomeness of the Christians, their intolerance, their censoriousness, their legalism, their arrogance, the blatant immorality of doctrines which they have accepted with equanimity, and the Christian Church's all too frequent resemblance to the Jewish Church which crucified Christ.[44]

Vidler admitted the dilemma that thus confronted many believers. How they responded depended on various factors. The most important (he believed) were two: (1) the enduring impression or impact made by "the person of Jesus as he is portrayed in the Gospels"; and (2) the believer's "participation in the Christian mystery as a present reality", by what they found "in the shared experience of the community of believers – it may be in the eucharistic sacrament or in the Friends' meeting house".[45] It would depend on whether or not they found "something there which despite all puzzlements" held them and spoke to their deepest level of being. The element of participation was crucial, and might (as the theologian Paul Tillich had reflected) offset the element of incertitude and doubt. At this point Vidler commented:

> And here I might interject that I often find myself more in sympathy or en rapport with non-Christians who have a sense of the strangeness and incertitude of our world and of the duty of a large measure of agnosticism than I do with Christians who are cocksure about their beliefs.[46]

He may have had in mind friends of his such as Malcolm Muggeridge or Anthony Powell.

In his book *20th Century Defenders of the Faith* (1965), Vidler revisited Catholic Modernism, as well as English Liberal Catholicism, Neo-Orthodoxy, and Christian Radicalism – styles of thought that he had studied and been influenced by, and some of which he had participated in. The book also served as a place of personal reminiscences, and reflection on the modern age. He seemed in sympathy with the judgment of the English Liberal Catholic scholar John Neville Figgis (1886-1919), who in *Civilisation at the Cross Roads* (1912) had said: "We live in an age of unparalleled anarchy both moral and intellectual". Modern intellectuals, Figgis thought, could agree in nothing but rejection of religion (a sweeping verdict but characteristic of *fin de siècle* thought). Scientific materialism was influential but not widely held as a creed. Beyond that, said Figgis, all was chaos: "Positivists, agnostics, idealists, pessimists, optimists, sceptics, theists, atheists jostle one another and nobody knows what his next-door neighbour thinks".[47]

In Figgis's view – and Vidler seemed to agree – religion had been undermined philosophically by the rise of naturalism, founded on the success of physical science. Naturalism postulated the uniformity of nature, and this predominance of a single method had created prejudice against Christian faith. However, this was too simple, Figgis said. The universe existed on different levels. Scientific naturalism was qualified to deal with the mechanisms of nature, but it was powerless to account for the deeper spiritual aspects of human existence:

> Either the whole world, seen no less than unseen, is conceived as personal, spiritual, alive, ever fresh... or else it is seen as mechanical, impersonal, dead... The one is the world of Catholic Christianity, the other that of Pagan philosophy or scientific fatalism and its more spiritual or at least decorative variety - Pantheism.[48]

Vidler had been involved with movements in England that were roughly described as Neo-Orthodoxy and Christian Radicalism. As he was at pains to point out, these were not at all organised or coherent movements as such, but rather a variety of trends and loose dialogues between people with diverse positions. Neo-Orthodoxy could be described as the predominant fashion in theology during the Second World War and for a decade or so afterwards. Its frame of mind as a biblical theology was to assume the foundations of theology to be secure, and then confidently to work at repairing or reshaping the superstructure. It focused not only on important matters such as the ecumenical movement and church unity, but also tended to become obsessed with issues of worship, ritual, ecclesiastical and episcopal matters.

Vidler encountered these preoccupations in his role as editor of *Theology* at the time. As he recalled:

> I used to say to my friends that I was disconcerted by the fact that theological students, the younger clergy and the like, when I conversed with them, never seemed to shock me by coming out with any startling novelties or disturbing thoughts: on the contrary, I could shock them by the things I said much more than they ever shocked me by anything they said. It should have been the other way on, as I was now a fuddy-duddy who should be allergic to new ideas.[49]

Of course what Vidler really thought was that much more fundamental questions had been addressed by thinkers of earlier decades, even centuries – historical matters that were no longer being thoroughly taught. True, some basic issues were being addressed abroad, as in the work of theologians such as Paul Tillich, Martin Buber and Dietrich Bonhoeffer (Bonhoeffer's papers from prison, written before his martyrdom by the Nazis, had been published in England in 1953): "But none of this seemed to make much difference to our English theological climate".[50]

Vidler was essentially a facilitator. He described how, soon after returning to Cambridge in 1956, he gathered together a group of younger theologians who felt much as he did "about the lethargic or ostrich-like condition of English, or at least anglican, theology".[51] They began meeting to discuss more radical ways of raising, if not necessarily resolving, fundamental issues. This culminated, as we have seen, in the publication of *Soundings* in 1962. The term "Christian Radicalism" was coined at this time, in the midst of the *Honest to God* debate. David Edwards used the term in an essay about the uproar. Vidler believed that the whole debate, which evoked strong reactions ranging from rejoicing to horror, at least raised hopes of a "new deal" in the honest presentation of the Christian faith, "a salutary upheaval in the Church".[52] From about this time he began to participate in television discussions of religion. Also at about the same time, the context of Christian debate was being significantly influenced by the appearance of searching new writings. Vidler thought Gregor Smith to be an original and radical thinker, while a more general impact was being made by the posthumous writings of Teilhard de Chardin. More tumultuous were the ongoing reforms in Catholicism initiated by Pope John XXIII, which had just culminated in the Second Vatican Council (1962-65).

Vidler had considerable sympathy with the new "subjectivism" that had come into theology from younger scholars (with earlier impetus from Bonhoeffer). This enabled ordinary Christians to escape from the more "objectivist", philosophically tough, theologies, preoccupied with grounds for belief in God or the problem of evil. It was now possible for Christians to understand their faith:

> … as an individual, subjective vision of the kind of life worth living, which they derive from Jesus, and which gives them insight and courage to encounter whatever comes to them day by day in their personal experiences and their personal relations.[53]

As H. E. Root suggested, these new voices were more in touch with deeper feelings in Christendom, and part of a wider reaction against organised religion. In Vidler's words:

> Christians who accept this point of view are enabled to feel as insecure and so, paradoxically, as much at home in this secular, empirical, changing world as anyone else. They are no longer burdened with a sense of being in this age aliens or survivors who need still to be buttressed by archaic beliefs and ruled by traditional or collective mores and sheltered in the sanctuary of a stable institution. There is exhilaration in knowing that you are free and open to whatever may come, and no longer wedded to doctrines that are liable to be shaken by evidence or argument and to an ethic that is based on law instead of love.[54]

This, it will be seen, was something of a retreat from his earlier emphasis on collectivity. Elements of Tyrrell's thought also surfaced here.

Vidler believed that religious studies should include all the options and available readings, not just the objectivist or subjectivist way of responding, but also sceptical, theistic readings and attention to the world's other religions, Hindu, Buddhist, Muslim and the rest. (This was prophetic of the way in which religious studies in modern universities have since gone.) Vidler refused to come down on one side or the other, always trying to see the validity in each school, affirming rather than denying (in Coleridge's famous maxim). Nor was he "selling out to secularism":

> I can see that we are at present sociologically conditioned to an almost exclusive preoccupation with the secular, and for that reason – and with the past and the future in mind, not to mention the eternal – I mean to keep myself open to the possibility that more is available to human experience than is comprised within the secular perspective.[55]

What made him tick, what in fact had always made him tick, was history. He remained always an historian:

> It is the whole Christian movement in history of which I am thankful to be an inheritor.... That is why of all the defenders of the Christian religion whom I have considered in these lectures it is the Roman Catholic Modernists with whom I feel most kinship, not least because they could not see the end of their enterprise.[56]

---

[1] *Oxford Dictionary of National Biography*, entry by Matthew Grimley and Sam Brewitt-Taylor.

[2]*Times* obituary (29 July 1991), p. 16.

[3] For his life see, in addition to the above sources, A. R. Vidler, *Scenes from a Clerical Life: An Autobiography* (London, Collins, 1977).

[4] David L. Edwards, "*Theology* under Dr Vidler", *Theology*, 68 (1965), p. 7 and passim. This was a special issue commemorating Vidler's work for *Theology*.

[5] A. R. Vidler, *The Modernist Movement in the Roman Church: Its Origins and Outcome* (Cambridge, Cambridge University Press, 1934), p. 208. The book deals mainly with Alfred Loisy (1857-1940) and George Tyrrell (1861-1909), but also includes English modernists such as von Hügel, Alfred Fawkes (1849-1930) and Maude Petre (1863-1942), a close friend and biographer of Tyrrell.

[6] A. R. Vidler, *The Church in an Age of Revolution: 1789 to the Present Day* (London, Penguin, 1961).

[7] Vidler, *Modernist Movement*, pp. 241-242.

[8] Vidler, *The Church in an Age of Revolution*, p. 52.

[9] Vidler, *Modernist Movement*, p. 243. *Lux Mundi* was a collection of essays by young High Church theologians, masterminded by its editor Charles Gore (1853-1932), a prominent Anglican theologian. The ideas in the book had been thrashed out over twelve years: "They saw God's revelation of himself as progressive, and this enabled them to accept not only the methods of biblical criticism but its assured results as they then seemed to stand. They were thus able to bring enormous relief to educated Christians": Vidler, *The Church in an Age of Revolution*, p. 192.

[10] Neville C. Masterman, "The Mental Processes of the Reverend F. D. Maurice", *Theology*, 68 (1965), p. 53.

[11] W. N. Pittenger,"Modernism", *Theology*, 68 (1965), p. 55 and passim. As Pittenger points out, Catholic Modernism arose largely in reaction against Harnack's narrow and culturally conditioned theology (e.g., in the work of Loisy and Tyrrell).

[12] Vidler, *Modernist Movement*, p. 251.

[13] *Ibid*, p. 255.

[14] *Ibid*, p. 261,

[15] *Ibid.*

[16] A. R. Vidler, *Secular Despair and Christian Faith* (London, Student Christian Movement Press, 1941), pp. 10-11.
[17] *Ibid*, pp. 12-14.
[18] *Ibid*, p. 15.
[19] *Ibid*, p. 24.
[20] Vidler in a later work quoted Barth on human frailties and folly. It was only when people had taken in the perils of their existence, only when they knew they were hopelessly lost, only then (said Barth) that the preacher could proclaim the Word of God, which came from beyond the horizons of this world: A. R. Vidler, *20th Century Defenders of the Faith: Some Theological Fashions Considered in the Robertson Lectures for 1964 (Glasgow University)* [London, Student Christian Movement Press, 1965], pp. 86-87. Vidler also expressed such sentiments, although he was by no means an uncritical follower of Barth.
[21] Vidler, *Secular Despair*, p. 81.
[22] *Ibid*, pp. 82-83.
[23] *Ibid*, p. 84.
[24] A. R. Vidler, *Christian Belief* (London, Student Christian Movement Press, 1954;1st ed., 1950), p. 10.
[25] *Ibid*, pp. 11-12.
[26] *Ibid.*
[27] *Ibid*, p. 13.
[28] *Ibid*, pp. 14-15.
[29] *Ibid*, p. 66.
[30] *Ibid*, pp. 66-67.
[31] *Ibid.*
[32] *Ibid*, p. 83.
[33] *Ibid.*
[34] *Ibid.*
[35] *Ibid*, p. 84.
[36] A. R. Vidler, "Editorial", *Theology*, 68 (1965), p. 2; and Edwards, "*Theology* under Dr Vidler", p. 11.
[37] Edwards, "*Theology* under Dr Vidler", pp. 4-5.
[38] Vidler, *Christian Beliefs*, pp. 71-72.
[39] *Ibid.*.
[40] *Oxford Dictionary of National Biography.*, entry on Vidler by Matthew Grimley and Sam Brewitt-Taylor. They add that *Soundings* was "the most intellectually heavyweight work that the 'radical ferment' in the theology of the 1960s produced, and caused a significant stir in the ecclesiastical press", though it did not turn out, in Vidler's later opinion, anything like as radical as originally intended.
[41] D. M. Mackinnon, H. A. Williams, A. R. Vidler, J.S. Bezzant, *Objections to Christian Belief* (London, Constable, 1963), pp. 8-9.
[42] S. D. J. Green, *The Passing of Protestant England* (Cambridge, Cambridge University Press, 2011), pp. 292-293. Green is recommended on the whole issue of religious decline from c.1920-1960.
[43] McKinnon, *et al, Objections to Christian Belief*, p. 65.

---

[44] *Ibid*, p. 74.
[45] *Ibid,* p. 76.
[46] *Ibid,* p. 77.
[47] Quoted from Figgis in A. R. Vidler, *20th Century Defenders of the Faith: Some Theological Fashions Considered in the Robertson Lectures for 1964* (London, Student Christian Movement Press, 1965), pp. 61-63. Vidler saw an affinity between the neglected Figgis and thinkers such as the Anglican P.T. Forsyth and the Catholic G. K Chesterton: "All three were highly rhetorical and addicted to startling epigrams. They supplied a wholesome challenge and corrective to prevalent trends in Christian apologetic, but they tended to depreciate the need for restating the grounds for Christian belief in as cool and lucid and precise a manner as was possible" (p.64). The reference to cool, lucid and precise gives an insight into Vidler's personality as well as thought (although he could be a combative public debater).
[48] *Ibid.*
[49] *Ibid*, p. 102.
[50] *Ibid*, p. 103.
[51] *Ibid*, p. 104.
[52] *Ibid*, p. 107.
[53] *Ibid*, p. 114.
[54] *Ibid*, p. 116.
[55] *Ibid,* pp. 120-21.
[56] *Ibid.*

11. T. S. Eliot: After Strange Gods

Thomas Stearns Eliot (1888-1965) is today famous as a poet and literary critic, a Nobel prize winner, paradoxically born of an old Boston family but, having emigrated to England at age 24, becoming almost more English than the English. He is remembered, of course, for poems such as *The Waste Land* (1922), *The Hollow Men* (1925) and the celebrated play *Murder in the Cathedral* (1935). Less well known today is the fact that he wrote profusely on religious and ethical topics, and about the state of western civilisation.

He saw himself as living in an age of moral decline. Like others around at the time, he campaigned for a re-Christianisation of society. If people like R. H. Tawney represented the left in this campaign, Eliot's position was essentially conservative. He stood for tradition, but not uncritically. Just sticking in the past was a fatal error. Tradition needed to be refashioned to meet modern needs, but its essentials and core values needed to be conserved.

He put some of these views in his literary criticism, in works such as *After Strange Gods* (1934), written, of course, at a fraught time for western culture with the rise of Fascist and Communist totalitarianism, rampant materialism and the obvious decline of religion. The book put into print a series of lectures that he had given in Virginia about writers such as D. H. Lawrence, Ezra Pound, W. B. Yeats and James Joyce. Eliot was rebelling against the amoralism of movements such as modernism, movements that he saw as repudiating communal values in favour of conceited or degenerate individualism. The decay of mainstream Christianity – much of which could be sheeted home to schismatic Protestantism – had resulted in an amoral Anglo-Saxon literature. Amongst writers, Eliot commented, "the rejection of Christianity –Protestant Christianity – is the rule rather than the exception".[1]

He openly acknowledged his intellectual debt to his former teacher at Harvard, Irving Babbitt, founder of "New Humanism", an anti-romantic in the Burkean mould politically.[2] But it was far from an uncritical admiration on Eliot's part. Babbitt, he felt, had moved too far from core Christian values. Babbitt had taught his Harvard students about French culture. He was "saturated" in it and was "thoroughly cosmopolitan" in thought and dialogue. Eliot approved, as he approved also of Babbitt's belief in tradition:

> He believed in tradition; for many years he stood almost alone in maintaining against the strong tendency of the time a right theory of education, and such effects of decadence as are manifest in [D. H.] Lawrence's work he held in abomination.[3]

And yet, to Eliot's mind, the very width of Babbitt's culture, and "his intelligent eclecticism, are themselves symptoms of a narrowness of tradition, in their extreme reaction of that narrowness". (Rather like G. K. Chesterton, Eliot was fond of paradox. This made his criticism difficult for readers.) Eliot continued: "His attitude towards Christianity seems to me that of a man who had had no *emotional* acquaintance with any but some debased and uncultured form".[4]

In discussing writers such as Babbitt and Ezra Pound, T. S. Eliot ventured to generalise that, with the disappearance of the idea of original sin and of the idea of intense moral struggle, the people being portrayed at the time in both poetry and prose – and especially by the more serious writers – tended to become less and less real. Why was this? Because:

> … it is in fact in moments of moral and spiritual struggle depending upon spiritual sanctions, rather than in those "bewildering minutes" in which we are all very much alike, that men and women come nearest to being real. If you do away with this struggle, and maintain that by tolerance, benevolence, inoffensiveness and a re-distribution or increase of spending power, combined with a devotion, on the part of an elite, to Art, the world will be as good as anyone could require, then you must expect human beings to become more and more vaporous.[5]

To illustrate this, tongue in cheek, Eliot professed to find the archetype of this sort of society in Ezra Pound's great work, his *Cantos*:

> It consists (I may have overlooked one or two species) of politicians, profiteers, financiers, newspaper proprietors and their hired men, *agents provocateurs*, Calvin, St. Clement of Alexandria, the English, vice-crusaders, liars, the stupid, pedants, preachers… bishops, lady golfers, Fabians, conservatives and imperialists; and all "those who have set money-lust before the pleasures of the senses".[6]

It was a Hell without tragedy, without dignity, in some ways admirable or comfortable. Eliot discerned three principles behind the apparent confusion of types. They could be broken down into "(1) the aesthetic, (2) the humanitarian, (3) the Protestant". If this Hell was affined to modern complacency, it had an essential fallibility: "If you do not distinguish between individual responsibility and circumstances in Hell, between essential Evil and social accidents, then the Heaven (if any) implied will be equally trivial and accidental".[7]

Eliot discusses another common feature of his age – one commented on by Chesterton, Tawney and others: the tendency to seek out, or to manufacture, "alternative" or *ersatz* religions to replace traditional ones. Eliot noted this key tendency in the work of W. B. Yeats. The problem arose, Eliot thought, out of Yeats's situation as an expatriate from Ireland, born of Irish Protestant stock but brought up in London. For him Ireland was rather a holiday home, which he romanticised and sentimentalised, turning it into a source of constructed myths. As Yeats himself reminisced in his autobiography:

> I was unlike others of my generation in one thing only. I am very religious, and deprived by [T. H.] Huxley and [John] Tyndall, whom I detested, of the simple-minded religion of my childhood, I had made a new religion, almost an infallible church of poetic tradition, of a fardel [bundle] of stories, and of personages, and of emotions, inseparable from their first expression, passed on from generation to generation by poets and painters with some help from philosophers and theologians.[8]

Eliot pictures Yeats:

> The rationalistic background, the Pre-Raphaelite imagery, the interest in the occult, the equally early interest in Irish nationalism, the association with minor poets in London and Paris, make a curious mixture. Mr. Yeats was in search of a tradition, a little too consciously perhaps - like all of us. He sought for it in the conception of Ireland as an autonomous political and social unity, purged from the Anglo-Saxon pollution.[9]

What was the result? At least for a long time, "a somewhat artificially induced poeticality... much of Mr. Yeats's verse is stimulated by folklore, occultism, mythology and symbolism, crystal-gazing and hermetic writings", beautiful but artificial and deliberately evoking a trance-like indifference to reality. This was to become repudiation, not merely of current civilisation, but of life itself, in favour of a supernatural world, "a world of symbolic phantasmagoria". Eliot added:

> It was not a world of spiritual significance, not a world of real Good and Evil, of holiness or sin, but a highly sophisticated lower mythology summoned, like a physician, to supply the fading pulse of poetry with some transient stimulant so that the dying patient may utter his last words.[10]

It was, Eliot flatly declared, simply the wrong supernatural world.

Eliot turns to D. H. Lawrence. Our first reaction may well be "wow: this is not the usual view of Lawrence". The author of *Lady Chatterley's Lover* is described thus:

> Lawrence lived all his life, I should imagine, on the spiritual level; no man was less a sensualist. Against the living death of modern material civilisation he spoke again and again, and even if these dead could speak, what he said is unanswerable.[11]

But it turns out that "the man's vision is spiritual, but spiritually sick". It seems that Lawrence's early belief in Life "may have passed over, as serious belief in Life must, into a belief in Death".[12] (This is of course, we may add, a variant on Freud's *Thanatos*, or death wish.) However Eliot felt that there was still much to be learnt from Lawrence, especially from his critique of modern materialistic capitalism:

> That we can and ought to reconcile ourselves to Liberalism, Progress and Modern Civilisation is a proposition which we need not have waited for Lawrence to condemn; and it matters a good deal in what name we condemn it. I fear that Lawrence's work may appeal not to those who are well and able to discriminate, but to the sick and debile and confused; and will appeal not to what remains of health in them, but to their sickness.[13]

People would tend to invent their own "Lawrencean" doctrines (some, we know, turned them into Fascist doctrines, and indeed Lawrence had his own inclinations in this direction).

Eliot then turned to a wider perspective on modern society:

> The number of people in possession of any criteria for discriminating between good and evil is very small; the

> number of the half-alive hungry for any form of spiritual experience, or what offers itself as spiritual experience, high or low, good or bad, is considerable. My own generation has not served them very well. Never has the printing-press been so busy, and never have such varieties of buncombe and false doctrine come from it.[14]

Eliot finished his Virginia lectures with a brief comment on writers. He and his fellow writers lived "in an age of unsettled beliefs and enfeebled tradition". For the "man of letters, the poet, and the novelist", it was a situation dangerous for themselves and their readers. Was tradition the saviour? Eliot was very aware of people who sentimentally admired some real or imaginary past, "fakers" of tradition:

> Tradition by itself is not enough: it must be perpetually criticised and brought up to date under the supervision of what I call orthodoxy.... Most "defenders of tradition" are mere conservatives, unable to distinguish between the permanent and the temporary, the essential and the accidental.[15]

In a final throw-away remark, Eliot attacked the cult of personality that had grown up about writers:

> The personality thus expressed, the personality which fascinates us in the work of philosophy or art, tends naturally to be the *unregenerate* personality, partly self-deceived and partly irresponsible, and because of its freedom, terribly *limited* by prejudice and self-conceit, capable of much good or great mischief according to the goodness or impurity of the person: and we are all, naturally, impure.[16]

His humble suggestion in the face of such deep cultural problems was to try to maintain standards of ethics and criticism. T. S. Eliot, to his credit, tried endlessly to do so.

---

[1] T. S. Eliot, *After Strange Gods: A Primer of Modern Heresy – The Page-Barbour Lectures at the University of Virginia* (London, Faber and Faber, 1934), p. 38.

[2] Irving Babbitt (1865-1933) was an American literary critic, based in Harvard and quite influential at the time. Eliot wrote an essay on Babbitt's 1924 book about democracy and leadership, in which he criticised Babbitt's humanism as not sufficiently receptive to Christian dogma, also referring to critics such as

Laski, Sinclair Lewis, Mencken and Edmund Wilson: "The Humanism of Irving Babbitt", in T. S. Eliot, *Selected Essays* (London, Faber and Faber, 1932; reprinted 1950), pp. 419-538.

[3] T. S. Eliot, *After Strange Gods*, p. 39.

[4] *Ibid.*

[5] *Ibid*, p. 42.

[6] *Ibid*, p. 43.

[7] *Ibid.*

[8] *Ibid*, p. 44, quoted from Yeats's *The Trembling of the Veil.*

[9] *Ibid.*

[10] *Ibid*, pp .45-46.

[11] *Ibid*, p. 60.

[12] *Ibid.*

[13] *Ibid*, p. 61.

[14] *Ibid.*

[15] *Ibid*, p. 62.

[16] *Ibid*, pp. 62-63.

12. C. S. Lewis: "Surprised by Joy"

C. S. Lewis is most famous for his Narnia stories. But at the time of his death in 1963 he was also regarded as a leading Christian apologist in the Anglo-American world. This was largely because of his wartime broadcasts for the BBC, and because of books such as *The Screwtape Letters* (1942), *Mere Christianity* (1952) and his autobiographical *Surprised by Joy* (1955). His reputation took a nosedive during the swinging sixties. This has been explained as due to such factors as rising secularism and philosophical movements like logical positivism. By the 1980s, however, a Lewis revival had taken place. His Narnia books became enormously popular, spawning films and TV series. Logical positivism was shoved aside by newer fashions, and there was a religious revival in the United States. Lewis was the right man at the right time. As the distinguished theological and Lewis scholar, Alister McGrath, has contended, Lewis had a knack, amounting almost to genius, for putting Christian essentials into accessible language using his remarkable literary talents and his insights into a broad western cultural tradition.[1]

He absorbed concepts abounding in the philosophical traditions of idealism and realism that were around in the late nineteenth century; and he made rich use of classical and Norse mythology (as did his contemporary and friend J. R. R. Tolkien). Lewis may be judged to have affirmed and expanded the existential appeal, and the philosophical grounding, of the Christian faith – no mean achievement in an age of growing unbelief and scepticism.

In this essay I would like to take a look at his book *Surprised by Joy*, in which Lewis tries to tell the story of his upbringing, early loss of faith, and a long and complex transition to theism and then conversion to Christianity. One focal point is his recurring sense of supra-rational reality, moments of revelation that aroused in him feelings of awe and a quest for meaning and the eternal. It was a sensation that had been experienced by many mystics and much written about in poetry and Romantic literature, subjects that Lewis taught at Oxford and Cambridge universities.

Brief Life

Clive Staples ("Jack") Lewis (1898-1963) was born in Belfast, the son of an Ulster Presbyterian solicitor, a loquacious eccentric with whom C. S. always had a prickly, at times impossible, relationship. He and his older brother Warren ("Warnie") escaped into a world of fantasy that they created in their picturesque surroundings and household. Their beloved mother, a maths and logic graduate of Queen's College, tragically died when Jack was nine, and he spent most of his following years unhappily in private colleges in England. After an innovative period of tuition under William Kirkpatrick in Surrey – a happy time that gave him a thorough grounding in the classics – he won a scholarship to University College, Oxford, in late 1916. He served in the trenches in 1917-18, until wounded in the battle of Arras in April 1918. Returning to Oxford after the war, he achieved brilliant results in classics and literature. At the same time he engaged with gusto in the glittering post-war intellectual milieu that he encountered there. In 1925 he was elected a fellow of Magdalen College, Oxford, tutoring in English language and literature. He was to spend the rest of his life in academia – thirty years at Magdalen, the rest as professor of English and Renaissance literature at Cambridge. In autobiographical musings, he remarked that this was the only occupation that he was any good at.

He wrote a number of highly regarded scholarly works. They included his medieval study *The Allegory of Love* (1936), his Bangor lectures *A Preface to Paradise Lost* (1942), his Durham lectures *The Abolition of Man* (1943), and his classic *English Literature in the Sixteenth Century* (1954).

The complex story of his religious transitions has been closely documented – ranging from an early austere Protestantism (that he felt damaged him for life psychologically) to teenage atheism; a growing need for something more than what he later called his "glib and shallow rationalism"[2]; then via prodigious reading in philosophy, poetry, romantic literature, mythology and fantasy to a reluctant theism; and finally, again painfully and fearfully, to Christianity, then on to his role as a leading Christian apologist. During the period 1936-1939, after his conversion, he and a number of friends – famously called The Inklings – met regularly in Lewis's Magdalen rooms and at an Oxford pub, The Eagle and Child, to discuss their writings and the eternal issues of life and death. The group included his long-time friend, and author of *The Lord of the Rings*, J. R. R. Tolkien, a key figure in his conversion (the other Inklings included Hugo Dyson, Nevill Coghill, R. E. Havard and Charles Williams).

Like other scholars at the time (and since), Lewis found that his popular writings, even the semi-scholarly ones, generated academic scorn, and certainly hindered his promotion to a chair at Oxford. His light-hearted *Screwtape Letters* (1942) – with wise-cracking exchanges between a senior devil and his apprentices – was a satire too far for many colleagues. Then came his famous *Chronicles of Narnia* (1950-1956), usually interpreted as Christian allegories for children, full of magic, imagination and adventures (*The Lion, the Witch and the Wardrobe*, 1950, being the best known).[3] After the success of his 1954 book on sixteenth century English literature, Lewis was headhunted for the Cambridge chair and later became a fellow of Magdalen College, Cambridge, where he remained until his death. Having overcome an early shyness, he became a gregarious, if eccentric, figure in Cambridge, and was nationally known, a broadcaster and public speaker. Like Chesterton, he enjoyed beer and food and convivial company. The death from cancer of his American wife Joy led him to write (under a penname) *A Grief Observed* (1961), the basis for the TV and film drama *Shadowlands*.[4] He died on 22 November 1963, just as the world's attention was focussed on the assassination of John. F. Kennedy.

Surprised By Joy

C. S. Lewis seems to have spent his life yearning for a sense of other-worldly joy and bliss. He attained this, momentarily, in his intense interest in Norse sagas, Wagnerian legends and music, George MacDonald's fantasy stories, and in flashes of landscape. He admitted, in his autobiography *Surprised by Joy* (1955), that for a long time he had made the mistake of too strenuously and consciously striving for this sense of transcendental joy. It was not to be attained in this way. It came unexpectedly. It was elusive. It came, not as the end-product of reading, acting, striving, imagining, but as a side-product of these things, something that just happened. Nor should you expect it to last. Trying to make it last didn't work. It faded away. It could not be captured. Many mystics had discovered this.[5]

In *Surprised by Joy* Lewis records that his first life-changing experience happened when he was about seven.[6] He had become a prodigious reader (his father, never explained, had a house full of books of all sorts). Jack and his older brother Warnie created imaginary "Animal-Land" worlds, full of adventures. But Jack also went in for "reverie, day-dream, wish-fulfilling fantasy". One summer day he had a very Proustian "memory of a memory". As he stood beside a flowering currant bush,

> … there suddenly arose in me without warning, and as if from a depth not of years but of centuries, the memory of that earlier morning at the Old House when my brother had brought his toy garden into the nursery. It is difficult to find words strong enough for the sensation which came over me; Milton's "enormous bliss" of Eden… comes somewhere near it. It was a sensation, of course, of desire;

> but desire for what? Not certainly, for a biscuit-tin filled with moss… and before I knew what I desired, the desire itself was gone, the whole glimpse withdrawn, the world turned commonplace again, or only stirred by a longing for the longing that had just ceased. It had taken only a moment of time; and in a certain sense everything else that had ever happened to me was insignificant in comparison.[7]

Lewis cited two other instances: a desire to possess the season autumn, sparked by a Beatrix Potter book; and being uplifted into "huge regions of northern sky" when he read a passage in Longfellow's *Saga of King Olaf.* What were the qualities common to these three experiences?

> … it is that of an unsatisfied desire which is itself more desirable than any other satisfaction. I call it Joy, which is here a technical term and must be sharply distinguished both from Happiness and from Pleasure…. I doubt whether anyone who has tasted it would ever, if both were in his power, exchange it for all the pleasures in the world. But then Joy is never in our power and pleasure often is.[8]

This experience faded from his mind during his agonising years at an English boarding school. *Surprised by Joy* gives an interminable description of his sufferings and loneliness, as well as a vividly unpleasant account of the dark side of the "Public School" system of the day (the pre-1914 years) with its "fagging", canings and whippings, pederasty and the rest. It was in these years that he embraced atheism, partly, as he admits, to empower himself against authority generally, but more specifically school authority. He described the Christian God as "a transcendental Interferer".[9] Lewis's imaginary life had become a "sandy desert". Authentic Joy had vanished from his life.

Then he stumbled upon Wagner's Siegfried and the Twilight of the Gods. It was a mere mention in a magazine. He knew nothing of the Ring nor of Wagner. Nevertheless: "Pure 'Northerness' engulfed me: a vision of huge, clear spaces hanging above the Atlantic in the endless twilight of Northern summer, remoteness, severity". He had met this long, long ago in Longfellow's elegiac poem *Tegner's Drapa.*[10] With that plunge back into his own past:

> … there arose at once, almost like heartbreak, the memory of Joy itself… that I was returning at last from exile and desert lands to my own country; and the distance of the Twilight of the Gods and the distance of my own past Joy,

> both unattainable, flowed together into a single, unendurable sense of desire and loss.... And at once I knew (with fatal knowledge) that to "have it again" was the supreme and only important object of desire.[11]

Thereafter, with characteristic obsessiveness, he immersed himself in the worlds of Wagner, Norse mythology and western literature. His intense romantic side was matched by a strong rational side, imparted first to him in an austere and almost autistic way by the private tutor his father sent him to study under in beautiful Surrey after the trauma of his school years. The retired Scottish headmaster William Kirkpatrick introduced him with ferocious intensity into the fascinating world of classical literature. Lewis became so expert that he easily won a scholarship to University College, Oxford in 1916. After his war service in 1917-18 (during which he was wounded, both physically and psychologically), Lewis went on (as we have seen) to a distinguished career in English literature in Oxford, and, in his later years, at Cambridge. He was often to remark upon the internal tensions he felt between his romantic and his classical rationalist sides.

By the time he had become an Oxford man he had tasted the temptations of materialism, the occult and sex. He finally became antipathetic to "everything occult", especially when at Oxford, "I came to meet Magicians, Spiritualists, and the like".[12] Sex was a pleasure but it was not Joy:

> You might sum up the gains of this whole period by saying that henceforward the Flesh and the Devil, though they could still tempt, could no longer offer me the supreme bribe. I had learned that it was not in their gift... I now knew that Joy did not point in that direction.[13]

Another of the life-changing incidents in his life that he recounts (as McGrath says, rather like Augustine pinning down incidents in his Confessions) was his encounter with George MacDonald's *Phantastes: a Faerie Romance*.[14] Lewis often recounted how, at some time before he went to the war, he bought *Phantastes* at a bookstall in Leatherhead Station and read it on a train trip in Dorking Valley. As we say these days, it "blew him away", bringing together many strands in his imaginative history. In his own words, it was as if:

> I had died in the old country and could never remember how I came alive in the new.... I did not yet know (and I was long in learning) the name of the new quality, the bright

> shadow, that rested on the travels of Anodos. I do now. It was Holiness.... It was as though the voice which had called me from the world's end were now speaking at my side. It was with me in the room, or in my own body, or behind me. If it had once eluded me by its distance, it now eluded me by proximity – something too near to see, too plain to be understood, on this side of knowledge. It seemed to have been always with me; if I could ever have turned my head quick enough I should have seized it. Now for the first time I felt that it was out of reach not because of something I could not do, but because of something I could not stop doing. If I could only leave off, let go, unmake myself, it would be there.[15]

There are obvious parallels here of course with Buddhist philosophy (as Joseph Needham experienced in his own odyssey).

Something else MacDonald did was to bring Lewis into closer touch with the palpable world of things: woods, cottages, bread on the table or coals in the grate. Now he saw:

> ... the bright shadow coming out of the book into the real world and resting there, transforming all common things and yet itself unchanged. Or, more accurately, I saw the common things drawn into the bright shadow.... That night my imagination was, in a certain sense, baptised; the rest of me, not unnaturally, took longer. I had not the faintest notion what I had let myself in for by buying *Phantastes*.[16]

He was progressively to realise that the human quest for meaning, the sense of awe and the eternal, the striving for a sense of supra-rational reality – the subject of poetry, Romantic literature and idealistic philosophy – all these were but tastes of Divine reality.[17]

Alister McGrath has written a perceptive study of Lewis's intellectual world. In it he analyses the impact upon the impressionable Lewis, during his early years at Oxford after the war, of "Oxford Realism", a philosophical movement now neglected. It was a reaction against the fashionable English Idealism of the Edwardian era associated with thinkers such as T. H. Green and Bernard Bosanquet. The "new realists" included famous names such as G. E. Moore and Bertrand Russell, but also lesser known ones such as G. F. Stout, John Cook Wilson (New College) and Lewis's tutor at University College, Edgar Carritt. Lewis had absorbed some Idealist values, including those of Plato and Hegel, ideas of a world of appearances here-and-now reflecting more eternal values in a higher world of the Absolute. However Lewis now reacted against such ideas in favour of the new school, which held that the universe known to the senses existed as reality, the only reality, independent of human knowledge of it. (Interestingly this preceded Einstein's thesis that the "reality" of the physical world varied according to the observer, to observation of the "facts"). McGrath shows how Lewis moved, sometimes erratically, through a number of contemporary controversies over logic, moral philosophy, and aesthetics in a complex transition back through idealism to theism, and eventually to Christianity. Many of the views that he later criticised, it turns out, he had himself held as a young man. He intimates this in *Surprised by Joy*.[18]

Back at Oxford, Lewis's generation was the generation of returned soldiers. Many of his friends were experimenting with all sorts of new (and also old) ideas. Lewis would spend long days and nights debating issues of ontology, aesthetics, psychology, ethics and religion with companions like Owen Barfield, Arthur Hamilton Jenkin, Neville Coghill and A. C. Harwood. Reading Henri Bergson turned him away from stark realism (the sort that could only end in what Lewis felt was a sterile behaviourism) into acceptance of a universal Whole: "… one Divine attribute, that of necessary existence, rose above my horizon". This was still far short even of Theism. Necessary existence was "attached to the wrong subject; to the universe, not to God", as Lewis later realised: "But the mere attribute was itself of immense potency".[19] He called his philosophy of the "New Look" a sort of Stoical Monism. It gave him great peace. It was the nearest thing he had had to a religious experience since his very early years.

To Lewis's horror his friend Owen Barfield had moved from scepticism to embrace a revised form of theosophy, Rudolf Steiner's anthroposophy, which explored new modes of spiritual perception. Steiner's philosophy was never acceptable to Lewis,[20] but Barfield forced him to confront some essential issues. He undermined Lewis's modernist "snobbery", that saw the present age as superior to all that had gone before (a crucial factor, given Lewis's later eminence as a Renaissance literary scholar); and Barfield convinced Lewis of the inadequacy of the ontology of realism. It was inconsistent and unsatisfactory as a theory of knowledge.

Lewis had by now given up realism and accepted The Absolute:

> It is astonishing (at this time of day) that I could regard this position as something quite distinct from Theism. I suspect there was some kind of wilful blindness. But there were in those days all sorts of blankets, insulators, and insurances

> which enabled one to get all the conveniences of Theism, without believing in God.[21]

The emotion that went with a sort of Hegelian Absolute Mind was religious, but it was a religion that cost nothing: "We could talk religiously about the Absolute: but there was no danger of Its doing anything about us". It was not God the Interferer (something he still feared). Nevertheless he had got from the Idealists one great wholesome thing. The Absolute represented:

> ... the reconciliation of all contraries, the transcendence of all finitude, the hidden glory which is the only perfectly real thing there is.... And so the great Angler played His fish and I never dreamed that the hook was in my tongue.[22]

Lewis was beginning to find in his omnivorous reading that the richest and most rewarding authors for him were not those he, in his modernist, sceptical phase, should have approved of, such as Shaw, Wells, Mill, Gibbon and Voltaire, but others: George MacDonald, Chesterton, Johnson, Spenser, Milton, Langland, Donne, Thomas Browne and George Herbert (as well as Plato, Aeschylus and Virgil among the classical writers). He loved them while dismissing their irritating tendency to have a bee in their bonnets about religion, or something like it. So many of them insisted on mediating life through "the Christian mythology":

> Absurdly (yet many Absolute Idealists have shared this absurdity) I thought that "the Christian myth" conveyed to unphilosophical minds as much of the truth, that is of Absolute Idealism, as they were capable of grasping, and even that put them above the irreligious. Those who could not rise to the notion of the Absolute would come nearer to the truth by belief in "a God" than by disbelief. Those who could not understand how, as Reasoners, we participated in a timeless and therefore deathless world, would get a symbolic shadow of the truth by believing in a life after death.[23]

Lewis's account of his final conversion is surprisingly brief, a bit vague at times, and omits much autobiographical detail. As scholars have also shown recently, his chronology is unreliable, like his memory (nor is it impossible that he had a covert agenda going on, as do many autobiographers). What does seem agreed is that his friendship in the twenties with J. R. R. Tolkien was crucial. As Lewis wryly noted, Tolkien broke down two of his prejudices: one, an Ulster prejudice against "Papists", and two, a distrust of philologists. Tolkien was both. Both men had also served on the Western Front and been profoundly affected by it, as reflected in their sagas, *Lord of the Rings* and *Narnia.*[24]

Lewis then described how a number of significant moves made in his imaginary chess match with God took place. Readings from disparate sources resulted in him being able to link up previously unconnected emotions and philosophies. Reading the *Hippolytus* of Euripides re-triggered the semi-mystical feelings he had for so long repressed: "...the long inhibition was over, the dry desert lay behind, I was once more into the land of longing".[25] Reading Samuel Alexander's *Space, Time and Deity* (1920) convinced him philosophically that having feeling about an object could not co-exist with introspection about that feeling. This solved the elusiveness of Joy. You could not hope for joy and think about hoping for it at the same moment:

> This discovery flashed a new light back on my whole life. I saw that all my waitings and watchings for Joy, all my vain hopes to find some mental content on which I could, so to speak, lay my finger and say "This is it", had been a futile attempt to contemplate the enjoyed.[26]

Synthesising this insight with his idealistic philosophy enabled him to see how Joy fitted into a more holistic awareness. We mortals had a root in the Absolute, the "utter reality":

> And that is why we experience Joy: we yearn, rightly, for that unity which we can never reach except by ceasing to be the separate phenomenal beings called "we". Joy was not a deception. Its visitations were rather the moments of clearest consciousness we had, when we became aware of our fragmentary and phantasmal nature and ached for that impossible reunion which would annihilate us or that self-contradictory waking which would reveal, not that we had had, but that we were, a dream.[27]

Having to tutor in philosophy, Lewis found his "watered Hegelianism" increasingly inadequate. He returned to Berkeley's theistic idealism. G. K. Chesterton's wide-ranging and visionary work *Everlasting Man* (1925) set out a Christian outline of history that made sense to Lewis in new ways. Then:

> … the hardest boiled of all the atheists I ever knew sat in my room on the other side of the fire and remarked that the evidence for the historicity of the Gospels was really surprisingly good…. If he, the cynic of cynics, the toughest of the toughs, were not – as I would still have put it – "safe", where could I turn? Was there no escape?[28]

One is reminded of Francis Thompson's Hound of Heaven. God follows the fleeing soul by His divine grace.

Then came a moment he was to recount often in later life. One day he was going up Headington Hill on the top of a bus. He became aware, out of the blue, that he was holding something at bay. It was as if he was wearing some stiff corset or suit of armour. He felt faced by a choice: unbuckle the armour or keep it on. Did he want to be "free"?

> The choice appeared to be momentous but it was also strangely unemotional. I was moved by no desires or fears. In a sense I was not moved by anything. I chose to unbuckle, to loosen the rein…. Then came the repercussion on the imaginative level. I felt as if I were a man of snow at long last beginning to melt…. I rather disliked the feeling.[29]

A fox dislodged from the Hegelian wood, he felt hounded on all sides, by everyone from Plato to Tolkien.[30]

Lewis decided on action. He must make an attempt at complete virtue: difficult given that, on self-examination, he found within himself "a zoo of lusts, a bedlam of ambitions, a nursery of fears, a hareem of fondled hatreds".[31] He needed continual conscious recourse to what he called "Spirit". Recourse to a pure Spirit rather than God proved appallingly difficult. The fine philosophical distinction between Spirit "and what ordinary people call 'prayer to God' breaks down as soon as you start doing it in earnest. Idealism can be talked, and even felt; it cannot be lived". It was as if "a philosophical theorem, cerebrally entertained, began to stir and heave and throw off its gravecloths, and stood upright and became a living presence".[32] There was horror in this revelation. It raised all his old fears about God the Interferer, and his "mad wish" to call his soul his own. His old ideal had been one based on a sort of Enlightenment Reason. But was God "reasonable"? Might not Lewis be asked to endure something "intolerably painful" in his search for virtue? Might not total surrender be demanded? "You must picture me alone in that room at Magdalen, night after night, feeling, whenever my mind lifted even for a second from my work, the steady, unrelenting approach of Him whom I so earnestly desired not to meet".

Finally, "I gave in, and admitted that God was God, and knelt and prayed: perhaps, that night, the most dejected and reluctant convert in all England".[33]

This "conversion", as Lewis admits, was only to Theism, not to Christianity. The details of just how he travelled the final steps to Christianity are only sketchily outlined in *Surprised by Joy*. In a sense he found that he had been "taken out of himself", and thus paid less attention to his own opinions and states of mind. Conversion led to less self-examination in his case. Hence we have only his woolly recollections of events. Still a theist, he began attending parish church and college chapel. He still had little fondness for churchmanship and ritual. His instincts were in a way evangelically individualistic, a matter of good people praying alone, or in small groups. But he did start comparing world religions and mythologies. In the end he concluded that pagan myths, Nordic and Greek legends – far from being incompatible with Christianity – were anticipations of the whole truth, the grand narrative or "big picture" that was offered by the Christian faith. They were glimpses, as he later wrote, of the very plot of the cosmic story: the theme of incarnation, death and rebirth.[34]

Lewis describes a revelatory moment, one that again he was to recount often:

> Every step I had taken, from the Absolute to "Spirit" and from "Spirit" to God, had been a step towards the more concrete, the more imminent, the more compulsive.... To accept the Incarnation was a further step in the same direction. It brings God nearer, or near in a new way.... I know very well when, but hardly how, the final step was taken. I was driven to Whipsnade one sunny morning.[35] When we set out I did not believe that Jesus Christ is the Son of God, and when we reached the zoo I did.[36]

Did Lewis continue to be "Surprised by Joy"? He would have us believe that he lost interest in the subject after he became a Christian. The moments of stabbing joy, the bitter-sweet moments, still came to him across the years. But they now seemed of less importance: "When we are lost in the woods the sight of a signpost is a great matter.... But when we have found the road and are passing signposts every few miles, we shall not stop and stare".[37]

---

[1] Alister McGrath, *The Intellectual World of C. S. Lewis* (Oxford, Wiley-Blackwell, 2014). McGrath has also published an acclaimed biography *C. S. Lewis – A Life: Eccentric Genius, Reluctant Prophet*, (Illinois, Tyndale House Publishers, 2013).

[2] McGrath *The Intellectual World of C. S. Lewis*, p. 139, comments that one of the reasons Lewis abandoned his shallow rationalism "was his growing awareness of its existential deficiencies. Access to what was logically true did not resolve the greater questions of life, which focused on identity, meaning, and value".

[3] Rowan Williams has explored the Christian implications of the seven-volume series in his *The Lion's World: A Journey into the Heart of Narnia* (London, SPCK, 2012). Williams speaks of how Lewis brilliantly conveyed "the disturbing otherness of what we encounter in the life of faith... a passion to communicate the excess of joy that is promised by the truth of God in Christ... the experience of surrender in the face of incarnate love" (book's dust cover).

[4] Lewis's love life has been the subject of much speculation, due in part to his secrecy on the matter. He had a long-term relationship – probably sexual, although no-one has yet proven this - with Mrs Janie Moore, the mother of a friend of his who was killed in the war. She seems to have been a combination of lover and mother figure to him, and they lived together from 1919 until her death in 1951. In 1956 he married an American woman, Joy Gresham, who shared his literary interests. It was a marriage of convenience, to allow her and her two sons residency rights in England, but it developed into a love match. These subjects are canvassed in A. N. Wilson, *C. S. Lewis: A Biography* (New York, Norton, 1990), an excellent read.

[5] Later, in his book *Mere Christianity*, Lewis combined the idea of needing to give up the *striving* for a transcendental experience with the idea of needing to give up self. In becoming a true Christian: "The very first step is to try to forget about the self altogether. Your real, your new self (which is Christ's and also yours, and yours because it is His) will not come as long as you are looking for it. It will come when you are looking for Him.... The principle runs through all life from top to bottom. Give up yourself, and you will find your real self. Lose your life and you will find it.": *Mere Christianity* (London, Fontana, 1955 (1st ed., 1952), p. 188.

[6] C. S. Lewis, *Surprised by Joy: The Shape of My Early Life* (London, Geoffrey Bles, 1955).

[7] *Ibid*, p. 22.

[8] *Ibid*, p. 24

[9] *Ibid*, p. 163. Rowan Williams explains that Lewis "readily adopted in his schooldays the language of revolt against the tyranny of 'orthodoxy' and imposed order, with God as the representative of this tyranny". He would later see God as in rebellion against "the oppressive clichés of the world", with the Devil's world being a tidy and orderly one: "Against this joyless order stands the unpredictable world of grace". This is a theme of the *Screwtape Letters*: Williams, *The Lion's World*, pp. 50-51; Lewis, *Surprised by Joy*, pp. 94-95. In the Narnia stories God is seen as a rebel. The state of transcendence is seen, not as unattainably far off, but something of "inexhaustible strangeness... this is expressed in terms of rebellion, the joyful overturning of a self-contained order in the name of an uncontrollable truth": Williams, *The Lion's World*, p. 139.

[10] Esaias Tegner was "the father of modern Swedish poetry", and "Drapa" is a death-song. Longfellow's poem was an elegy for both Tegner and Balder the

Beautiful, the God of the summer sun. One line goes: "I saw the pallid corpse/ of the dead sun/ Borne through the Northern sky".
[11] Lewis, *Surprised by Joy*, pp. 74-75.
[12] *Ibid*, p. 168.
[13] *Ibid.*
[14] George MacDonald (1824-1906) wrote fantasy stories that influenced many writers, including Lewis Carroll, Tolkien, Chesterton and Auden. A Scottish poet and minister, he also wrote Christian apologetics, rejecting his Calvinist background and putting forward a more forgiving and optimistic doctrine of "Christian Universalism". In 1947 Lewis wrote an introduction to an anthology of MacDonald's work.
[15] Lewis, *Surprised by Joy*, p. 169.
[16] *Ibid*, p. 171.
[17] As Rowan Williams says of Lewis's repeated appeal to the experience of joy: "There are moments in our experience when we know that we are overtaken by a fulfilment of desire so overwhelmingly more than we could have expected that we can only think of it in terms of contact with a life or an agency immeasurably in *excess* of what we can otherwise imagine". *The Lion's World*, pp. 107-108.
[18] McGrath, *The Intellectual World of C. S. Lewis,* especially pp. 36-42.
[19] Lewis, *Surprised by Joy*, p. 193.
[20] He admitted later that, rather unfairly, he equated Steinerism with some of the mumbo-jumbo versions of theosophy that were rife at the time. Madame Blavatsky and Annie Besant were best sellers, and there was much lampooning in intellectual circles of fads about séances, spirit-rapping and poltergeists.
[21] Lewis, *Surprised by Joy*, p. 198.
[22] *Ibid*, p. 199.
[23] *Ibid*, p. 203.
[24] Joseph Loconte, *A Hobbit, a Wardrobe and a Great War: How J. R. R. Tolkien and C. S. Lewis Rediscovered Faith, Friendship and Heroism* (Nashville, Thomas Nelson, 2015).
[25] Lewis, *Surprised by Joy*, p. 205.
[26] *Ibid*, p. 207.
[27] *Ibid*, p. 209.
[28] *Ibid*, p. 211.
[29] *Ibid*, p. 212.
[30] Rowan Williams explains this fear of accepting joy and God as a fear of losing self-possession: "What we finally see reflected in the face of truth is *both* the depth of our hunger for joy and the tangle of ingenious strategies that we devise because we fear the dissolving of our self-possession that joy brings with it". *The Lion's World*, p. 108.
[31] Lewis, *Surprised by Joy*, p. 213.
[32] *Ibid*, p. 214.
[33] *Ibid*, p. 215. The timing of Lewis's "conversion" here is problematic. Lewis remembered it as happening in the summer Trinity Term of 1929. However, McGrath has convincingly dated his change of belief as occurring a year later, in

1930. In 1931 a conversation with Tolkien over the nature of myth "led Lewis to embrace Christianity… his process of intellectual realignment was essentially complete by the summer of 1932, when he penned *The Pilgrim's Regress…*": McGrath, *The Intellectual World of C. S. Lewis*, p. xi (also fully documented in his *C. S. Lewis: A Life*, pp. 131-151).

[34] See McGrath, *The Intellectual World of C. S. Lewis,* ch.3, "A Gleam of Divine Truth: The Concept of Myth in Lewis's Thought".

[35] This was probably in September 1931, after his discussion with Tolkien about the nature of myth. Lewis seems to have merged his memories of two, quite different, visits to Whipsnade, one in September 1931 and a second in June 1932: details in McGrath, *The Intellectual World of C. S. Lewis,* p. 21.

[36] Lewis, *Surprised by Joy*, pp. 223-224.

[37] *Ibid.*

13. Joseph Needham: Reflections on The Holy and Society

Joseph Needham was a famous bio-chemist who went on to bring to the world's attention the great inventiveness and brilliance of Chinese civilisation – a civilisation that far exceeded the west for centuries before the rise of modern science and capitalism in Europe. But Needham also had fascinating ideas about The Holy and society, incorporating Christian and socialist principles into his vision of a better human future. This essay will explore some of these ideas.

Brief Life

Described by a colleague in 1997 as "one of the greatest scholars in this or any country, of this or any century" and intellectually "a bridge builder between science, religion and Marxist socialism", Joseph Needham (1900-1995) was the son of a Harley Street specialist and "an artistically gifted" Irish mother.[1] Needham in his life possibly unconsciously tried to arch over the tense gap between his parents, almost a "Two Culture" gap in C. P. Snow's terms, his mother musical and volatile, his father a rational and scholarly man with classical and Francophile tastes and a perhaps paradoxical interest in theology and philosophy, in his youth active in the Anglican Oxford Movement. Needham's lifelong attachment to a broad and tolerant Christianity, and deep interest in other religions (such as Buddhism and Taoism), may surely be traced back to his youth, to his father's wide-ranging and open-minded interests,[2] and to the influence of the historic independent school he sent him to, Oundle School in Northamptonshire. It taught a broad and diverse curriculum that encompassed science, the humanities and philosophy. Its orientation was strongly Anglican, emphasising Christian ethics (which later infused Joseph's socialism, not unlike that other historian R. H. Tawney). Needham veered towards a religious vocation, trialling for two years as a novice in the Oratory of the Good Shepherd (an Anglo-Catholic order), and also active in the Guild of St Luke, promoting Christian ethics in the medical profession.

Needham progressively devoted his research interests to bio-chemistry after he entered Gonville and Caius College, Cambridge, in 1918, becoming a stellar performer and world figure. (He remained a member of this college for the rest of his life, being appointed Master from 1966 till 1976). As Mansel Davies remarked: "Needham matured at Cambridge in the presence of J. J. Thomson, Ernest Rutherford, Arthur

Eddington [another religious scientist], Edgar Adrian and Charles Sherrington, not to mention some ten other Nobel laureates from Blackett and Bragg to C. T. R. Wilson".[3] At twenty-five Needham edited a book, *Science, Religion and Reality*, which covered comparative religion, history and philosophy, and had essays by the anthropologists Bronislaw Malinowski and Charles Singer and the controversial Anglican divine W. R. Inge ("The Dismal Dean" as he was dubbed). Needham compressed his views on the relation between science and religion in two collections of essays: *The Sceptical Biologist* (1929) and *The Great Amphibium* (1931).

Politically he was a strong advocate of social justice, a socialist Labourite, and like many during the Depression years he was drawn to intellectual Marxism, but not to its totalitarian extremes. He joined activist groups of leftist scientists working for change within the universities during the thirties. Others included J. B. S. Haldane, his close friend J. D. Bernal and Laurence Hogben, working in groups such as the Association of Scientific Workers in the thirties.[4] Needham incorporated Marxist insights into his magisterial multi-volumed history *Science and Civilisation in China* (1954+). This history of Chinese science was a project that occupied most of his later life. However his activities were many and varied. They included playing a vital role in having a science component incorporated during the founding of UNESCO after the Second World War; and also helping to found the history of science as an academic discipline.

In the atmosphere of the Cold War, Needham's pro-Russian and Chinese sympathies, his anti-imperialist and anti-war activities, aroused distrust in the west, especially in the US. He got into hot water during the Korean War when he participated in an international commission of inquiry, instigated by the Chinese, into claims (false it has since emerged[5]) that the US had been using biological weapons. The commission found a guilty verdict, and Needham publicised it: "Widely denounced in parliament and the [British] press as a traitor and a stooge, he had to weather a furious storm of calls for him to be removed from his academic posts, and he became *persona non grata* in the United States".[6] He was denied a visa to visit the US until the mid-1970s, and was only grudgingly given proper academic recognition in the UK for many years. One turning point came with his setting up of the Needham Research Institute (as it became) from 1976, dedicated to the history of East Asian science and technology. In his later years Needham continued to work, along with a growing team of co-workers, many young Chinese scholars, on his massive China science project, which has been continued by other hands since his death. He was renowned for conducting informal seminars and debates at his home in Cambridge until the end. I remember strolling past his street, near Grange Road, many times on a study leave in 1992, but only learning after his death in 1995 about his Sunday soirees, open to all apparently, and wishing that I had been able to attend. His final years were wreathed in laurels.

His Ideas: Marxism, Christianity and More

Needham's essential attitude to Marxist thought was, it seems to me, utilitarian. He used Marxist insights and analysis (as have many anthropologists, sociologists, and historians) as useful tools in his historical work but was never ideological about it. As a committed Christian throughout his life, he opposed the totalitarian and Godless aspect of Marxism. He included spiritual and non-materialist values within his overarching human philosophy, and did not see these values as simply a by-product, or epiphenomenon, of economic forces, the modes of production. He embraced a very wide-ranging methodology. Indeed the Japanese scholar Nakayama described him as an "organic philosopher".[7] He has also been categorised as a monist, embracing "a kind of epistemological pluralism".[8] He himself described his approach as synthetic and syncretistic, combining the radical ideas of the early Christians with Buddhist and other Asian religious philosophies.

Needham's world-view in this respect has been acutely analysed by Gregory Blue in an important article.[9] Blue agrees that Needham had a "deep and abiding" relation to Marxism during his long career. He used concepts derived from historical materialism in his history of science, treating them as "fruitful lines of analysis": concepts about class warfare, socio/economic factors underlying the development of science, and so on. But Blue sees his relation to the Marxist tradition as "an innovative and discerning one", finding some insights valid, others less useful or irrelevant. He was never an orthodox Marxist historiographer, differing from Soviet and Chinese historiography in significant ways. Blue puts this down to a range of factors, including early intellectual influences upon him, especially religious and philosophical, and "partly to his commitment to synthesize insights from a wide range of sources, including several repudiated in more orthodox Marxist historiography".[10]

Blue unearthed an unpublished piece by Needham, a draft of a talk he was thinking of giving to a BBC forum in 1967 celebrating the centenary of Marx's *Das Kapital.* He finally decided against participating in the talks. In these notes he discussed his ambivalence about using Marxist theory in his science history. His monumental history asserted the pre-eminence of Chinese science and technology well before the rise of modern western science. The great issue he raised – and one which is still being vigorously debated – was why Chinese science failed to develop further and ultimately succumbed to the rise of western science. As Needham wrote:

> I do indeed believe, in accordance with "historical materialism", that the fundamental factors which prevented the rise of modern science in China (and India) were sociological and economic, and it was factors of this kind too which brought it about that during the previous fourteen centuries Chinese science had been applied to human welfare far more efficiently than in Europe. On the other hand, there are various other theories of Marxism which I do not accept, e.g., the conception of a rigid universal succession of social structures, and its views of the nature and role of religion.[11]

Needham always staunchly opposed the so-called "internalist" school of science history, which focussed almost exclusively on "internal" logical and epistemic factors driving the progress of science. By contrast he argued that science theories and knowledge were culturally conditioned, varying with changing historical contexts. (My own studies of Darwinism have confirmed me in such views.[12])

In answer to critics who put him simplistically into a doctrinaire communist camp, Needham made some interesting observations in his 1967 notes. Blue summarises them:

> On the political front, he observed simply that he had been an "equalitarian socialist" long before reading the classics of Marx and Engels, and he reaffirmed (as he did until the end of his life) that he still adhered to the Christian Socialism of his youth, though in a version influenced in his early adulthood by friends like [the French biologist] Louis Rapkine and [Polish-born neurobiologist] Liljana Lubinska, Marxists (he said) of an "undogmatic and unorthodox" sort, brought up originally in Jewish and anti-clerical traditions.[13]

He agreed that he had been influenced by colleagues who embraced a dialectical materialist philosophy, such as J. B. S Haldane, J. D. Bernal and Roy Pascal. But Needham maintained an independent, "personal, non-exclusive" style of thinking. He wrote of his "world view of faith", expressed in many "syncretistic" essays in his early career: "I combine Marxist thought with the revolutionary Christianity of Conrad Noel, the philosophy of religion of Rudolf Otto and R. G. Collingwood, and the emergent evolutionism of Lloyd Morgan and Samuel Alexander. Teilhard de Chardin I came to know and admire only after the second world war.[14]

***The Great Amphibium* (1931)**

In the aftermath of the Darwinian revolution of the mid-nineteenth century, there was much talk of a "war" between science and religion, between Evolution and Christianity. Recent historiography has tended to play down this so-called "warfare". Historians cite the significant traffickings and continuities between science and religion. They argue that the Darwinian paradigm had less than radical religious and social repercussions, that (at least for a long time in Britain) Darwinism was rendered less threatening by making it containable within existing paradigms.[15]

Joseph Needham took a more traditional line. He spoke of a "war" between science and religion in his early book *The Great Amphibium* (1931).[16] In four lectures given to the First General Conference of the Student Christian Movement at Derbyshire in July 1931, he gave a wide-ranging analysis of the differing world-views of science and religion, warning against the bleak domination of an amoral scientific world-view. Coming from an eminent scientist, he hoped it would carry weight, but the book was hardly a best-seller, and is now very rare. (I managed to consult a copy that had been squirreled away in the library of Adelaide's St Alban's Priory).

History, in Needham's mind, had been marked by the inescapable presence of great forms of human activity in the realm of thought. Great ideas systems struggled "like leviathans" against each other: "No opposition has been more violent and long-continued in the past than that between the organised apprehension of the world's ultimate mystery, which we call religion, and the organised investigation of the world's apparent mechanism, which we call science". Much evil had been caused by this profoundly tragic strife. In the present age, one of obvious secularisation, the world was increasingly dominated by scientific thought.[17]

Needham was not saying that this followed inexorably, or logically, from scientific methodology or epistemology. But, in practice, in popular versions of science, scientific values and mind-sets tended to be very invasive: "A great organised form of experience such as science carries with it a mass of subsidiary ideas, feelings, beliefs and conventions, which you can easily strip off it when you begin reducing it to its essence, its minimum claims". Thus it was not philosophically necessary that scientists be determinists, but in practice it was their typical state of mind, and this undermined liberal ideas such as free will. Science, with its maths and statistics, also tended to collectivity of mind, not individualism. In an age of rising totalitarianisms, this was alarming. Science was increasingly controlling nature and natural processes.[18]

Needham was no Luddite. He appreciated the positive gains made by technology, but he also warned against the unknowns and possible perils that went with (say) population control or genetic engineering. Mindless Millenarianism, the Doctrine of Progress wedded to Science, was an illusory dream. In an interesting comparison, Needham saw militant communism as a variant of virile millenarianism, a substitute religion: "The communist is in one sense the direct descendant of the nineteenth century scientist, detesting mystery and determined to control the material world in the interest of man". Marx had warned against religion as the "opium of the people". Needham warned that science could itself become the opium of the people. He had no faith in the wishy-washy do-gooder clerics of the day (an echo of Chesterton?). In a dramatic flourish he declaimed that only:

> … a virile mysticism will know how to estimate the golden promises of a scientific millennium at their true worth. Beauty is transient, Death inevitable, and escape will never be possible from the essential tragedy of life.[19]

Needham also had a problem with "the ethical neutrality" of science. Of course science needed to approach its materials, to approach Nature, objectively and to conduct experiments without bias. This was at the core of modern scientific methodology. But too many scientists were unconcerned with the social implications of their work. Needham was arguing here along the same lines as the "Responsibility in Science" movement that was started in the late 1920 and 1930s by the "Visible College" of reform-minded scientists such as Bernal, Haldane, Hogben, Levy and others. It was to reach its apogee in anguished reactions to the atomic bombing of Hiroshima and Nagasaki towards the end of the Second World War, and was to continue with a strong anti-nuclear movement among scientists, and others, thereafter.

Needham was already alarmed in 1931. Scientists, with their air of "detachment", had done much work that would become incorporated into the armaments industry and be used with disastrous effects in warfare. In the course of their chemical experiments, for instance, "somebody stumbled on the substance we now know as 'mustard gas', and in spite of the properties of this substance, no doubt felt it both his duty and his pleasure to go on investigating it and even to prepare a number of compounds very similar to it or even worse. At this point the men of evil will stepped in, the military intelligence came into operation, and the forces of disunion, envy, hatred, and malice" were unleashed.[20] Like Pontius Pilate, the scientists washed their hands of any guilt for this outcome:

> It is as if the house of the spirit, which was previously inhabited by the genius of religion, always preoccupied about God, Man, the Good, the Holy, the Right, were thoroughly spring-cleaned, swept, and garnished, leaving nothing but the empty rooms and bare walls of scientific ethical neutrality, whereupon seven other demons, all worse than the first, including war and pestilence, enter in and take up permanent residence there.[21]

Needham strongly felt that science, along with other forces, was undermining the distinction between good and evil, undermining the traditional foundations of social morality. He painted a dark vision of a future amoral world. People were laying aside ethics, thinking only of pleasure, gratification, personal gain and power. In a long discussion that ranged from Epicurus to Schleiermacher, Needham dissected the scientific attitude, which implied "a total lack of reverence, a complete absence of awe"[22] – qualities indispensable to religion: "It must be frankly admitted that the sense of the holy cannot flourish in the atmosphere of defiance, power, irreverence, and impiety, which science quite legitimately has to cultivate."[23] Needham was pessimistic about the capacity of the churches to counter the intractable problems that they faced. Just as the golden age of the Hellenistic world had disappeared, and the Gods of Olympus had faded away: "So it is with us. Our religious period has gone, and gone for good. The Christian Middle Ages can never return… for the religious age of Western man will not recur."[24] He predicted a sort of inverted Middle Ages to come, with science playing the key role that religion had once occupied in western culture.

He himself was not prepared to run with this current. He believed that every culture needed heroic individuals who opposed the dominant ethos:

> If now, as individuals, we give up religion, we hand ourselves over like passive logs to the flood-waters of history, and transform ourselves into fundamentally one-sided creatures… man was not born to be hypertrophied in one special direction…. The best man is the man who is friendly to, even if he himself cannot enter into, each of the great forms of human experience…. This is why it seems to me that it is now more necessary than ever before to participate actively in religious rites, and to maintain firmly

> the fundamental validity of the religious experience as a characteristic activity of the human spirit.[25]

Needham tended to disclaim any expertise in philosophy, but he made many comments in passing concerning philosophical issues. He had encountered recent philosophical trends during his time at Cambridge, as had most intellectuals of his generation, the generation of philosophers such as T. H. Green, R. G. Collingwood, Edward Caird, Samuel Alexander, A. N. Whitehead, Ernst Mach, Ludwig Wittgenstein and others. There was plenty to choose from: dialectical materialism, neo-Hegelianism, pragmatism, scientific humanism, early existentialism, linguistic analysis, logical positivism, and so on. Then there were the theological movements associated with names like Kierkegaard, Barth, Niebuhr and Tillich. Theologies ranged from the Oxford Movement and its Anglo-Catholic offspring to Liberal Protestantism, Catholic Modernism and Bergsonian intuitionism to crisis theology.

Needham seems closest to a philosophical trend at the time claiming that the world of discourse of science and the world of discourse of religion, art and literature were distinct. They spoke of different things and were not subject to the same critical criteria. Baldly, science spoke of facts, religion and the arts of subjective matters and values. Needham ultimately equated science with materialism (although he agreed that this was not a necessary connection). Materialism simply neglected issues such as God, Freedom and Immortality. It placed such subjects in the realm of "the unspeakable". They were not subject to logical or scientific analysis. (Wittgenstein and Hogben influenced him here. Wittgenstein was noted for his anti-scientism). In an apt phrase Needham said "it is worth while to persist in trying to communicate the incommunicable and to speak the unspeakable".[26] He often described religion as "numinous experience".[27] He said:

> Not how the world is, but that it exists at all in the form which we know, is the mystical. Scientific thought stands completely helpless before that profound element of arbitrariness which characterises the world. Logic exists in the world and fills the world, but the world itself is at bottom alogical, arbitrary, inscrutable, affording no possible answer to the question why it should be as it is and not otherwise.[28]

This seems to border on Zen.

Did scientists have a sense of wonder about the universe, even a hint of numinous experience? Needham conceded that this occasionally occurred, but it was rare. He saw science and religion (together with the arts) standing on polar opposites. Science was mathematical, quantitative, generalising, reductionist, and simplifying. Natural objects and processes were torn from "the matrix of sense-experience" and the facts thus obtained sorted into boxes, classifications,

> … all their properties being subordinated to the one property upon which we are focusing our attention… the incredible richness of the so-called real or raw world which furnished the metrical data remains out of the scientific field of vision.[29]

Science always had a leaning towards the mechanical and the deterministic, because these concepts were central to the scientific frame of mind. Being orderly and analytical, it hated mystery and hence was:

> profoundly incompatible with poetry, religion, metaphor, and symbol. A mystery stimulates a scientific worker to clear it up, not to worship it, and the fact that "God moves in a mysterious way, his wonders to perform" is almost sufficient reason for his having a disrespect for the deity.[30]

If science faced the question of the meaning of the universe, it could but assert that it had no meaning. We live in a meaningless world. Science was anti-teleological:

> The concept of purposiveness is distasteful to the scientific worker…. Nor has anyone so far suggested a mathematical formulation for a final cause which should prove itself of any practical value in investigating nature… science is impersonal and studiously avoids any consideration of the possible destinies of man, his fears, hopes, and premonitions of other modes of existence.[31]

What of that polar opposite, religion? It was "concerned with the sense of the holy just as art is concerned with the appreciation of the beautiful".[32] Needham was inclined to describe religion as preoccupied with the numinous: unintellectual, other-worldly,[33] simply indifferent to science and the world of facts. This of course did not describe all the religious-minded people he knew, who included intellectuals and scientists, as we have seen. It was as if he was putting forward an archetypal mystic, as opposed to the rationally-minded or socially engaged clerics who were certainly around at the time (William Temple was one). Needham wavered on the issue. Let us look at what he was saying in 1931.

The bio-chemist Needham was more than ready to admit that there was a mysterious core to the universe, that there was beauty and enchantment to behold. (Darwin himself took this view, as modern commentators have pointed out, and so at the time did thinkers such as Aldous Huxley and even his brother, the biologist Julian. Needham often quoted Aldous).[34] Needham said:

> … the world to the religious state of mind is nothing if not mysterious, for to fathom its nature is as impossible as not to worship the maker of it. The religious man knows that in the last resort "the whole creation is a mystery", as Sir Thomas Browne said, and that there is nothing logical or rational about the universe, except the logic and reason of the gods, whose ways are not our ways nor their thoughts our thoughts.[35]

Needham was contemptuous of the Deists and "bloodless" ethicists who tried to bridge the gap between science and religion by emptying God from the equation:

> In these times it will be well for us to remember that the essential component of religion is mystery and mystical experience…. The numinous sensation of shuddering fear and joy, the sympathetic understanding of all creation, the dark night of the soul, the supernatural sense of peace and illumination, the peculiar beneficent effects of rites, the whole range of experience, in fact, which makes up religious mysticism, is what we have to deal with when we speak of religion.[36]

(One can detect here the later attraction Buddhism would have for him.)

It followed that religion was antagonistic to features of science such as its emphasis on measurability:

> To weigh the mountains in a balance or to measure the heavens with a rod was deemed impossible…and when religion thinks at all, it puts its emphasis upon individual things, unique things, incalculable and spontaneous things, qualitative entities having no exact counterpart anywhere in the universe. It is thus wiser than science and akin to history.[37]

Religion was also teleological:

> Nothing is so characteristic of the religious view of the world as this preoccupation with the purpose of things; why everything should be as it is, why evil should exist, why God should have made the world, are primarily religious questions, and only afterwards philosophical ones. The scientific worker leaves them on one side as insoluble conundrums in which he is not interested.[38]

Needham wrote eloquently of:

> the austere realm of the scientific spirit, which is continually subsuming one thing under something else, and arranging the myriad phenomena in hierarchies of importance and laws of ascending generality. It is in this way that religion is akin to art, and especially to poetry, being profoundly non-analytical and concrete, content to accept objects and events as they come and caring nothing about their relations with other preceding or succeeding events.[39]

There is an interesting sub-text in all this, in that Needham could in fact empathise with both the scientific and the religious mind-sets. After all he was a scientist and valued the methodologies that science used in its quest for knowledge, just as he valued the riches of the numinous. So we continually encounter underground tremors in his writings, hidden ambivalences, when he commented on such matters. If he was satirical and scathing at times about science and scientists, with their tunnel vision, so could he be sarcastic and critical about the foibles of the religious. He was only too aware of the difficulties of passing from one world of experience to the other. Enough, he said, to deter most of us from even think of leaving the realm where we are most at home.

Given the seemingly intractable differences between science and religion, could the two be melded together in some higher philosophical synthesis? Some thinkers had suggested this. It would be a sort of higher Hegelian synthesis of lower theses. Needham ridiculed such an idea. This would only result in the loss of what was most valuable, most central, in both worlds of discourse. "It is flatly impossible", he declared, "to give a coherent account of the universe which shall include what all the forms of experience have to say about it."[40] Better to accept the strengths and weaknesses of each discourse:

> It is more likely that we shall do better to accept, for instance, a sort of materialism inherent in the scientific mind, rather than strip it remorselessly of its favourite errors and demonstrate how weak fundamentally it is. We shall do better to follow each road out to its farthest end, and to accept the Lucretian estimate of the world in the laboratory as well as that of St Augustine or St Teresa at other moments and in other places. All alike are partially false, none means exactly what it says, save only that of philosophy, which, unfortunately, can say practically nothing.[41]

Needham concluded *The Great Amphibium* with an endorsement of the Greek ideals of moderation, balance and harmony. The best human community, as he saw it,

> … would be that which possessed the largest number of harmonious souls within it, the fewest fanatical ascetics, the fewest hide-bound, hard-boiled scientific minds, the fewest aesthetes cultivating art for art's sake, and perhaps, but I not sure of this, the largest number of philosophers.[42]

Time: The Refreshing River (1943)

The 1930s were a time of hectic engagement and frenetic activity for Needham. Based in the Department of Bio-chemistry at the University of Cambridge, he became a world figure in chemical embryology. Unusually in such a field, he wrote big books, filled not only with hard science but broader cultural reflections and attention to historiography. *Perspectives in Biochemistry* appeared in 1937, *Biochemistry and Morphogenesis* in 1942. He gave prestigious lectures at places like Stanford and Yale, as well as in Britain and Europe, while becoming deeply engaged in political and science reform movements, anti-war movements, and, as an Anglo-Catholic, religious affairs. He was part of the religious community run by the revolutionary socialist cleric Conrad Noel in Thaxted, Essex. He often attested to Noel's formative influence upon his thinking. Inspired by the Soviet papers presented at the 1931 London International Congress on the History of Science (which inspired a number of scientists of the left, including Desmond Bernal), Needham began writing history. It started with a short book on the seventeenth century Levellers and culminated in his massive history of Chinese science.

Eric Hobsbawm writes that Needham was perhaps the most interesting mind amongst a "constellation of brilliant 'red' scientists" of the thirties. These inter-war scientists had an incredible range of knowledge and interests, the Renaissance men of their day (a type that, sadly, no longer seems to exist):

> They also tended to combine the imagination of art and science with endless energy, free love, eccentricity and revolutionary politics.... No man belonged more obviously to it than Joseph Needham....[43]

Malcolm Muggeridge often reminisced about the naturist and nudist recreations of the "Croydon socialists" of his father's generation (the vegetarian Bernard Shaw is perhaps a founding father of such things, offshoots of the "return to nature" movement of the late nineteenth century.) Needham's pastimes included cavorting in the nude and Morris dancing (characteristically he wrote about its history). A little later in life, he was to be part of a *ménage a trois*, with his wife Dorothy (herself an eminent biochemist) and a young Chinese woman scholar Lu Gwei-djen. Lu was one of an exodus of young scholars who fled the Japanese invasion of China in 1937, and it was she who probably inspired his interest in China. The trio stayed together for the rest of their lives.[44]

It is clear that, by 1935, the year he wrote an essay entitled "Science, Religion and Socialism", Needham's empathy with institutionalised religion, even indeed with orthodox Christianity, had diminished. This essay was an early piece in his collection of essays that would be published in 1943 as *Time: The Refreshing River*.[45] Needham had come under the influences of sceptical rationalist philosophies, biblical criticism undermining the literal accuracy of the scriptures, and a growing interest in Eastern religions. Also we must add to that Marxist-Leninist theory, culminating in an almost romantic faith in the spiritual potentialities of Soviet communistic society and culture. He adhered to this – in a way that was characteristic of the British left at the time – despite the evidence-based criticisms of Soviet despotism made by leftist commentators such as George Orwell and Malcolm Muggeridge.

The essay contained an interesting insight into Needham's developing ethical philosophy. His early work was liberally sprinkled with moral judgments. But there was little explicit analysis of the basis for his ethics. The impression given was that his moral codes rested quite often upon some absolute basis, such as a supernatural authority or agency. He often evoked God or the wisdom of ancient authorities; and seemed to imply an indwelling moral sense in humanity. However by 1935 he seemed to be at least experimenting with a form of evolutionary ethics. He was taking Darwin's view that human ethics was a product of the evolutionary process, rather than being something transcending or apart from natural development. Needham said:

> The good seems to arise out of the evolutionary process rather than to have been in it from the beginning. But the good is an immediate datum, and the holiness of good actions is an immediate datum. These are the occasions of modern religion. From this point of view, the bonds of love and comradeship in human society are analogous to the various forces which hold particles together at the colloidal, crystalline, molecular, and even sub-atomic levels of organisation. The evolutionary process itself supplies us with a criterion of the good. The good is that which contributes most to the social solidarity of organisms having the high degree of organisation which human beings do in fact have.[46]

Needham became increasingly outspoken about Church deficiencies. The difficulty about religion, he wrote, was that it could not be considered apart from organised religion as embodied in institutions: "In practice, its effects throughout the world are, in the present social context, largely harmful".[47] Needham distanced himself a little by talking about modern perspectives about religion, but it was obvious that he shared many of them himself, if with qualifications. He discussed the debate of the time in terms such as this:

> How far religion can be transformed without the disappearance of the old vessels is a very disputable matter. [Chesterton was fond of the metaphor of old wine in new bottles.] The detailed beliefs of the past – verbal inspiration, eternal damnation, magical efficacy of prayer for "particular mercies"…, miraculous intervention, ascription of psychological states to God, and so on, are of course irrevocably of the past, not of the present or future. None of them are relevant to true religion. Religion is [nowadays] seen not as a divine revelation, but as a function of human nature…. Theology, indeed, comes off badly in our modern survey. In so far as it is a codification of the experiences of religious mysticism it is an attempt to reduce to order what cannot be so reduced. In so far as it is a description of such experiences, it is engaged on the fruitless task of describing the indescribable. And, in so far as it is occupied with

> cosmology, anthropology, and history, it is trespassing on legitimate fields of scientific activity.[48]

Needham decried a fashionable trend towards a vague mysticism. Although he had gently pilloried such a thing before, you can sense his personal sympathy for mysticism, intensified by his explorations of Eastern mysticism. He cited a number of current scholars, including Julian Huxley and John Middleton Murry, who saw the essence of religion being in the sense of the holy:

> Religion thus becomes no more and no less than the reaction of the human spirit to the facts of human destiny and the forces by which it is influenced; and natural piety, or a divination of sacredness in heroic goodness, becomes the primary religious activity.[49]

Ethics and spirituality were thus divorced from any dependence upon God. Religion without God was becoming the fad. (Julian Huxley tried to manufacture such a "new religion" in the form of Evolutionary Humanism.) Many modernist and liberal theologians had almost reached such a point (George Tyrrell and Stewart Headlam sprang to his mind).

Needham however was wary of divorcing religion completely from traditional concepts of God and rituals. That was emptying the baby out with the bathwater. As he commented, an acquaintance with the life of religion from the inside:

> … convinces one that the sense of the holy cannot be ordered about at will, unhooked from one thing and hooked on to something else, or simply detached from ancient traditions and poured into the cold vacuum of our modern mechanical world. The poetic words of the Liturgy, for instance, philosophically meaningless though they may be, cannot be separated from the numinous feeling which has grown up with them. Though built upon the basis of a world-view which we can no longer accept today, they retain, for some of us, enough symbolism of what we do believe, to make them of overwhelming poetic value.[50]

Naively, as it now appears to us, Needham saw the Soviet Union as a source of the "New Dispensation", a new development of social emotions. Was not a new numinous feeling to be found among the Russian proletariat in its system of communal ownership?[51] Take drama for example. Drama, as was well known, had religious origins, "and it is surely significant that in the Soviet Union, the first great socialist state the world has ever seen, drama, poetry, and all cognate arts flourish as never before".[52] It was statements like this that made Orwell and Muggeridge – who knew better – shudder.

In the west, Needham saw people like himself who continued to cherish the central values of Christianity as an embattled minority. It was appallingly difficult for people to combine traditional religious life with the life of social and political action that was needed in the present time:

> Those of us who have loved the habitation of God's house and the place where his honour dwells would be well content if the traditional forms of rite and liturgy could survive the coming storm. We would like to fill the old bottles of Catholic doctrine with new wine. The words of the Fathers on equality and social righteousness seem more likely to be fulfilled than we had hoped.[53]

However, if this revivification of the ancient faith could not be accomplished, "those of us who love both the spirit and the letter will not complain if the spirit be taken and the letter left".[54] Had not that great German theologian Rudolph Otto shown the universal existence of a sense of the numinous? In the great religions of the world it formed the essential backbone of the experience of the worshippers. Here at least there was consolation.

Although Needham seemed now to have abandoned any absolutist basis for ethics, and was more and more sceptical about the tenets of institutionalised religion, he retained faith in what he called "creatureliness, the unescapable inclusion of man in space-time, subject to pain, sorrow, sadness and death".[55] Even the Marxist dream of abolishing evil by a revolutionary change in the class structure of society was an illusion. The problem of evil would remain, just as tragedy and sorrow would always be with us. The Old Testament and thinkers like Thomas Browne were right. We live with death and die not in a moment (Browne); dust we are and unto dust shall we return (Bible):

> The whole realm of thought and feeling embodied in these phrases is fundamentally natural and proper to man, and there is little to be gained by trying to replace it by a eupeptic opium, derived from too bright an estimate of the possibilities of scientific knowledge. Driven out, it will return in the end with redoubled force.[56]

He kept warning that the "opium of religion" was in danger of being replaced by the "opium of science".[57]

Needham reiterated and developed his analysis of the perils of "scientific opium". Not only was science blind to some of the greatest forms of human experience, numinous experiences, religious experiences, it also threatened to permit ominous forms of totalitarianism. Reluctantly Needham included Soviet scientific socialism as possibly open to such tyrannies. Already the Russian Revolution had "broken heads", as Lenin had famously said was necessary. A certain degree of ruthlessness was necessary "when the people are defending themselves against the final attack of the possessing class which sees itself on the verge of expropriation".[58] But there was a danger (Needham admitted) that scientific ruthlessness could be taken to non-Christian lengths. Christians of conscience, even Christian socialists, were obliged:

> … to plead for the retention of certain Christian principles in dealing with people…. As long as aberrant individuals are not permitted to be a danger to the socialist state, the greatest tolerance should prevail. There is no need for Marxists to follow the example of those many unchristian Christians who manned the Inquisition, the witch-hunting tribunals, and the boards of godly divines in Geneva, Westminster and Massachusetts.[59]

This was true of western science as well:

> The ruthlessness with which a biologist throws out an anomalous embryo useless for his immediate purpose, the ruthlessness with which the astronomer rejects an aberrant observation, may all too easily be applied to human misfits and deviationists….[60]

Aldous Huxley's *Brave New World* (1932) had brilliantly dramatised such dangers to humanity.

In *Time: The Refreshing River*, Needham gave an interesting analysis of Social Darwinism. He argued (in an address of 1941, "Pure Science and the Idea of the Holy") that Darwinian theory had been socially conditioned, and that Darwinism had been distorted in politically motivated ways to justify capitalism and class inequality. In this he followed the lead of Marx and Engels.[61] Needham wrote:

> The principle of natural selection necessarily implied a struggle for existence among animal species for food and

> reproductive facilities, and also among the individuals in any one species. It is no criticism of this theory to point out, as Engels did, that it was a reflection on to the animal world of the competitive conditions prevailing in the economic world of nineteenth-century capitalism. In the animal world it happened to be to a large extent true, and the principle of natural selection is today held to account very substantially, if not entirely, for the phenomena of organic evolution. The obvious conclusion was that if competitive capitalism was so like the sub-human world, that was just too bad for competitive capitalism. Like the dinosaurs, it was getting a little out of date.[62]

However, the Victorian apologists of capitalism took quite another slant: "All they could see was that the struggle for existence was, as they would have put it, the universal law of life, and that the more red in tooth and claw life could be made in the industrial areas, the more would human civilisation benefit".[63]

Needham, like a host of reform-minded Social Darwinists, reminded his readers that Darwin had emphasised the importance of the "co-operative" element in both animal and human evolution. This was a synergetic factor in evolution. Darwin emphasised the ability of humans to progress via their altruistic and ethical capacities to a higher, more peaceful and civilised stage of development. Needham cited the alternative readings of the Russian anarchist Peter Kropotkin in his famous *Mutual Aid: A Factor of Evolution* (1902 – a precursor of mutualism as a theory, and other thinkers such as Henry Drummond). Needham concluded with a flourish:

> And as for human society, Marx and Engels, by their historical analysis, showed that capitalism had not always existed, and that there was no reason whatever to think that free competition in exploitation of commodities and labour was more than a stage in man's evolution towards a planned and rationally controlled society.[64]

This wartime address contains what is perhaps Needham's most blatantly apologetic account of Soviet science. He waved aside the alarms of other scientists about the politicisation of science under Stalin. He was suspiciously silent about the infamous Lysenko phenomenon, where biological data was manipulated to fit Soviet dogma about the transmission of acquired characteristics. Scientists who opposed this genetic heresy were shot.

Finally, let us look briefly at Needham's essay, "Integrative Levels: A Revaluation of the Idea of Progress", The Herbert Spencer Lecture at Oxford in 1937. He was clearly ambivalent about Spencer. At one level Needham saw Spencer as an innovative global theorist who combined sociological with biological insights. Both Spencer and Needham were also railway geeks. Needham liked Spencer's anti-aristocratic, progressive middle class energy, and approved of his anti-imperialist, pacifist stance. But Needham judged Spencer to be trapped in a time-warp. Needham believed that Spencer's ruthlessly individualistic *laissez-faire* ideas, his anti-welfare and anti-poor sentiments, were rooted in a dated and romantic attachment to bourgeois culture. Spencer wrongly thought that social evolution had reached a dead-end with bourgeois capitalism. Needham was more attached to Marx's theory that bourgeois capitalism was inevitably fated to be supplanted by a more advanced stage of social evolution: the classless society, attained by a proletarian revolution. This was the real direction of human evolution. And it must be said that Needham was even more romantic than Spencer in prophesying an idealised classless society of the future.

Like Spencer, Needham justified his position from biology, drawing many analogies from his own extensive knowledge of bio-chemistry. The forces of biological and social evolution were converging. Needham asserted: "… there is a natural affinity between millenarism and evolutionary naturalism".[65] There was a lesson for humans in the developmental nature of social organisation (a principle present in all biological data). Why should we think that our present condition of civilisation was "the last masterpiece of universal organisation, the highest form of order of which nature is capable"? On the contrary, he argued, there were many grounds for seeing in collectivism a form of organisation as much above that of middle class nations as their form of order was superior to that of "primitive tribes".

> It would hardly be going too far to say that the transition from economic individualism to the common ownership of the world's productive resources by humanity is a step similar in nature to the transition from lifeless proteins to the living cell, or from primitive savagery to the first community, so clear is the continuity between inorganic, biological and social order. Thus, on such a view, the future state of social justice is seen to be no fantastic utopia, no desperate hope, but a form of organisation having the whole force of evolution behind it.[66]

Evolution of course could be regressive. Humans were capable of retrogressing (as Darwin himself admitted). But for Needham, the driving dynamic of social evolution was relentlessly towards "a co-operative commonwealth of humanity".[67]

He stuck to this, despite the clouds of global war looming in 1937. Perhaps taking his cue from J. A. Hobson, he saw dark phenomena such as imperialism and Fascist totalitarianism as last-ditch rescue operations for capitalism. Ultimately these dark forces would be defeated, or simply fade away. Grimly he conceded the possibility that humanity might have to suffer a long period of totalitarian repression if the Axis powers should prevail in a war:

> It may mean the enslavement of whole peoples for many generations, the destruction of culture and learning over a wide part of the world… the martyrdom of many thousands of our best and noblest friends…. To speak of the inevitability of our higher integrative level is to say nothing of when it will come.[68]

However he hammered away on the theme that ultimately a higher order of human society would emerge. What I say amounts to this, he said: "that evolution is not finished, that organisation has not yet reached its highest level, and that we can see the next stage in the co-operative commonwealth of humanity, the socialisation of the means of production".[69] As human consciousness progressed, it must exert more control over human affairs. This was Needham's answer to the pessimism of Freudianism and other philosophies of the early twentieth century with their emphasis on the centrality in human behaviour of irrationality. It followed, Needham argued, "that the more control human consciousness has over human affairs, the more truly human, and hence-super-human, man will become":

> Now the common ownership of the means of production implies the consciously planned control of production. No longer is production to be governed by the self-acting mechanism of profitability; it is to be carried on for communal use. No longer, at a given conjuncture of the world-market, will so many dozen factories automatically go out of action in some far corner of the earth, throwing some thousands of workers into immediate poverty, and diverting the energies of the owners into other channels. No longer will thermodynamic efficiency and geographic common sense alike be turned upside down at the

> irrationalities of a profit-making system. By the deliberate decisions of a central planning body the production and distribution of goods will be consciously organised.[70]

Our present civilisation was manifestly not a state of stable equilibrium. Modern science – itself largely the product of "the middle-class economic system of which Spencer was the representative" – had made capitalism an anachronism:

> Nothing short of the absolute abolition of private ownership of resources and machines, the abolition of national sovereignties, and the government of the world by a power proceeding from the class which must abolish classes, will suit the technical situation of the twentieth century.[71]

Spencer had been an apostle of the famous Doctrine of Progress. But so too, it turned out, was Joseph Needham, if in a dramatically different way.

Within the Four Seas (1969)

The elder Joseph Needham, while retaining the essentials of his earlier world-view, seemed to be moving towards the stance of that other global thinker, the historian Arnold Toynbee. In his multi-volumed *A Study of History*, Toynbee postulated that great ethical and timeless truths were encapsulated in the "higher religions", Christianity, Islam and Buddhism. These truths transcended the time-bound limitations of these religions, limitations that sprang from their institutionalisation.

Let us look at a perspective of 1961, expressed in a speech Needham gave at a Cambridge Union Society debate, given the title "Science and Religion in the Light of Asia", published in 1969 in a set of his essays called *Within the Four Seas*.[72] In this debate Needham conceded many of the points made in an advancing tide of secularism and popular disenchantment with orthodox Christian religion in the west. Science had succeeded in undermining many naïve religious beliefs, the flat-earth misconceptions of a "limbo of the past". It needed to be admitted that unforgivable atrocities had been committed by humans in the name of religion: witness the Crusades, pogroms against Muslims, Jews and Albigensians, and much more. There were also the psychological miseries caused by repressive Latin and Puritan versions of Christianity and "rigid ecclesiastical prohibitions", or by clergy "preaching personal salvation instead of social regeneration". But had not science also been associated with atrocities, Hiroshima being only one example? And, underlying everything remained the fact "that there is also the worship of the 'greater than ourselves', the 'mysterium tremendum', the 'wholly other', the immanent".[73]

Needham said:

> Religion, the distinctive sense of the holy, the application of the category of the numinous, attached as it has been in its most developed form to the highest ethical principles known to man, altogether transcends the particular manifestations of it familiar in our parochial and limited experience.[74]

The advance of science had to lead to "the increasing purification of religious philosophy and to new interpretations of theology". Broader insights had to be explored from the great diversity of religions, and especially for Needham – The Man Who Loved China – from eastern religions and philosophies. Religion, for example, did not necessarily imply "a doctrine of a creator god at all". Needham had absorbed this from eastern religion. From Confucianism – "a this-worldly ethic" - we could take the possibility of finding how to live together in harmony and happiness all the days of our life. Confucianism rejected sacerdotalism, the authority of a priesthood, yet could be genuinely spiritual. Needham spoke here from personal experience, and this essay contains some moving accounts of the deep impact made upon him when he had visited and meditated within Confucian and Buddhist temples in China and other regions of Asia. "I can testify from personal experience", he wrote, "that I have nowhere felt the presence of the numinous more strongly than in Confucian temples"; and he lauded the ancient Chinese tradition that conceived of liturgy and sacramental acts "as mystically instructive and profoundly beneficial poetry".[75] In the great religion of Buddhism,

> … once again we find no theology of a creator god, or any kind of supreme deity, no insistence on miracles daily renewed, no priesthood and no claim to infallibility…. Here the numinous is again most deeply associated with ethical insights, and the salvation, though in a way personal, is primarily from self…. Again from personal experience in Buddhist temples – Lankatillaka, Gadaladeniya, Abhayagiriya, Mihintale – evocatively beautiful Sinhalese names – or in China at Hua-Thing Ssu or on Chin-Yun Shan no less – not the most exquisite cathedral of all

> Christendom can inspire in the visitor and the worshipper a more profound sense of the numinous.[76]

How will science affect this religion? Needham asked: "The mythological system and even the belief in reincarnation may crumble, but the liberation of the self by the practice of compassion, with all its psychological justification, will remain, and hence the worship of the Enlightened One".[77]

What Needham was saying - and it was at one level a repeat of what he had been saying in the interwar years - was that only through true religions, or truly religious values, "the holiness of 'mercy, pity, peace and love'", could the world save itself from the very real threats posed by a capitalist-based and sponsored science. Science had long striven to be value free, "objective". It was as if disengaged scientists had sleepwalked through the disasters of the twentieth century. And in 1961 this unawareness of the tragic side of life "seems to me far more dangerous than in the pre-atomic age". Sceptical scientists, dismissing religious experience as nonsense, thinking only of themselves as mathematical or experimental geniuses, "are truly in danger of becoming 'hashishin', assassins…, the destroyers of the innocent on a scale infinitely exceeding Herod". He noted vividly how, in merely turning over the pages of the *Scientific American*:

> Science for war is dominant; "automatic accurate attack", "electronic equipment for missile launching", "skybolt deterrent", "heat shields for ICBM nose-cones". Calculating machines, rocket propulsion, orbiting satellites, cybernetic devices, substances injurious to plants and animals, new drugs, cloud-seeding, subliminal instruction – for what, for what? We are now invited to throw religious sanctions out of the window; we had better be careful that this does not end in kicking ethics downstairs. For ethics and the appreciation of the numinous are intimately and inextricably associated.[78]

Ever since Needham had made his personal discovery of East Asia, he had fulminated against "the unjustifiable cultural pride" of the west. This cultural myopia was dangerous because it prevented a full appreciation of the essential unity of humanity, and even threatened world peace. In a sermon he preached at his college in 1961, he celebrated the fundamental parallels between the most spiritual Christian values and those of other cultures. Unfortunately few in the west perceived this. There was precious little sign of western humility. This *hubris* vitiated all contacts between western civilisation and other peoples: "this may truly be called 'spiritual wickedness in high places'... the spirit of evil in things heavenly".[79]

The psychology of dominance had derived from the rise of modern science in the west from about the beginning of the seventeenth century. The advanced technology of armaments had enabled imperial conquest and ultimately a sense of cultural superiority. With it came the debauching of Christendom: "Cultural and religious humility seemed to die, and still lie a-sleeping".[80] Westerners still felt superior, despite the fact that Asia was now embracing western science, technology and industry, and was undergoing a Renaissance of culture and religion. Asia would soon enough challenge the dominance of the west. Western peoples were living in a sort of time bubble, still attached to outdated cultural norms: "Today the balance of power is quickly changing, but we Westerners are still slaves of this idea that our culture and our religion is in some way 'superior' to those of our brothers and sisters in the great countries of Asia".[81]

What was Needham's advice to fellow Christians? Celebrate your religion certainly, but be humble, give up trying to missionise great civilisations such as China and India, and embrace a policy of greater fraternity and mutual understanding between people. Focus on Christian essentials, not on the accidental incidentals of the faith but on its eternal values:

> If we only knew the treasures of human experience of God contained in cultures which because we will not work to understand them seem so foreign to us, we should hug them to our breasts and cry out in amazement at the work of the Holy Spirit under all meridians.[82]

His concluding message was one of hope: "If heaven is where the good are, and where good things are done, perhaps the invisible Church already covers the broad earth without our knowing it, most truly one spirit, under one God and Father of all".[83]

"History and Human Values" (1976)

In the agitated years of the 1960s and 1970s, the time of the Vietnam war, student protests and terrorist bombings, Needham borrowed time when he could from his all-consuming Science and Civilisation in China project to prophesy about the human future. In various talks, he gave what he hoped would be helpful advice on how the world might benefit from Chinese science and values. He asked: "what clues can we get about the help which the Chinese tradition and contemporary China could perhaps give for the ethos and operation of the World Cooperative Commonwealth of the future?"[84] This seemed the right time. Needham detected an avid new interest in China, a new "Chinoiserie" period.

In his "History and Human Values" paper of 1976, Needham was not only quietly promoting the achievements of the communist revolution in China and his own *magnum opus*. He was also penning a philippic against the fashionable "counter-culture" movement of the time, a movement associated with people like Theodore Roszak (*The Making of a Counter-Culture*, 1968). This movement expressed the widespread alienation of youth from the prevailing establishments of the west and especially the science that had produced evils such as nuclear weapons. Needham of course sympathised with much of this, as we have seen, but he had a strong residual faith in science as a component of the highest civilisation. Science had been an epic story of mankind, but its control had to be ethical and political. Mere psychological distaste for science and dehumanising technology, or a retreat to nature or a romantic past, was not enough.

Needham had obviously studied with care, and appreciated the strengths of thinkers such as Roszak and Victor Weisskopf. Their attack on the scientific world-view as a cerebral and ego-centric mode of consciousness, "completely heartless in its activity", certainly rang a bell with him. The real meaning behind the anti-science movement, he speculated, was the conviction that science should not be taken as the only valid form of human experience. Many philosophers, and especially the poet William Blake with his hatred of "single-vision", had already made the point. As Weisskopf himself admitted:

> There is a scientific way to understand every phenomenon, but this does not exclude the existence of human experience that remains outside science… the nature of most human problems is such that universally valid answers do not exist, because there is more than one aspect to each of them.[85]

Needham continued this line of thought by arguing:

> … the only way forward is the existentialist realization that the forms of experience, which have a habit of contradicting each other flatly, are all basically inadequate ways of apprehending reality, and can only be synthesized within the individual life as lived.[86]

Confucianism, Buddhism and Christianity understood this. He cited Julian of Norwich, who declared in 1373: "By reason alone we cannot advance, but only if there is also insight and love". Needham worried that this lesson had been lost in the modern scientifically-based world-view, with its belief "that it is quite proper for the results of science to be applied in a rapacious technology often at the service of private capitalist profit". So widespread had such callous and insensitive values become that they seemed "quite beyond the power of traditional codes of religion and ethics to modify".[87]

Needham made some prescient warnings about the dark potentialities of future science. Developing science and technology could threaten not only world peace – through nuclear weapons, chemical and biological warfare – but also human individuality and freedom. Even in 1976 he could visualise the perils of genetic engineering, cloning, designer babies and other forms of a "new eugenics", gene manipulation, organ transplants, euthanasia, artificial intelligence, robotics, state or private control of reproduction, visions of Aldous Huxley's *Brave New World* or H. G. Wells' *The Island of Dr Moreau* coming alive. Humanity needed constant vigilance and ethical control over such science. It could be good for mankind, but who could ensure that powerful vested interests, such as arms or pharmaceutical manufacturers would respect ethics?

It was here that Needham proposed China as an ethical model. Having elaborately analysed Eastern philosophies and religions over many years, he saw possible answers to western dilemmas, answers that were embedded in a great culture that was over two thousand years old. Chinese philosophers had always considered justice and righteousness as arising directly out of what in the west was called "the inner light".

> If the world is searching for an ethics firmly based on the nature of man, a humanist ethic which could justify resistance to every dehumanizing invention of social control, an ethic in the light of which mankind could judge dispassionately what the best course to take will be in the face of the multitude of alarming options raised by the ever-growing powers the natural science give us, then let it listen to the sages of Confucianism and Mohism, the philosophers of Taoism and Legalism. … what matters is their underlying faith in the basic goodness of human nature, free from all transcendental elements and capable of leading to a more perfect organization of human society.[88]

Needham also thought that the Chinese respect for nature was eminently relevant to a western world intent on destroying natural resources. He blamed the western idea of "feudal or imperialistic domination" of nature as arising from the Hebrew/Christian tradition, the tradition of the People of the Book. Compare that with the Chinese philosophy:

> … for the Chinese the natural world was not something hostile or evil, which had to be perpetually subdued by will-power and brute force, but something much more like the greatest of all living organisms, the governing principles of which had to be understood so that life could be lived in harmony with it.[89]

This might be called an "organic naturalism". Humanity was central, but not the centre for which the universe was created. Man's function was to act in conjunction with, not in disregard of, "the spontaneous and interrelated processes of the natural world".[90]

Chinese culture acted in accordance with the principle of Ying and Yang, balancing a masculine dominating attitude with a more patient and caring feminine attitude. Chinese tradition warned against the depletion of natural resources, for instance against deforestation (although it had undoubtedly occurred), against over-fishing or water wastage. Their great water engineering feats of the past were in accordance with nature as far as possible:

> For example, if water was wanted at 50 feet above the level of a river, it was much better to take it off by a derivative lateral canal some miles upstream and follow the contours, rather than laboriously lift it by water-raising machinery at the spot.… It was a profoundly right instinct that to use Nature it was necessary to go along with her.[91]

The Man Who Loved China thus characteristically ended one of his later commentaries on the human future and religion by commending the Chinese example. It could make an outstanding contribution for the future guidance of the human world. In a final word to Christians he said: "Nothing that I have been saying denies the 'Everlasting Gospel' of the two great commandments; but it is time that Christians realized that some of their highest values may be coming back to them from cultures and peoples far outside Christendom".[92]

Needham had thus moved from a strong, if not entirely orthodox, Christianity in early life to a broadly ecumenical or universalist religious world-view by his later life. He continued to fight against the vices of materialistic secularism or unrestrained capitalism. He defended science against the counter-culturists, while agonising over "the Pandora's box" of technology. And through it all he preserved his sense of The Holy. Science had much to say, much to contribute. But, like Immanuel Kant, Needham was hungry for the "inaccessible beyond".

---

[1] Mansel Davies, "Joseph Needham", *British Journal History of Science*, 30, 1 (1997), pp. 95-100. For biographical material, I have also drawn on Needham's entry in the *Oxford Dictionary of National Biography* (by Gregory Blue), and other sources.

[2] Needham in an interview late in life attested to his father's religious influence. As Gary Wersky writes: "During his life the elder Joseph had passed through the Anglo-Catholicism of the Oxford Movement, the mysticism of the Quakers, ending up with the rationality of Christian modernism. The final tendency was ably expressed every Sunday morning at the Temple Church in London, where Bishop E. W. Barnes presided. For many years, the two male members of the Needham family would faithfully attend these services, thereby enabling the son to listen to 'discourse on the pre-Socratic philosophers and medieval scholasticism and all kinds of things which would not normally come into sermons'": see Gary Wersky, *The Visible College: A Collective Biography of British Scientists and Socialists in the 1930s* (New York, Holt, Rinehart & Winston, 1979), p. 71 (interview with Needham in 1968).

[3] Davies, "Joseph Needham", p. 95.

[4] On this generally (and also on Needham), see Wersky, *The Visible College*, especially chapter 4. Wersky describes Needham as "a tall, lumbering, bookish Englishman, given to introspective ruminations" (p. 68).

[5] As Simon Winchester comments: "communist spymasters and agents, it turned out, had pitilessly duped him". Secret Soviet documents subsequently published show that the sites to which Needham and his scientific colleagues on the International Commission were taken during their investigations "had all been *created artificially* by, or with the help of, intelligence agents from the Soviet Union": Simon Winchester, *The Man Who Loved China* (New York, Harper, 2009), p. 212, and for the whole affair, chapter 6.

[6] *Oxford Dictionary of National Biography.*

[7] Shigeru Nakayama, "Joseph Needham, Organic Philosopher", in Nakayama and N. Sivin, eds., *Chinese Science: Explorations of an Ancient Tradition* (Massachusetts, M.I.T. East Asian Science Series, 1973), pp. 23-44.

[8] McKenzie Wark, "Extrapolation, not Acceleration": www.publicseminar.org/2014/09, p. 2.

[9] Gregory Blue, "Joseph Needham, Heterodox Marxism and the Social Background to Chinese Science", *Science & Society*, 62, 2 (1998), pp. 195-217.

[10] Blue, "Joseph Needham", pp. 195-196.

[11] 1967 Notes, quoted Blue, "Joseph Needham", p. 198.

[12] See Paul Crook, *Darwin's Coat-Tails: Essays on Social Darwinism* (London, Peter Lang, 2007), where I argue that Darwinist theory was highly conditioned by the British Industrial Revolution.

[13] 1967 Notes, quoted Blue, "Joseph Needham", p. 199.
[14] *Ibid*, pp. 200-201.
[15] I discuss this in my book *Darwin's Coat-Tails*, Essay 4.
[16] Joseph Needham, *The Great Amphibium: Four Lectures on the Position of Religion in a World Dominated by Science* (London, Student Christian Movement Press, 1931). Three of the lectures had appeared in journals. The term "Amphibium" is rare. Needham took it from Thomas Browne's verse reference to "MAN that great and true Amphibium, whose nature is disposed to live, not only like other creatures in divers elements, but in divided and distinguished worlds".
[17] *Ibid*, p. 11.
[18] *Ibid*, p. 12.
[19] *Ibid*, pp. 17-18. In an essay of 1935 Needham expanded on the dangers of "the scientific spirit" (or the "opium of science"). Science led to the tacit belief that the problem of evil could be solved by social engineering, and it fostered the process of secularisation: "The principle of ethical neutrality leads to a general chaos in the traditional system of morals, and hence to decay in the religious emotion formerly attached to the performance of certain actions.... And, above all, in actively interfering with the external world, in persistently probing its darkest corners, science destroys that feeling of creaturely dependence upon, and intimate relation to, a transcendent and supernal Being, which has certainly been one of the most marked characteristics of the religious spirit": Joseph Needham, *Time: The Refreshing River: Essay and Addresses, 1932-1942* (London, Allen and Unwin, 1943), pp. 70-71.
[20] Needham, *The Great Amphibium*, p. 23.
[21] *Ibid*, pp. 24-25.
[22] *Ibid*, p. 35.
[23] *Ibid*, p. 37.
[24] *Ibid*, p. 40.
[25] *Ibid*, pp. 41-42.
[26] *Ibid*, p. 57.
[27] He may have got this concept of the "numinous" from the book by the German theologian Rudolf Otto, translated as *The Idea of the Holy* (1923; published in German 1917). "Numinous" implies an association with the divine or transcendence, and has a sense of mystical revelation, awe and dread mixed with mysterious fascination. The term was used later by Carl Jung and C. S. Lewis. A perceptive reviewer in 1933 remarked of Needham: "Science is conceived *a la* Eddington as quantitative, general, abstract; religion *a la* Otto as 'numinous experience'": Gregory Vlastos (Queen's University, Ontario), "Review of *The Great Amphibium*", *Journal of Religion*, 13, 1 (1933), pp. 100-101.
[28] Needham, *The Great Amphibium*, p. 84.
[29] *Ibid*, pp. 138-139.
[30] *Ibid*, p. 145.
[31] *Ibid*, pp. 147-148.
[32] *Ibid*, p. 160.
[33] He felt that this other-worldliness, this tendency to withdraw from everyday life, had as one danger that it alienated the committed social reformer: "It is

probable that this attribute will bring about the death of organised religion in the west within the next two or three centuries" (*Ibid*, p. 163). Rowan Williams analyses this drawback of monasticism in his fascinating book *A Silent Action: Engagements with Thomas Merton* (Louisville, SPCK Publishing, 2013).

[34] On Darwin's deep love of nature and natural beauty, even his Romanticism towards it, see George Levine, *Darwin Loves You* (Princeton, Princeton University Press, 2006). I have discussed Julian Huxley in my book *Darwin's Coat-Tails*. Also see R. S. Deese, *We Are Amphibians: Julian and Aldous Huxley on the Future of our Species* (Oakland, University of California Press, 2015).

[35] Needham, *The Great Amphibium*, p. 150.

[36] *Ibid*, p. 151.

[37] *Ibid*, pp. 152-153.

[38] *Ibid*.

[39] *Ibid*, pp. 158-159. Not all commentators have fully appreciated Needham's belief in the deep antagonisms, the seemingly intractable differences, between science and religion. Eric Hobsbawm certainly misconstrues this in his otherwise perceptive essay, "Mandarin in a Phrygian Cap: Joseph Needham", in his *Fractured Times: Culture and Society in the Twentieth Century* (London, Little Brown, 2013), chapter 15. Hobsbawm asserts that Needham "certainly did not believe [religion] was in conflict with science, although he approved of Confucius's view that the existence of gods and spirits must be accepted, but kept at a distance" (p. 189).

[40] Needham, *The Great Amphibium*, p. 162.

[41] *Ibid*, p. 161.

[42] *Ibid*, p. 165. McKenzie Wark has recently offered a synthetic account of Needham's thought. He sees a strikingly contemporary aspect of Needham's work in that "he comes very close to a kind of epistemological pluralism, where different kinds of knowledge might co-exist, each with its own aims, methods and criteria. Initially he seems to have thought of different modes of knowledge as separate but parallel. Later, his thought turns to the problem, not of their synthesis, but of their relation to each other. He remained sceptical of any way of knowing that claims to be the royal road to knowledge or total worldview." Needham was opposed to philosophies such as logical positivism, which was wilfully ignorant of history and art; but he was equally opposed "to that tendency in literature represented to him by D. H. Lawrence that belittled the scientific worldview and put irrationalism in command. In each mode of knowledge what was of value was that which supported both autonomy and communion with other modes" (Wark, "Extrapolation, not Acceleration", p. 2). (It is worth noting, however, that Needham quoted approvingly quite often from Lawrence, especially when Lawrence claimed the legitimacy of modes of thought that transcended empiricism.) Wark is a critical/cultural/situationist theorist .

[43] Hobsbawm, *Fractured Times*, pp. 185-186.

[44] See Simon Winchester, *The Man Who Loved China*; published in the UK as *Bomb, Book and Compass*. Another of the "red" scientists, or Visible College, was Desmond Bernal, a serial womaniser with unorthodox marital arrangements.

When I was doing some research on Bernal's wartime activities, I consulted his papers at Cambridge University Library. There was one collection marked "Sealed". When I asked about it I was told that this was a large archive containing his love letters, not to be opened until 2021. My research was published as "The Case Against Area Bombing", chapter 10 in Peter Hore ed., *Patrick Blackett: Sailor, Scientist and Socialist* (London, Frank Cass Publishers, 2003); a shortened version of my "Science and War: Radical Scientists and the Tizard-Cherwell Area Bombing Debate in Britain", *War & Society*, 12 (1994), pp. 69-101.

[45] Needham, *Time: The Refreshing River.* The essay referred to was first published in a book of essays entitled *Christianity and the Social Revolution* (London, Gollancz, 1935).

[46] Needham, *Time: The Refreshing River*, p. 56.

[47] *Ibid*, p. 57.

[48] *Ibid.*

[49] *Ibid*, p. 58.

[50] *Ibid.*

[51] He adds a little later: "The Christian who becomes a communist does so precisely because he sees no other body of people in the world of our time who are concerned to put Christ's commands into literal execution". *Ibid*, p. 64.

[52] *Ibid*, p. 60.

[53] *Ibid.*

[54] *Ibid.*

[55] *Ibid*, p. 65.

[56] *Ibid*, p. 66.

[57] *Ibid.*

[58] *Ibid*, p. 69

[59] *Ibid*, p. 70.

[60] *Ibid.*

[61] I discuss this in my book *Darwinism, War and History* (Cambridge, Cambridge University Press, 1994), p. 13. On the demonisation of Social Darwinism in popular culture, see my piece "Social Darwinism: Myth and Reality" in the online science journal *This View of Life: The Evolution Institute* (September 2015).

[62] Needham, *Time: The Refreshing River*, p. 115.

[63] *Ibid.*

[64] *Ibid*, p. 116.

[65] *Ibid*, p. 240.

[66] *Ibid*, p. 235.

[67] *Ibid*, p. 236.

[68] *Ibid*, p. 269.

[69] *Ibid*, p. 260.

[70] *Ibid*, p. 263.

[71] *Ibid*, p. 265.

[72] Joseph Needham, *Within the Four Seas: The Dialogue of East and West* (London, Allen and Unwin, 1969). The title came from a Confucian poem of the fifth

century B.C: "He who respects the dignity of man, and practises what love and courtesy require – for him all men within the four seas are brothers". Needham's speech of 9 May 1961 was in reply to a motion "Where Science Advances, Religion Recedes".
[73] *Ibid*, pp. 196-197.
[74] *Ibid*, p. 189.
[75] *Ibid*, pp. 190-191.
[76] *Ibid*, p. 193
[77] *Ibid*, p. 194.
[78] *Ibid*, pp. 195-199.
[79] Joseph Needham, "Christianity and the Asian Cultures", a sermon preached in Gonville and Caius College, 22 January 1961, in *Ibid,* p. 201.
[80] *Ibid*, p. 202.
[81] *Ibid*, p. 203.
[82] *Ibid*, p. 204.
[83] *Ibid*, p. 205.
[84] Joseph Needham, "History and Human Values; A Chinese Perspective for World Science and Technology", *Centennial Review*, 20 (1976), pp. 1-35 (quote p.1). This was based on a talk he gave to the Canadian Association of Asian Studies in May 1975. His mentor, the priest Conrad Noel, often used the term World Cooperative Commonwealth to mean the immediate goal of human social evolution.
[85] *Ibid*, p. 12.
[86] *Ibid*.
[87] *Ibid*, p. 13.
[88] *Ibid*, p. 22.
[89] *Ibid*, p. 31.
[90] *Ibid*, p. 32.
[91] *Ibid*. Needham believed (perhaps wanted to believe) that the Maoist regime still respected the conservationist values of older tradition, for example being conscious of the dangers of pollution. He argued that a socialist economy could better regulate such matters than a free-wheeling capitalist one. Late in life he was dismayed by the industrial pollution and destruction of historic heritage sites in Chinese cities that he visited: see Winchester, *The Man Who Loved China*.
[92] Needham, *Time: The Refreshing River*, p. 35.

14. Social Darwinism: Myth and Reality

When I first encountered Social Darwinism as a student, my first reaction, I'm afraid, was something like this: Oh, Social Darwinism, wasn't that used to justify ruthless capitalism, militarism, imperialism and racism, using Darwin's "survival of the fittest"? - something that ended up in Nazi eugenics and the elimination of the Jews in the death camps?

One would have hoped that these simplistic stereotypes would have been supplanted by more nuanced views in this day and age, at least in academic circles. Sadly, it seems not. I have heard such clichés hurled around almost as knee-jerk reactions at history conferences, whenever Darwinism is evoked in debate. Hopefully symposia such as this one[1] will help to rectify the situation. One can always hope. But I am struck by the resilience, the sheer survival power, of such stereotypes, even when contradicted by overwhelming scholarly evidence. The question that needs to be asked, it follows, is what social and cultural conditions reinforce and serve to preserve such misconceptions? I know that there are young scholars attempting to plumb such depths at the moment.

Darwin's concept of struggle was fascinatingly complex, full of ambivalences. He recognised that it was multi-layered. I am using it, he said, not in a rigorous scientific sense (which he regretted) but "in a large metaphorical sense". He distinguished many types of struggle, ranging from violent predation and savage killing of prey, to struggle for resources, to ecological dependence:

> I shall use the word struggle… including in this term several ideas primarily distinct, but graduating into each other, as the dependency of one organic being on another… the agency whether organic or inorganic of what may be called chance… and lastly what may be more strictly a struggle, whether voluntarily as in animals or involuntary as in plants.

Thus in the *Origin of Species*[2] we are given many possibilities: conflict, dependence, chance; not only brutal victory or dominance, but also coadaptation and coexistence. He used vivid metaphors such as the web of nature, the tree of life, the tangled bank, to represent a grand and integrated biological system that was life, holistic and interdependent as well as undeniably "red in tooth and claw". His struggle metaphor, as that luminous thinker Gillian Beer put it, "expresses his unwillingness to give dominance to a militant or combative order of nature".[3]

If there was grandeur in this view of life, as he famously said, there were also myriad usages, validations, interrogations, illuminations, subversions that filtered from it into politics, religion, social thought and philosophy, to name a few discourses. Because of its ambivalences, Darwinism was infinitely adaptable for use in an amazing galaxy of ideas, agendas, and ideologies. They ranged from the epistemically pure and supposedly "hard science" to pseudo-science and outright propaganda. Darwinian science was undeniably culturally conditioned to start with – Darwin took many metaphors and terms from industrial and imperial Britain – and the Social Darwinisms that followed were also culturally conditioned, varying from nation to nation, culture to culture. This can be found in debates on such topics as the nature of capitalism, Man and God, race, war and human violence. Just as people had raided the Bible to sustain their particular world-view, so they raided the *Origin of Species* to the same end. And the spectrum of people and parties was dizzying: Robber Baron capitalists, laissez faire theorists, militarists arguing the survival of the fittest to utopian (sometimes even revolutionary) socialists, mutual aid Kropotkinites, technocratic Fabians, and pacifists appealing to the cooperationist side of Darwin, his unwillingness to give dominance to a combative or militant order of nature.

Yet it is that dark one-sided perspective of Darwinism that has come to prevail in the public imagination. The mental association is of a Godless, amoral, ruthlessly self-interested, unequal world based on greed, force and survival at all costs. If we dig deep enough we find that this dark Darwinian image was frequently the creation of its numerous critics. (Paradoxically they were willing enough to use Darwinism themselves when it suited their purposes.) The historical reality is that buccaneering dog-eat-dog capitalist apologetics and stark force-based imperialist and militarist rhetorics gained surprisingly little traction in the nineteenth century Anglo-American world. If we take war theory (something I have looked at in some detail), of course there were those who argued that humans were biologically-programmed fighting animals, and saw war as an adaptive response to long-term evolutionary pressures. But historians have underestimated an alternative discourse of "peace biology". It derived from Darwin's cooperationist ideas and his predictions that humanity was likely to evolve into a higher, more ethical and peaceful stage of its history. This discourse was more amenable to traditional moral culture, and conventions of order and legitimacy, than was unpleasantly ruthless militarism. Even in one of the more blatant militaristic national systems of the pre-1914 period, Wilhelmine Germany, it seems to me that war doctrine was less dependent upon biological justifications (despite General Friedrich von Bernhardi's "war is a biological necessity") than upon nationalistic and realpolitik factors.

It was Allied propaganda during and after World War I that magnified out of all proportion the demonic role of Prussianised Social Darwinism in causing the war.[4]

Social Darwinism has routinely been linked with the rise of imperialism. I tested this supposed linkage in the instance of British imperialism during its massive expansionist phase, examining books, periodicals and political speeches from the 1880s to 1914, the age of the "New Empire".[5] To my surprise, the textbook orthodoxy proved almost totally fallible. Very few people used sustained or serious "Darwinian" reasoning to justify empire, that is using central biological concepts such as natural selection or differential reproduction. (One exception was the biometrician and eugenist Karl Pearson.) "Darwinian" themes were used, when used at all, primarily as slogans and catchcries ("survival of the fittest" being the most popular), or as simplistic propaganda, crude theatre and cultural extravaganza. By far the most common and sustained defences of empire were couched in traditional geo-political, economic, nationalistic and – hard for us to imagine today – moralistic terms: Britain's moral mission to confer the benefits of its western and Christian civilisation upon less fortunate colonial peoples. Again, it was the critics who largely created the myth of a Darwinised imperial discourse; critics such as the "New Liberal" J. A. Hobson who feared the authoritarian implications of biological determinism and biology-based social science, fears writ large in his classic *Imperialism: A Study*.[6]

As for Charles Darwin himself, he was no redneck reactionary or heartless neo-con. He best fits the category of liberal progressive. Through his grandfather Erasmus, his roots were in the Enlightenment. He wanted to improve the human condition by means of education and gradualist reform. I see him as essentially an optimist. Unlike some of those who came to evoke his name, he did not take a "pitiably low view of human nature". He admitted the possibility of human decline and extinction, because evolutionary history was full of extinctions, failures to adapt to crises. He could be bafflingly vague and ambivalent at times, swinging for example between physical and cultural evolution as motors of human evolution. Ultimately his emphasis came down on cultural evolution as the prevalent mode of human change. On race – although he was not uninfluenced by current Victorian stereotypes – he saw *Homo sapiens* as one species, probably descended from a common ancestor. Differences in group traits, such as skin colour, were minor, best explained in terms of adaptation, divergence and geo-political isolation. The dominant "races" of any era had got there largely by dint of superior social organisation. There were no guarantees that (say) the Anglo-Saxon races would stay top-dog forever. It was quite possible that (say) Asian peoples would supplant them, if they became more socially efficient.

True, Darwin did flirt with the eugenical ideas of his cousin Francis Galton towards the end of his life. He shared some of the anxieties of the period about a swarming population of the less intelligent lower classes, and about the danger of lowering selective pressures because of welfarist reforms. One possible solution was to improve the human stock by selective breeding. But Darwin remained an ethical and humane man. He did not approve of cruel exploitation of workers for profit, and he welcomed improved living conditions as a sign of advancing civilisation. Ultimately he had faith that humanity possessed the capacity to evolve to higher levels of civilisation, becoming more peaceful, altruistic and just. Both biology and culture could contribute towards this. His later classic *The Descent of Man* exhorted its readers to extend their "social instincts and sympathies", firstly "to all the members of the same nation", then, having reached this point, there were only artificial barriers to prevent their sympathies extending to the people of "all nations and races" The virtue of sympathy, "one of the noblest with which man is endowed", would eventually be extended "to all sentient things".[7]

---

[1] "Truth and Reconciliation for Social Darwinism", online symposium, September 2015: evolution-institute.org.

[2] Charles Darwin, *On the Origin of Species by Means of Natural Selection, or the Preservation of Favoured Races in the Struggle for Life* (New York, D. Appleton & Co., 1859). The above quote is based on "Struggle for Existence", chapter III of *Origin of Species.* The exact wording I have taken here from his later extended version (unpublished in his lifetime) called *Natural Selection*, ed. R. C. Stauffer (Cambridge, Cambridge University Press, 1975), pp. 186-188.

[3] Gillian Beer, "Darwin's Reading and the Fiction of Development", in D. Kohn, ed., *The Darwinian Heritage* (Princeton, Princeton University Press, 1985), p. 70.

[4] See Paul Crook, *Darwinism, War and History (Cambridge, Cambridge University Press, 1994).*

[5] Paul Crook, "Historical Monkey Business", *Darwin's Coat-Tails: Essays on Social Darwinism* (Oxford, Peter Lang, 2007),Essay 12.

[6] J. A. Hobson, *Imperialism: A Study* (New York, James Pott & Company, 1902).

[7] Charles Darwin, *The Descent of Man* (London, John Murray, 1871, reprinted 1901), p. 185.

1. The Politics of Heredity: Essays on Eugenics, Biomedicine and the Nature-Nurture Debate. By Diane B. Paul (Albany: State University of New York Press, 1988).

Here we have a collection of revisionist essays by one of the more discerning scholars in this history of science discourse. Two essays at least have been justly described as minor classics. Diane Paul was originally a political science PhD who then turned to the apparently disparate field of biology. The interaction of science and politics has proven to be most fruitful, so that she speaks of the political dimensions of science with professional authority. (Some historians of science are resistant to the whole idea of science being conditioned by politics, while others are too ideological and sweeping, some just too local in their politics.)

Paul made her name with a 1984 essay on "Eugenics and the Left" (one of the "minor classics" mentioned above). She documented the undeniable attraction of eugenics to (mainly British) socialist-reformist intellectuals. After all there had been an ameliorationist wing of the eugenics movement that had leftist leanings in Britain from the days of Francis Galton and Karl Pearson. These people (including Bernard Shaw and H. G. Wells) were fatally attracted to the ideal of protoplasmic engineering, wanting a superior proletariat for the future socialist utopia. They wanted socialism to have a modern and scientific image, echoing Lenin's "scientific socialism". This was in contrast to the supposedly *laissez-faire* "Social Darwinism" of earlier times (something of a furphy, but Paul doesn't get into this dust-up). Paul shows that reformist "eugenics" and hereditarianism continued to have an underground existence in the 1930s and 1940s, despite the usual textbook equation of eugenics with reaction and Nazism.

Throughout the book there are illuminating discussions of the changing usage of the term "eugenics". Its level of acceptance varied with political factors and the historical context. Contrary to accepted wisdom (until recently), this had surprisingly little to do with advancing scientific, especially genetic, knowledge. As Paul shows in her other classic paper, "Did Eugenics Rest on an Elementary Mistake?", eugenics came under serious theoretical attack as early as 1917. The work of Edward M. East and R. C. Punnett using the Hardy-Weinberg formula (a feared phrase for many members of the English Eugenics Society) seemed to suggest that policies of segregation or sterilisation would have only limited impact in eliminating feeble-mindedness, given the large numbers of "invisible" carriers of the alleged recessive gene for mental defect.[1] Yet – despite this strong scientific evidence – eugenics flourished in the 1920s, and indeed was even more widely applied in the 1930s (the period when it was supposed to have died out under the blows of a more sophisticated genetics, plus Nazi race hygiene – both problematic cases).

As Paul brilliantly shows, the whole matter was complex, and judgments on the generally agreed scientific facts were based on different values than today: "The Hardy-Weinberg theorem meant different things to different people". For many, and this included Lancelot Hogben, Herbert Jennings and E. G. Conklin – usually seen as critics of eugenics – even a small reduction in incidence of feeble-mindedness, and prevention of propagation, was worth the effort. Paul carefully unravels the mathematics of the debate, giving credence to Ronald A. Fisher's work, often debunked as eugenic propaganda. Ronald Fisher versus J. B. S. Haldane may have been right versus left, but in the end they basically agreed that compulsory sterilisation could probably cut the supply of mental defectives by about ten per cent.

What has happened since (Paul suggests) is that revulsion against Nazi atrocities, a trend towards patients' rights in medicine, and the rise of feminism have made reproductive autonomy a dominant value in our culture. Paul questions the social implications of this commitment and she foreshadows shifts in it as global conditions change. Do read her "PKU Screening", which asks why major resources have been devoted to screening for a rare recessive disorder leading to mental retardation, and why so much hype has been given to a diet treatment widely portrayed as a success story when, alas, it is not. One answer is that both "enthusiasts for genetic medicine and critics of genetic determinism have come to find the story useful". Shifts in political culture explain many otherwise inexplicable mutations in scientific and biomedical perspectives. She explains, in one example, why carrier detection was viewed in the interwar years as a way of rooting out defective genes, and in the postwar period as a means of masking their effects.

These are important ideas meant to have an impact upon our time and issues such as genetic engineering and biomedical interventions. The essays are also written in a lively and entertaining style. One is reminded of Stephen Jay Gould's popular essays, or – to take a wilder comparison – of John Sutherland's literary sleuthing in Victorian literature ("Is Heathcliff a Murderer?" etc). Scientific sleuthing can also be fun.

---

[1] I discuss these matters in detail in Paul Crook, "Eugenics, Genetics and Feeblemindedness", *Darwin's Coat-Tails: Essays on Social Darwinism* (New York, Peter Lang, 2007).

2. The Dictionary of Nineteenth-Century British Philosophers. Ed. W. J. Mander, Alan P. F. Sell, *et al.* (Bristol: Thoemmes Press, 2002), 2 volumes.

This is a sequel to the successful Thoemmes dictionaries on seventeenth and eighteenth century British philosophers. These works meet a pressing need, as there is no comparable reference work in this area, although the new *Oxford Dictionary of National Biography* covers major thinkers. The great strength of the Thoemmes dictionary is its amazing comprehensiveness. Not only are the "usual suspects" there, the best-known philosophers (from Whewell, Hamilton, McTaggart and Dugald Stewart to Green, Bosanquet, Sidgwick, Whitehead, Schiller and Russell), but also main thinkers in a wide range of discourses, plus a great swag of "lesser, even quite obscure, authors" on the grounds "that they indicate the scope of the intellectual environment in which those who have become household names worked". This is a great boon to anyone interested in British intellectual history. Far too often we have to scratch around for information on minor figures, while there is a surfeit of material on the big names.

Purists may quite likely object that the editors have stretched the term "philosopher" to breaking point (indeed they give no exact definition of the term). They seem simply to have included anyone who is deemed to have made a contribution to British philosophy. Many entries relate to areas other than "pure" philosophy (whatever that is), and to people who ranged across a rich diversity of fields. There are political theorists: e.g. Bagehot, Bentham, Engels (why not Marx?), Gladstone, Godwin, Hobhouse, Kropotkin, the Mills, Morris, Owen and Spencer – just to list them is to indicate the problem of categorisation; social theorists (Arnold, Carlyle, Carpenter, Cobbett, Galton, George, Harrison, Kidd, Ruskin, the Webbs, Wells); theologians and religious thinkers (Balfour, Butler, Drummond, Gore, Maurice, Newman, Paley, Pattison, Pusey); economists (Cairnes, Bain, Cobden, Jevons, Malthus, Marshall); scientists (Darwin, Huxley, Babbage, Faraday, Lyell, Clerk Maxwell, Wallace); colonial theorists (Bryce, Buller, Dicey, Froude, Seeley, Wakefield); legal thinkers (Austin, Brougham); anthropologists (Lubbock, Maine); artists and aesthetes (Ford Madox Brown, Holman

Hunt, Pater, Whistler); writers on women's issues (Fawcett, Edgeworth, Martineau, Schreiner); historians (Grote, Lecky, Macaulay); and literary figures (the Brownings, Disraeli, Blake, Byron, Coleridge, George Eliot, Gissing, Wordsworth).

Overall there are more than 600 entries by 160 authors, mainly from Britain and North America. And here I should state an interest in that I wrote one entry (on Benjamin Kidd). The essays on major figures – their lives and ideas – are reasonably, but not excessively, detailed, a sensible decision given the ready availability of monographs on them. The editors have handed some big names, not to the usual authorities, but to younger scholars and people in related discourses, with some refreshing results. Flexibility has been the goal, flexibility in respect of chronological limits, the concept of Britishness and disciplinary boundaries: "In selecting entries for this dictionary we have sought to have in mind the nineteenth century's broad understanding of the nature and scope of philosophical thought".

My judgment of specific items upon which I have knowledge is that high standards have been achieved. However I have some reservations. The production is sumptuous but the format itself is rather stodgy. In this day and age one expects something more vivid and user-friendly. For example, the reader needs constantly to juggle between the volumes, given that the list of contributors is at the start of volume one and the index is at the end of volume two. Why not simply print the contributor's name at the close of the entry? However this has been a monumental project and the work of the editorial team has been fruitful and valuable. I look forward to seeing the next volumes on the twentieth century.

3. Crossing Borders: Political Essays. By Bernard Crick (London, New York: Continuum, 2001).

I came to know Bernard Crick when he was supervising my PhD at LSE (The London School of Economics, London University) in the early 1960s. He was then best known for his book *The American Science of Politics* (1959), a London doctoral thesis reshaped after a four-year teaching stint at Harvard and McGill universities in the US, and much influenced by the "Chicago School" of Charles Merriam and Harold Lasswell. Echoing Alexis de Tocqueville and Gunnar Myrdal (who argued that America was conservative but the principles conserved were liberal), Crick contended that political science there was not value-free, but was based upon democratic idealism. Politics was treated as an agreed implementation of an agreed set of values within a closed political system. Bernard became a prolific writer on political theory and practice, including reform of the British parliament, the Labour party and socialism, Northern Ireland, Scottish devolution, and (perennially) citizenship, an ideal he might be said to have spent a fruitful lifetime trying to invigorate. His classic works are probably his long-running bestseller *In Defence of Politics* (1962) and his *George Orwell: A Life* (1980).

Following in Orwell's footsteps, Crick has made the political essay an art form, aimed at educated readers and concerned citizens. In his seventies, when this collection appeared, and loaded down with public laurels (but still active at the time, heading a group of experts reporting to the Home Office on the degree of English knowledge needed by those seeking naturalisation), he was still busy publishing other collections of essays on politics, literature, polemics and much else. This 2001 effort crossed borders: academic borders, genre borders, and personal borders between England, Wales, Ireland and Scotland. Living in Edinburgh for the last twenty or more years of his life, he became almost an honorary Scot. He was proud that his fellows had honoured him rather as a "lifelong gadfly" than as a conventional (too often constricted) scholar. This certainly comes out in his penetrating, irreverent and often provocative comments on a wide spectrum of topics – from his substantial pieces on Britishness, Englishness, and Scotchness ("The Sense of the Identity of the Indigenous

British" as one essay is entitled) to essays on Loyalist Unionism, multiculturism, postmodernism, New Labour (which he warned was potentially authoritarian), the decline of political writing, and some delightful papers on his favourites such as Hannah Arendt, Isaiah Berlin, Bernard Shaw, Orwell; and those great forerunners of his at LSE: Harold Laski on the left of the political pendulum, and Michael Oakeshott at the other end. He often spoke kindly of his departmental head Oakeshott to me, even though they disagreed fundamentally on political doctrine.

I would love to delve into these topics but space forbids. The early essays foreshadow the ideas that he planned to investigate fully in his magnum opus on *The Four Nations* (but which, alas, he never completed). It was essential, he argued, that Englishness not be confused with Britishness, but be seen as one culture within laws originally framed for four nations. Crick was hopeful that devolution, etc., need not spell future disaster. In fact the various communities, old and new, in the UK might deal more justly with each other if it were better understood how historically Britain had been a multinational and multiethnic state. This theme is argued with a deft sense of history, and sensitive subtlety. [It is fascinating to speculate what he would have had to say about the recent events centrally concerned with national identities, such as the independence referendum in Scotland and the Brexit upheaval].

Crick's style enabled him to be impressively nuanced (possibly too nuanced for the supposed general reader). Orwell famously advised the use of simple English. His biographer was more than capable of observing this maxim in the breach. He was fond of long parentheses, asides, qualifications, thinking aloud, idiosyncrasies, even (heaven forbid) prolixities, interspersed with pithy and accessible encapsulations. As a style it can be an acquired taste, but it can also be addictive.

[I wrote this in 2003. Born in 1929, Bernard Crick died in December 2008. He was a great character, a fine, if also flawed, man, who was a greatly influential public intellectual. As a scholar I am immensely in his debt.]

4. War Against the Weak: Eugenics and America's Campaign to Create a Master Race. By Edwin Black (New York, London, Four Walls Eight Windows, 2003).

Eugenics, although born in Britain (the brainchild of Francis Galton), was formidably implemented in the United States. From there it was exported to the world, and most infamously to Germany, where sterilisation and "euthanasia" of the "unfit" or "undesirables" turned into genocide. The US was the engine-room for Hitler's eugenic programme, although by the 1930s Germany had taken the lead and American eugenists were openly envious about the thoroughness of Nazi "race hygiene". After the war American eugenists conveniently distanced themselves from the Nazis. Historians such as Mark Haller, Kenneth Ludmerer, and even Daniel Kevles, absorbed the official line that hardline eugenics and racist science were largely confined to a lunatic fringe of American right-wingers. Eugenics was supposed to have lost scientific respectability during the 1930s.[1]

However a new generation of revisionist historians of science, including Garland Allen, Barry Mehler, Allan Chase, Stephen Trombley, Robert Proctor, Paul Weindling and a number of younger German scholars, have challenged this orthodoxy. Eugenics has been shown to have had much greater survival power than expected, and to have been widespread within American scientific, medical and social elites. (In my own research I have encountered very general adherence to eugenic thinking amongst medicos in Britain, and this was true also of Australia.) There were strong ideological affinities and a mutually supportive relationship between American and German eugenics during the Nazi period, as convincingly shown and brilliantly analysed in Stefan Kuhl's *The Nazi Connection: Eugenics, American Racism and German National Socialism* (Oxford, New York, Oxford University Press, 1994).

This revisionist trend has been strongly reinforced in this book by investigative journalist Edwin Black, author of *IBM and the Holocaust.* Black has used an army of (mostly volunteer) researchers to ransack archives in the US, Britain, Germany and elsewhere, governmental, organisational, corporate and private. Most notably Black has explored hitherto unused American material from state, county, local and institutional archives. This was essentially where the invasive eugenic programmes took place that targeted, trampled the civil rights of, and in effect tried to wipe out "the submerged tenth" in the name of respectable science:

> The victims of eugenics were poor urban dwellers and rural "white trash" from New England to California, immigrants from across Europe, Blacks, Jews, Mexicans, Native Americans, epileptics, alcoholics, petty criminals, the mentally ill and anyone who did not resemble the blond and blue-eyed Nordic ideal that the eugenics movement glorified.

Black recreates the roles in all this of scientists, academics, universities, schools, business, bureaucrats, politicians, the press, philanthropic institutes such as Carnegie and Rockefeller, doctors, psychiatrists, mental testers, and of course the eugenic societies and journals. The American section is the most original part of the book, although much interesting new material is presented on Britain and Germany. By using overseas records Black was able to recover materials that had been "cleansed" from American files. His use of the Rockefeller archives sheds extra light on the foundation's crucial funding of the Kaiser Wilhelm institutes, and thus Hitler's master race project. Would the Holocaust have happened without Rockefeller?

Black vividly recreates the horrendous Nazi narrative. The 550 page work is indeed full of narrative power. It is not as analytically sophisticated as Kuhl's work (which is not sufficiently acknowledged). One could argue that Black is too one dimensional in his view of eugenics. It was in reality multi-valent, diverse and complex. But that is to miss the point. This is not a history of science work. It is investigative journalism of the highest calibre, designed to inform, to jolt our consciences, to show how immense abuses of power and shameful injustices can occur even in supposedly democratic countries. Black's warning about the capacity of genetic engineering to become a reincarnation of eugenics is particularly well timed.

---

1 I discuss these issues in Essay Fifteen, "American and Nazi Eugenics: Flawed Alliance" in Paul Crook, *Darwin's Coat-Tails: Essays on Social Darwinism* (New York, Peter Lang, 2007).

5. Perceptions of Race and Nation in English and American Travel Writers, 1833-1914. By Erik S. Schmeller (New York, Bern, Oxford, Peter Lang, 2004).

By examining the work of twelve travel writers Schmeller hopes to reconstruct the interaction between factors of race and national identity in the Anglo-American world in a formative period from 1833 to the outbreak of the First World War.

Edward Abdy, a Cambridge graduate, saw America through a humanitarian lens. He deplored slavery, seeing racism as the defining trait of American identity. His 1835 travel journal reviled American manners and materialism, while justifying English class values. He spoke of America's "foetid atmosphere of mock equality", whereas the British breathed "the pure air of liberty". This was a sort of blend of Frances Trollope, who wrote a famous (or infamous) book on the manners of the Americans, and English Whiggery. Lady Emmeline Wortley portrayed vigorous commercialism and money-worship as more significant than race in defining national identity. Her account anticipates today's Wall Street world: "they must win, do or die, and the dead on the field are trodden under foot by their eager comrades and competitors, hurrying onward" (1851). She reinforced the idea of a "natural gentleman" by reference to the "true hero-nature" living within the Americans of the great West. This was in line with a growing tendency in the US and elsewhere to romanticise the Frontier and The West (ignoring genocide of the Native Americans, widespread outlawry – think Billy the Kid – and the violence of an emerging gun culture). Mary Seacole, the daughter of a Scots soldier and a liberated slave in Jamaica, combined pride in her race and gender with a strong perception of Englishness that was superior to the expansionist racism of the Americans (based on the American adventurers she encountered in Panama in the 1850s).

Alexander Mackenzie avoided race in his *The American in England* (1836): "we are ourselves but Englishmen in another hemisphere", a common theme. He anticipated hereditarian ideas by suggesting that the English poor and blacks shared genetic defects. Less consistently he maintained that a mobile American society had produced a more virile working class. This assumes of course that nurture was at least as important as nature in shaping human abilities. William Wells Brown and David Dorr were black travellers, a rarer breed of writers. Brown's *American Fugitive in Europe* (1855) saw race as defining both American and English national identity. A novelist, abolitionist and pacifist, Brown became an Anglophile: "no sooner was I on British soil, than I was recognised as a man, and an equal". He strove to show Americans that racial harmony was possible. Dorr's *A Colored Man Around the World* (1852) was ambiguous, given his confused status as a travelling companion, actually slave, to his globetrotting master (who later reneged on a promise to free Dorr).

Schmeller argues that racism became more entrenched in Britain and America after the Civil War, due to Darwinian ideas, nationalism and imperialism, and that this was reflected in the travel literature. For white visitors to America such as Henry Latham (1866) and Lady Mary Hardy (1879-80), "racial attitudes were no longer a source of difference between England and America but of unity". Both were patronising, with Latham stating that blacks had failed to develop beyond the mental age of fourteen. The black English composer Samuel Coleridge-Taylor was living reproof of this claim, but even he – whose tours of America in 1904, 1906 and 1910 were great successes – relied upon his educated English accent to "overshadow the color of his skin for Americans".

There is sparser evidence for Schmeller's thesis from American travellers cited for this period. The black Thomas L. Johnson put English racial tolerance so far above American that he became a British citizen in 1900. Mary Krout's *A Looker On In London* (1899) focused on women's issues, but did raise what she saw as a growing awareness that American society was becoming more multi-racial than British. Hiram Collier's *England and the English from an American Point of View* (1909) celebrated male Anglo-Saxonism, but warned of English racial decline. This was symptomatic of "degenerationist" discourse at the time.

This book was originally a thesis and it shows, with mechanical organisation and a rather perfunctory nod towards theory. Its value lies in the travel information provided. Some of the contemporary observations are great reading, even today. However there are methodological problems entailed in Schmeller's limited sample.

6. Darwin's *Origin of Species*: A Biography. By Janet Browne (Crow's Nest, Allen and Unwin, 2006).

Charles Darwin's *Origin of Species* is an obvious choice for inclusion in a series called "Books that Shook the World". As Janet Browne says, Darwin's writings "challenged everything that had previously been thought about living beings and became a crucial factor in the intellectual, social and religious transformations that took place in the West during the nineteenth century". This delightfully readable little book is a brilliant work of compression, simplification and explanation for general readers not versed in the history of science.

The story has all the ingredients so familiar to Darwin scholars: young Charles born into a professional provincial (Shrewsbury) family, with the early evolutionist Erasmus Darwin on his father's side and the industrial Wedgwoods on his mother's; an education that combined the medical-scientific traditions of Edinburgh with Cambridge intellectualism; the influence of figures like John Henslow, Adam Sedgwick, William Whewell, John Hershel, Alexander von Humboldt and William Paley's natural theology (whose ideas of Godly design Darwin ultimately denied); the catalyst of the *Beagle* voyage (Browne rehabilitates the often demonised Captain Fitzroy – the two did not quarrel over religion, and Fitzroy was the one who gave Darwin a copy of Charles Lyell's provocative *Principles of Geology*); the early insight of 1837 that matured into the articulation of natural selection after a reading of Thomas Malthus (she doesn't mention that Charles had read Malthus in 1833, with less effect); the uproar over Robert Chamber's *Vestiges of the Natural History of Creation* that deterred Charles from premature publication of his 1844 paper on evolution; his years of research into pigeons and barnacles (rather like doing a PhD thesis, something he felt he needed to do); the panic over Alfred Wallace's abstract encapsulating the concept of natural selection, and the double publication of their papers for the Linnean Society in 1858; the rushed publication of the *Origin of Species* by 1859; the sheer power of the book (its cunningly crafted arguments are carefully explained); its turbulent reception, "one of the first genuinely public debates about society to stretch across general society"; the triumph of a vigorous lobby orchestrated by younger Darwinians, such as T. H. Huxley and Joseph Hooker, over a divided opposition (a contrast to today's creationist movement); the later works including the cautiously argued *Descent of Man* (1871).

It is to be expected that Janet Browne, a biographer of Darwin, should deal well with his life. It is less expected that she should be so enlightening on post-Darwinian developments and his legacy for today's worldview. She covers the decline of natural selection theory after the rise of genetics in the late nineteenth century. Karl Pearson's biometricians squabbled with William Bateson's Mendelians (an often petty and personal dispute). Other types of evolutionary thought, such as Lamarckian and teleological, threatened to eclipse Darwinism (Peter Bowler has written well on this). Problems arose out of C. Lloyd Morgan's chromosome work, molecular biology and the displacement of naturalist field studies by laboratory research, problems that were not resolved until the brilliant work of Darwinians like Ernst Mayr, Sewell Wright and Gaylord Simpson put into place a "modern synthesis", publicised by Julian Huxley in 1942.

Browne discusses topics such as the interaction of science, politics and religion, Social Darwinism, eugenics, palaeontology, atavism, feeblemindedness, criminality and social deviance, race "science", ecology, nature versus nurture, evolutionary ethics and socio-biology, down to today's world of the "selfish gene", advertising's "alpha males", cloning and creationism.

Of course there are problematic issues where specialists will differ in their interpretations. In my own areas of interest, I would have liked more on the industrial and imperial context in which Darwinism arose. Darwin's metaphors reflected the world of business, factories and the empire ("profit and loss", "workshops", and ecological niches described as "colonising enterprises"). Browne is conventional on Social Darwinism and eugenics, ignoring recent revisionist research. The evidence suggests that Darwinism was surprisingly marginal in discourses such as capitalist ideology, militarism and the "new imperialism". There is perhaps too much emphasis on the "revolutionary" aspects of Darwinism and not enough on the subtle ways in which it was accommodated into existing paradigms. (I canvass such issues in my book *Darwin's Coat-*

Tails). Overall however this is a splendid and enjoyable book.

7. The New Eugenics? The Ethics of Bio-Technology

Is Human Nature Obsolete? Genetics, Bioengineering, and the Future of the Human Condition. Ed. Harold W. Baillie and Timothy K. Casey (Cambridge, Massachusetts and London: The MIT Press, 2005).

Liberal Eugenics: In Defence of Human Enhancement. By Nicholas Agar (Oxford, Malden MA., Blackwell, 2004).

The history of eugenics is getting tricky. Once regarded as an initially idealistic concept that degenerated into the monstrous Nazi race hygiene project or into an American sterilization assault against the disadvantaged and racially "inferior", eugenics was deemed to have died after World War Two, utterly discredited by better biological science and more enlightened social ideas. However recent research has shown that eugenics was more variegated than once thought – there were leftist and "reform" eugenists as well as "mainline" or reactionary eugenists, with dedicated opposition coming more from liberal and religious quarters. Ingrained into contemporary structures and social issues such as demography, welfare, race and gender, eugenics proved more resilient and widespread than previously thought. Historians were slow to recognize its pervasive influence in Scandinavia, Latin America and Asia, where local variants evolved as adaptations to local culture and conditions. And it has persisted to the present day. In welfarist Scandinavia, eugenics has been repackaged as reproductive autonomy or "medical" measures.[1] In Communist China it is alive and well in sterilisation programmes and the one baby policy.[2] More than this, critics allege, it has been resurrected in the "new genetics" of recent times.

Geneticists have historically been strong supporters of eugenics as a way of scientifically improving (now read "enhancing") the genetic quality of the human race. As I have argued in another place, during the inter-war period they failed properly to scrutinize methodologies and data used to support sterilisation of mental defectives[3], and it is contendable that social and ideological factors have continued to play a role – alongside epistemic factors associated with the expansion of genetic knowledge – in the motivations of biological scientists, although of course they routinely avoid the term "eugenics".

The Human Genome Project unleashed a tide of triumphalism about bio-technology[4]. But it also unleashed criticism, ranging from moderate philosophy to doomsday prophecy. Some scenarios were of the stuff of science fiction: human clones, androids, cyborgs, super-intelligent-strong-creative humans, post-humans, a world divided into a genetically enhanced elite and genetically deprived proles[5], etc, etc. There is talk of a loss of "humanhood" and the human meaning of life, of scientists "playing God" – of interfering with nature, of being morally unconcerned with the social consequences of their research: understandable enough, given the poor historical track record of scientists (there have been some honourable exceptions) in this respect, as the history of the atomic bomb suggests. The emotionality of claims both for and against human enhancement seems to have calmed down perceptibly as the Genome project has steadily advanced. Perhaps it is because we have become quietly conditioned to accept what was once unthinkable. Perhaps it is because the medical focus has been trained upon the practical benefits of specific research into congenital diseases, while the more grotesque prophecies have not yet eventuated. While the power of bio-engineering has by no means diminished, there has emerged a more realistic understanding of the limitations adhering to genetic manipulation. Nevertheless ethical concerns continue to be raised about issues such as the destruction of embryonic life in stem cell research, cloning and so on. Given that we are dealing with possibly the most dramatic scientific breakthrough in history, one that could change the human future massively, ethical debate is inevitable. It is also vital, not least because technology is threatening to quarantine itself from ethical (or any other) scrutiny.

Book titles on the ethics of bio-technology radiate a sense of concern: for instance Paul Ramsay's *Fabricated Man* (1970); John Harris's, *Wonderwoman and Superman* (1992) and *Clones, Genes and Immortality* (1998); Bernard Rollin's *The Frankenstein Syndrome* (1995); Robert Cook-Deegan's *The Gene Wars* (1996); Jeff Lyon and Peter Gorner's *Altered Fates*

(1996); Ted Peter's *Playing God?* (1997); Jon Turney's *Frankenstein's Footsteps* (1998); Bryan Appleyard's *Brave New Worlds* (1998); Thomas Shannon's *Made in Whose Image* (2000); Francis Fukuyama's *Our Posthuman Future* (2002); Leon Kass's *Human Cloning and Human Dignity* (2002); Stephen Hall's *Merchants of Immortality* (2003); Bill McKibben's *Enough: Staying Human in an Engineered Age* (2003); and Van Huyssteen's *Alone in the World?* (2006).

Debate has centred on the concepts of nature and human nature: "the questions ultimately raised by genetic engineering itself and the prospect of constructing our bodies and the bodies of future human beings are ones that go to the heart of our humanness and place in the larger scheme of things, and thus can be ignored only at our peril". Thus comments Timothy Casey in a wide-ranging set of essays aptly titled *Is Human Nature Obsolete?*[6]

Critics of human enhancement tend to argue – with varying degrees of subtlety – against interference with the order of nature, especially human nature, which is seen as a "given" or sacrosanct, stable and coherent. To meddle with its stability and complexity is to invite disaster, to distort the inherent meaning of things. Some would see it as subverting the inherent moral order of things. As the philosopher Mark Sagoff remarks, the concepts of nature and the natural carry enormous importance and emotional force: "Nature is the object of responsibility, respect, stewardship, love, rights, and reverence".[7]

One problem with this view is that humans have been obviously "interfering" with nature for ever. It is contendable that what gives a special character to the human family (including some hominids) is its capacity to adapt to, alter and control its natural habitat by means of brainpower, language, tools, etc. Since the scientific and industrial revolutions of the sixteenth century onwards (the Anthropocene era as it has been called[8]), the human capacity to control and dominate nature has risen to new, even terrifying heights, explaining scientific hubris and setting off a variety of counter movements, including the modern environmentalist and green movements. Clearly technological change has had both beneficial and harmful effects. Ethicists would presumably agree, for example, that European exploration of the New World brought valuable new resources into Europe but also introduced damaging illnesses to indigenous peoples. If a technology brings good outcomes – e.g., making people healthier, more intelligent, etc – why shouldn't we use it? We have been "enhancing" humans for a long time through education. Why not by means of bio-technology?[9] Advocates of bio-technology argue forcibly that all we need to do is to make utilitarian assessments of the outcomes of genetic manipulation. We essentially add up the possible costs and benefits. Other approaches can be dismissed as either flawed (e.g., naturalistic ethics), or antediluvian (e.g., religious), or impossibly romantic (e.g., environmentalist). Bio-ethicists such as Leon Kass or the environmentalist David Suzuki counter that this approach is not enough – it is too instrumental and hubristic. Nature is more than a system of utilitarian calculations. Sagoff summarises: "Nature may be useful, but more important, it is majestic, beautiful and sacred, either because of its randomness and spontaneity or its intricate design and balance".[10]

Darwinian history raises some interesting issues in this respect. Some early Social Darwinists used the model of a competitive struggle-based nature to justify what we now regard as morally unedifying or problematic stances, such as exploitative capitalism, militarism and racism. "Laissez faire" Darwinism based ethics on nature. People should follow the example of nature with its harsh natural selection and selection of "fitter" types. Not to do so would court disaster. They were taken to task by critics who were appalled by the violence and bloodshed of nature: Tennyson's "nature red in tooth and claw". Some critics simply substituted a more benevolent model of nature (e.g., Kropotkin's mutual aid model). However others disputed the philosophical basis of naturalistic ethics. They appealed to a long-standing tradition which claimed that "is" does not logically entail "ought" (or description entail prescription). This goes back to Hume but was given influential expression in G. E. Moore's *Principia Ethica* (1903), which sought to quarantine science from ethics. In such views it was illegitimate, a "naturalistic fallacy", to derive morals from the "is" of nature. Humans needed to put themselves "above" nature and adhere to human-derived moral codes. Clearly this is one way of validating genetic manipulation of the human genome. Sagoff notes that the advance of bio-technology has thrown into confusion "the settled distinction between nature and artifact". Bio-science could transform people from created to "fabricated" beings. This could be thought to be a bad thing: "Alternatively, one could view nature as a war of each against all – as having no moral purpose, course or direction – and so believe that by separating itself from nature, culturally and biologically, humanity fulfills its ethical potential".[11]

Interestingly the early eugenists also rejected "laissez faire" Darwinism, although more on the grounds that human interference (through social reform, welfarism, etc) was thwarting natural selection and causing human degeneration. Galton's followers advocated systematic control of human reproduction to improve the genetic quality of the stock. This led to what has been called "authoritarian eugenics", essentially led by state agencies. The abuses that resulted led to accusations that eugenics threatened the very notion of humanhood. This is still the basis of criticisms of bio-technology, but it is now directed also at concepts of "market-driven" enhancement, with private consumers driving demand for "designer babies", and so on.

Sagoff is clearly sensitive to such concerns. Is medical technology not only making irreversible interventions into the human germ line itself, but treating genomic materials, embryos, life itself as commodity? Thinkers like Kass answer yes.[12] Sagoff makes an interesting distinction between two medical traditions, one seeking to work within natural limits, the other (more dominant) concerned with conquering nature. The first would accept germ line therapy or enhancement, provided it respects "what is already present or implicit in the individual's genomes". For proponents of the opposite view, "the human genome must be reckoned with, not respected. It imposes practical limits, not moral constraints".[13]

The theological response to such latter views is understandably less than enthusiastic. Although there are significant disparities across the Catholic-Protestant-Jewish spectrum, no one (to my knowledge) accepts a genetic free for all. The Catholic theologian Karl Rahner sees the human genome as God-given and not to be meddled with in its essentials. Although human nature is "open and undetermined", to surrender the genome to the technologists would threaten inherent human freedoms. These would include the rights and autonomy of future "fabricated" individuals – a concern shared by some liberals. Other Catholic theologians allow a certain scope for genetic therapy but rule out manipulations that treat individuals "instrumentally rather than as ends in themselves". The Protestant theologian James Nash allows interventions "for the sake of perfecting or redeeming creation, but not for reshaping it to human purposes". Ronald Cole-Turner, however, rebuts this view: "To think of genetic material as the exclusive realm of divine grace and creativity is to reduce God to the level of restriction enzymes, viruses, and sexual reproduction".[14]

The Christian ethicist Jean Elshtain willingly takes the risk of being tagged a technophobe or Luddite. She defends concepts of human finitude against the threat of very powerful cultural demands – fuelled by the profit interests of large bio-tech companies – for "perfecting" the human body and privileging wealthy elites over the ordinary or the "imperfect". This constitutes a threat to the idea of Christian freedom, which (as Bonhoeffer argued) turns on recognition of relationships and natural limits to human "beingness". As Elshtain notes:

> There is a big difference between enacting human projects as cocreators respectful of a limit because, unlike God, we are neither infinite nor omniscient and, by contrast, those projects that demand humans embrace God-likeness for themselves, up to the point of displacing God himself.[15]

Spin-offs from our increasingly hedonistic and amoral culture include indifference to destruction of bodies and life (abortion, the death penalty) and the harvesting of body parts. Genetic screening and enhancement can lead to discrimination against those with inherited genetic "faults" (as is already happening with the American insurance industry). Parents who have "abnormal" children (Down syndrome, autism, the disabled, the "unchosen") are already reporting medical and popular prejudice.[16] Are we that far away from eliminating the mentally and physically inferior, as did the Nazis? Of arrogantly deciding which culturally determined types of humans should be allowed to exist at all? Elshtain detects a siege mentality among critics forced to fight a rearguard battle against powerful forces. She fears: "Too many theologians, philosophers, and cultural critics have become reticent about defending insights drawn from the riches of the Western tradition".[17]

The Boston theologian Lisa Cahill puts a similar case. She accepts that it is difficult to rule out genetic interventions by reference to an "inviolable" human nature. Nevertheless "many of us feel almost instinctively – or on the basis of cumulative moral experience that we find hard to put into the form of a logical argument – that some genetic engineering should be off-limits".[18] Leon Kass (the head of George W. Bush's Council on Bioethics) has argued that instinctive "repugnance" is our best guide in cases such as cloning of humans. It is "the emotional expression of deep wisdom, beyond reason's power to fully articulate it".[19] Cahill however rejects such essentialism and prefers an ethical argument based on social justice and cooperative relationships (as found in traditional Catholic social teaching). On such grounds, "regardless of whether or not cloning is intrinsically evil in itself", it should be regulated or even banned:

> Commercialized, technology-driven reproduction affects the social institutions of family and parenthood in deleterious ways because it makes basic, intimate human relations and communities subject to individualism, commodification, and exploitation".[20]

For their part the philosophers Casey and Sagoff seem to opt for an existential acceptance of human indeterminacy. Given that there is no going back to natural law tradition – "that is to say, to any kind of ahistorical conception of nature whose laws and structures are fixed for all time" – Casey sees us as "enmeshed, fully and without recourse, in the turbulence of history". We must either acquiesce in a biological determinism "along cybernetic lines", or we resist "the thoughtless equations of freedom with technical control and wisdom with technical expertise". Above all we will need to learn "what it means to be at home in our homelessness, and so to thrive in a world that despite our best efforts and no matter how powerful our techniques can be made neither wholly comfortable nor ultimately reassuring".[21]

Sagoff feels that bio-technology offers us both possibilities and punishments. There are real threats to human identity. He cites the British philosopher Alan Holland who explains the distrust of genetic engineering as representing what he calls a "metaphysical fear" that "centers on concerns over the implications of this technology for conceptions of identity, integrity and origin which are foundational to our world view and to our ability to classify individual beings".[22] Sagoff argues that the concept of nature that sees it as existing independently of human action or intention (one view of nature that John Stuart Mill identified) is meaningless as a scientific notion, but nevertheless "carries a great deal of force in arguments having to do with what we ought or ought not to do". Its force may depend however "on how one judges the moral worth of nature – for instance, whether one condemns nature as a gruesome war of each against all or reveres it as what God has made". But to sever nature from humanity is to invite a sort of human fatalism. The temptation is to absolve humans of responsibility for events: "In dealing with great tragedies and taking up heavy burdens, people console themselves with the thought that their plight is God's will or that it couldn't be helped". No one is to blame. This fatalism is dangerous, especially when it is used to refer to what should not be changed:

> To place nature beyond human blame or responsibility is simply to recognize the limits of our knowledge and powers. To suppose that nature has itself a moral order or purpose we should respect, in contrast, is for us to impose limits on those powers.[23]

Any appeal to a fixed nature, nature that is the source of human norms, is increasingly problematical as technology transforms the life process itself.[24] Sagoff concludes that the problem with engineering the human genome "is not so much that it will alienate or separate us from our human nature – from what is given or contingent – but that it will increasingly make us responsible for it".[25]

Nicholas Agar argues eloquently for a middle position based upon traditional liberal principles in his bravely titled *Liberal Eugenics: In Defence of Human Enhancement.* An ethics philosopher who teaches at Victoria University of Wellington, Agar feels that both advocates of enhancement technologies and their critics have a duty to take responsible stances. Advocates cannot simply assume a right to proceed (as many do) but ought to furnish "morally transparent" descriptions of their technologies. But critics are also under an obligation to show "that their criticisms are properly directed at the technologies, not merely at caricatures of them".[26] (Such caricatures are readily found in sci-fi films such as *Gattica* and *Star Wars: Attack of the Clones.*)

Agar's "liberal eugenics" is essentially market-based eugenics with safeguards to ensure individual and social rights. As opposed to authoritarian eugenics, this system would focus upon giving choices to people. The state would simply foster development of a wide range of enhancement technologies "ensuring that prospective parents were fully informed about what kinds of people these technologies would make. Parents' particular conceptions of the good life would guide them in their selection of enhancements for their children".[27] Agar uses classical liberal reasonings (especially those of John Rawls) to justify eugenic freedom in the same fashion as other liberal freedoms. However he recognizes that procedures such as somatic cell nuclear transfer have the potential to alter humans in a powerful way. Thus he stresses the need for limits to be imposed to prevent obviously unethical outcomes, such as those related to the quality of life of the individual offspring themselves. Scrutiny will be needed also of social and economic realities within liberal societies that may subvert "individual enhancement choices".[28] Limits on eugenic choice may also be needed to counter pressures towards racist, homophobic or grossly inegalitarian social outcomes (given that the expense of bio-technology would seem to favour the rich and powerful). Agar carefully considers ways of pragmatically ensuring ethical outcomes but warns that "liberal eugenicists should be open to the idea that some uses of enhancement technologies are just wrong and should be banned".[29]

How does one make such decisions? Agar uses the method of "moral images" to test cases.[30] This method reduces the "strangeness" of bio-technologies by applying moral judgments from the familiar to the unfamiliar. Moral scenarios are set up of particular test situations: these must resemble the practices at issue in relevant respects; and "we should have secure moral intuitions about them".[31] For those concerned about foundations for all this, Agar supplies detailed analysis of consequentialist, Kantian and other ethical systems. His method (he says) is not designed to displace such (sometimes differing) moral principles. Its purpose is practical, "to direct us to the wide variety of moral concerns provoked by enhancement technologies". Moral images will give the Kantians, utilitarians and other moralists a way to express their concerns: "They will propose different moral images, each of which can be assessed in terms of its closeness to the practices of enhancement".[32]

Among his major categories are the moral images of Therapy, Nature and Nurture. Overall he holds that parents should be permitted but not obliged to enhance their children. Hence he opposes the authoritarian view (as with the Nazis) that would oblige parents to enhance offspring "according to a single eugenic template".[33] This type of "therapy" supports obligations rather than permissions. Hence Agar suggests strictly limiting the scope of therapy to the prevention or treatment of disease. Agar addresses criticisms of bio-technology based on the view that humans are products of nature – "nature's handiwork" – whether by divine design or by processes of evolution, and that genetic interventions threaten these processes (or usurp them). Francis Fukuyama typifies this approach.[34] Agar responds that the moral image of nature actually supports a restricted prerogative to enhance. He relies on the conditional claim "that if it is morally acceptable to leave in place a given natural genetic arrangement associated with enhanced ability, then it is morally acceptable to engineer an arrangement with the same effects".[35] He cites "the nature principle", that moves from a permission not to act, to permission to act.[36] He also has a "nurture principle": "If we are permitted to produce certain traits by modifying our children's environments, then we are also permitted to produce them by modifying their genomes".[37] Agar rejects genetic determinism, which so often infects enthusiasts for bio-technology. He is aware that this threatens to subvert socially progressive projects (such as educational reform) on the grounds that they are a waste of time and money, given that we are prisoners of our genes. There is in fact widespread theoretical acceptance that human development is the product of profoundly complex interactions between genes and environment (including upbringing and education). This approach can be used to counter ethicists, such as Kass, who fear that genetic engineering will "manufacture" humans, and thus dehumanise and depersonalise them. Personalities are in reality "made" by environments as well as by genes.

What are Agar's "liberal safeguards"? Despite his touching faith that systems based upon individual choices are more likely to produce good outcomes than state-based systems (historians might well be sceptical on that point), he accepts the dangers of poor or unethical choices being made:

> We will need to make educated guesses about how our rationally and morally imperfect descendants will react to the widespread availability and use of genomics, genetic engineering and cloning.[38]

He concedes that there are future dangers of (1) "polarisation", where genetic change results in different sub-groups – even perhaps sub-species – evolving to the point where the social bonding that is integral to liberal society becomes impossible; and (2) "homogenisation", where citizens become so similar "that liberal protections of diversity will become redundant"[39] and we will be fated to live in a suffocating monoculture. Agar is not alarmist about such fears. He devises safeguards, mainly along the lines of ensuring the right of the child to make meaningful choices about the course of its life and countering differential access to genetic technologies. This (he urges) would be consistent with traditional liberal strategies of ensuring a just distribution of goods needed for a good life, as Rawls argues, and thus prevent a widening of the gap between rich and poor. Diffusion of technology would hopefully lower costs and enable wider access to medical procedures. Much of this is, of course, problematic. Are modern health systems becoming cheaper and more readily accessible, or is the trend the other way? How feasible are "just distribution" aspirations in (say) an American political system that is outspokenly anti-welfare? Agar is a philosopher, not a political scientist, and he does not searchingly interrogate such political issues.

Agar is a "pragmatic optimist". While recognizing that bio-technology is unbelievably complex, and that there are serious risks in genetic change, he considers the potential benefits to outweigh harms. He is to be commended for a thoughtful analysis of a plethora of ethical scenarios, treated with respect, an awareness of reality and common sense. His humane liberalism is cogently argued and admirable. Yet at times he seems to be standing in the path of an engulfing tsunami. And there is a depressing sense in his final chapters that ultimately little can be done about some major threats to humanity coming out of bio-technology. On the contentious ethical issue of full human cloning, for example, he seems essentially to have conceded the battle before it has begun. He virtually rules out legislative prohibition in liberal democracies, on the grounds that cloning would happen anyway: either as research is driven underground with private funding; or as cloning is given the green light in countries such as China and Korea. Brave New World indeed!

---

[1] Gunnar Broberg and Nils Roll-Hansen, eds., *Eugenics and the Welfare State: Sterilization Policy in Denmark, Sweden, Norway, and Finland* (East Lansing, Michigan State University Press, 1996). On South America see Nancy Stepan, "The Hour of Eugenics": *Race, Gender and Nation in Latin America* (Ithaca, New York, Cornell University Press, 1991) and Julia Rodriguez, *Civilizing Argentina: Science, Medicine and the Modern State* (Chapel Hill, University of North Carolina Press, 2006).

[2] Frank Dikötter, *Imperfect Conceptions: Medical Knowledge, Birth Defects and Eugenics in China* (New York, Columbia University Press, 1998).

[3] Paul Crook, *Darwin's Coat-Tails: Essays on Social Darwinism* (Peter Lang, Oxford, New York, 2007), essay 16 "Eugenics, Genetics and Feeblemindedness". See essay 15 "American and Nazi

Eugenics: Flawed Alliance" for more on the historiography of eugenics.

[4] There are a number of groups (mostly in the US) who embrace ideas of redesigning humans (intellect and psychology), finding eternal youth and beauty, merging the human and the technological ("cyborgisation") and colonizing other planets. They include the World Transhumanist Association with its *Journal of Transhumanism* and less reputable cults such as the Extropians and the Raelians (who claim to have produced human clones, aim at eternal life and source the human race to a process of cloning by aliens from space). On this see ch.14 in Harold W. Baillie and Timothy K. Casey, eds., *Is Human Nature Obsolete? Genetics, Bioengineering, and the Future of the Human Condition*, (Cambridge, Massachusetts and London, MIT Press, 2005), chapter by Langdon Winner, entitled "Resistance is Futile: The Post human Condition and its Advocates". A popular example of the posthumanist genre is Hans Moravec, *Robot: Mere Machines to Transcendent Mind* (Oxford, New York, Oxford University Press, 1999).

[5] As in Lee Silver's predicted division of the world into "GenRich" and "Naturals" in three hundred years' time: Remaking Eden: *Cloning and Beyond in a Brave New World* (Avon, New York, Harper, 1997).

[6]. Baillie and Casey, *Is Human Nature Obsolete?*

[7] *Ibid*, p. 74. Interestingly some voices have called for a truce between science and religion in order to save nature and the planet from global warming. The socio-biologist E. O. Wilson – usually aligned with secularists such as Richard Dawkins in attacking religion – has just written a book *The Creation: An Appeal to Save Life on Earth* (London, New York, W. W. Norton, 2007) emphasizing human responsibility to preserve bio-diversity, and asking for religion to assist science in averting natural disaster.

[8] As Jonathon Silvertown says: "The current geological era has been dubbed the Anthropocene in recognition of the fact that, since the Industrial Revolution about 200 years ago, human influence on the environment has become planetary in scale. Now 40 per cent of plant growth each year is appropriated for human use": review of David Beerling, *The Emerald Planet: How Plants Changed Earth's History* (Oxford, Oxford University Press, 2007) in *Times Literary Supplement* (23 November 2007), p. 29. Beerling criticizes James Lovelock's well known Gaia theory that the earth is a self-regulating system as too restrictive. It is (he says) a theory "suspended uncomfortably between tainted metaphor, fact and false science".

[9] John Harris, *Clones, Genes, and Immortality: Ethics and the Genetic Revolution* ((Oxford, Oxford University, 1998), pp. 171-172. Harris develops his ideas in a book just out: *Enhancing Evolution: The Ethical Case for Making Better People* (Princeton, Princeton University Press, 2007).
[10] Baillie and Casey, *Is Human Nature Obsolete?* p. 87.
[11] *Ibid*, p. 69.
[12] Leon Kass, *Life, Liberty and the Defense of Dignity: The Challenge for Bioethics* (San Francisco, Encounter Books, 2002); *Human Cloning and Human Dignity: The Report of the President's Council on Bioethics* (New York, Perseus Books, 2002).
[13] Baillie and Casey, *Is Human Nature Obsolete?* p. 79.
[14] *Ibid*, pp. 82-85.
[15] *Ibid,* p. 156.
[16] Hans S. Reinders*, The Future of the Disabled in Liberal Society* (Notre Dame, University of Notre Dame Press, 2000).
[17] Baillie and Casey, *Is Human Nature Obsolete?* p. 168.
[18] *Ibid*, p. 342.
[19] Leon Kass, "The Wisdom of Repugnacnce", *New Republic* (2 June 1997), p. 20; quoted in Nicholas Agar, *Liberal Eugenics: In Defence of Human Enhancement* (Oxford, Malden MA, Blackwell, 2004), p. 56. Agar dubs this the "yuck" factor and objects that this places moral conclusions beyond reason's reach.
[20] Baillie and Casey, *Is Human Nature Obsolete?* p. 346.
[21] *Ibid,* pp. 60-61.
[22] Alan Holland and Andrew Johnson, eds. *Animal Biotechnology and Ethics*, (London, Chapman & Hall, 1998), p.239
[23] Baillie and Casey, *Is Human Nature Obsolete?* p. 89.
[24] *Ibid*, p. 8.
[25] *Ibid*, p. 90.
[26] Agar, *Liberal Eugenics*, p. 23.
[27] *Ibid,* p. 5.
[28] *Ibid,* p. 6.
[29] *Ibid,* p. 15.
[30] *Ibid*, chapter 3.
[31] *Ibid,* p. 3.
[32] *Ibid,* p. 39.
[33] *Ibid,* p. 33. Agar is opposed to the "intrusive" approach adopted in Allen Buchanan, Dan Brock, Norman Daniels and Daniel Winkler, *From Chance to Choice: Genetics and Justice* (Cambridge, Cambridge University Press, 2000).
[34] Francis Fukuyama, *Our Posthuman Future: Consequences of the Biotechnology Revolution* (New York, Farran, Straus & Giroux, 2002): "In the end, biotechnology will cause us in some way to lose our humanity – that is, some essential quality that has always

underpinned our sense of who we are and where we are going…". Agar, *Liberal Eugenics,* p. 101.
[35] Agar, *Liberal Eugenics*, p. 89.
[36] *Ibid,* pp. 99-100.
[37] *Ibid,* p. 113.
[38] *Ibid,* p. 133.
[39] *Ibid,* p. 134.

8. War in Human Civilization. By Azar Gat (Oxford, Oxford University Press, 2006).

Azar Gat's books on the history of military thought broke new ground. He has now moved on to a massive new subject. It is not a history of warfare but a study of the causation of war in human nature and history. War, with its shocking human costs, has been deplored by civilized writers since the Greeks. Less recognized have been its benefits, which were often shameful to admit (such as conquering other people's territory, or capturing women and impregnating them so as to spread one's genes). Gat argues compellingly for evolutionary explanations of war rather than the culturist (or cultural-materialist) approach that has tended to be taken by modern anthropologists and sociologists, although he freely concedes the complex role of culture in shaping aggressive behaviour. War is seen as essentially springing out of basic human drives and embedded desires that function to acquire resources needed for survival (food, land, women, etc). This "motivational complex" has been shaped by selective forces that go back to the beginning of life on earth.

Gat's method is perhaps best seen in the considerable attention he gives to the "first two million years", justifiably so given that humans led a hunter-gatherer life for 99.5% of their evolutionary history, which is responsible for their genetic inheritance. He demolishes the Enlightenment-Rousseau view of peaceful natural man in favour of Hobbes's "nasty, brutish and short". Just as intra-specific killing is now known to be widespread in nature, so was it for the human family, from hominids to the various *Homo* species. Warfare was not, as the romantics would have it, a later product of agriculture or industry or the rise of states (although it may be said that Gat sometimes slides surreptitiously from terms like fighting and conflict to warfare). Brilliantly using a vast array of evidence from a range of disciplines, Gat shows that from Palaeolithic hunters on, there was fierce competition for, and guarding of, rich ecological niches of the world, a contrast to older views of peaceful co-existence within spacious countrysides. Kin selection factors explain the willingness of related groups to fight for each other against non-kin, the "other", as he says, "the deeply engrained evolutionary root of ethnocentrism, xenophobia, patriotism and nationalism". In the Darwinian cost analysis, high mortality rates in conflict were offset by gains in subsistence resources and mates and a lessening of population pressure within the group. These are primary motivations for Gat, whereas factors such as gaining prestige, power and revenge are second-level aims. Like explanations based on sorcery or cannibalism, they can be traced back to more fundamental evolutionary motives. He describes early "arms races" – that have continued until the nuclear age. They had real justifications but also escalated and became self-perpetuating: "Warfare can thus become a self-fulfilling prophecy" with net losses for all. Gat tellingly uses scenarios borrowed from games theory, such as the "prisoner's dilemma" and the "Red Queen effect".

He goes on to apply his method to the growth of agriculture, the rise of the state, modern class systems, "Machine Age War" and liberal democracies to the world of nuclear deterrence and terrorism. Despite strong peaceful tendencies arising from modernity, are our embedded predispositions still driving us towards global violence or even destruction? Gat hedges his bets. It is "anybody's guess" how future developments will shape our potential for conflict.

Gat will be criticized for not writing a more conventional book, for leaving out politics and much of traditional diplomatic or military history, for projecting images of primal violence upon modern warfare or for being "reductionist". Certainly he sails too close to biological determinism for my liking at times. Evolutionary rationales and scenarios can all too readily be imagined to account for almost any complex behaviours. However Gat claims to be building up a comprehensive framework across disciplines. Overall I find his thesis persuasive, based on mind-boggling scholarship, sophisticated and nuanced analysis. This is an awesome book on an awesome subject.

9. Enhancing Evolution: The Ethical Case for Making Better People. By John Harris (Princeton and Oxford: Princeton University Press, 2007).

The US government calls "waterboarding", a form of torture, an "enhanced interrogation technique". Critics of genetic modification might be forgiven for thinking that its proselytes are using similar sleight of hand when they refer to human "enhancement". John Harris, however, defines enhancement as a way of making humans better: living longer, healthier, happy lives, making us smarter, stronger, more resistant to disease, even super or post-human in our capacities and qualities. If genetic manipulation results in demonstrable human improvement it is, by definition, good. If not, it is bad (or possibly neutral?) The logic of this is impeccable (if possibly trivial as he admits), but it also has the effect of giving a rhetorical advantage to one side in the debate.

Harris is comfortably at home with advancing biotechnology and skilled at philosophical analysis. Here he elaborates and recycles positions he took in his *Wonderwoman and Superman* (1992), *On Cloning* (2004) and other works. If humans have been enhanced over eons by the evolutionary process, have enhanced themselves by cultural evolution (including education and social change) and this is ethically acceptable (one might observe that there has been much ethical debate about some at least of these changes), then (argues Harris) there is no ethical difference in humans rejecting stick-in-the mud concepts of a sacrosanct nature and enhancing themselves by consciously directing their evolution through such methods as genetic engineering, embryonic splitting, implantation, stem-cell research, cloning, life extension, nanotechnology, performance enhancing drug use, etc. He clinically dissects the ethical issues involved in such technologies and exposes misconceptions about them. He makes his case impressively while ruthlessly demolishing critics (unfortunately this sometimes degenerates into unnecessarily insulting language, as in the case of Leon Kass). Doing nothing when benefits are possible is morally inferior to enhancements, which become a moral duty: "they make us better, not simply by curing or ameliorating our ills, but because they make us better people, less the slaves to illness and premature death, less fearful because we have less to fear, less dependent, not least upon medical science and on doctors". Harris makes an eloquent plea for the right of citizens freely to choose enhancements. This is not only self-evidently sensible but is enshrined in the moral and political theory of liberal democracy, whereas state prohibitions – unless justified by clear evidence of general harms – are illiberal. The onus of proof is thrust upon those doomsayers who have predicted everything from calamitous changes to human nature to a world dominated by drug companies and wealthy elites able to afford the new technologies (involved in, say, designer babies). They must show in a realistic balancing of probabilities that harms outweigh benefits. Harris has superhuman optimism about the results of his felicific calculus.

Harris is long on logic but short on historical imagination. To take one instance, he brilliantly defends the ethics of vastly increasing human longevity (essentially an extension of life-saving medicine) but hardly scratches the surface when it comes to the social consequences of an elite of "immortals" (shades of Shaw's Ancients) coexisting with "mortal" people. To be fair he does recommend "commensurate work in ethics and social policy" to cope with such problems. Harris seems not really to grapple with the disturbing social implications of commodification and exploitation of the building blocks of life. He might well try Nicholas Agar's use of "moral images" to elucidate more complex ethical scenarios.[1] Agar also spells out more clearly the sources of his ethical theory and position vis-à-vis major philosophical schools than does Harris. Finally, although this will seem Luddite to Harris, do we really want to live in a world that celebrates (say) "drug cheat" cyclists winning the Tour de France? (Ask Cadell Evans.)

[1] Nicholas Agar, *Liberal Eugenics* (Oxford, Malden MA., Blackwell, 2004).

10. Design and Destiny: Jewish and Christian Perspectives on Human Germline Modification. Edited by Ronald Cole-Turner (Cambridge, Mass., and London: The MIT Press, 2008).

There is a stereotype that religion is almost totally opposed to genetic modification of the human germline. This excellent collection of essays by religious scholars (mostly Americans) sets the record straight. The views presented are rich and nuanced.

Elliot Dorff explains that Judaic tradition honours medicine and sees humans as God's partners in creation. Gene therapies are welcome as an answer to suffering, as long as other conditions are met: that cures are available to all who need them; that the essence of God's world is preserved; that we maintain humility about what we can know and do; and that the worth of people being "modified" not be undermined. Overall the aim should not be to create superior elites or to fulfill narcissistic desires for super bodies or babies. Rather, in Maimonides' words, we should maintain health in order to keep our souls upright, "in a condition to know God". We need to be cautious that we are not creating "physical, social or moral monstrosities".

In Catholic teaching also the value of medical research is balanced by an ethical perspective based on a coherent vision of the person (body and spirit). Thomas Shannon feels that:

> … the ethical foundation of permissible research is – absent a few explicit warrants – identical with mainstream research ethics: informed consent, an acceptable risk-benefit ratio, appropriate research design, the promise of benefit.

Intervention is taboo where it breaches the right to life from conception, human dignity (that of persons endowed with a soul, with moral responsibility and who are called to beatific communion with God) or is not within God's created order. These areas include experimentation on embryos that is not directly therapeutic, harvesting ova from women, cloning human embryos for stem cell research or reproduction, risky gene therapies, etc. Some fine discriminations are drawn. Transplants of functional organs, such as kidney, heart, lungs, are okay, but those threatening some change in the identity of the recipient (such as brain tissue transplants) are problematic and to be assessed case by case. Shannon's exposition is illuminating, but not likely to convince enthusiasts for "enhancement". He himself suggests philosophical problems with the assumption that fertilization is a discrete moment (at which personhood begins) rather than a process.

James Walter usefully rehearses the range of theological arguments available to Catholics. He uses an evolving concept of material nature to take a prophetic view that therapies are not in principle contrary to God's creative and redemptive purposes. The Protestant theologian Ronald Cole-Turner adopts a similar position. Lisa Cahill's concept of human nature includes rationality, free will and sociality in order to advocate restraints on manipulation of the germline. She highlights the perils of consumer-oriented marketing of genetic enhancements. Given the expense of therapies, the pathetic state of the American public health system, and the terrifying power of the drug companies, who can believe that the benefits of genetic medicine will not go disproportionately to the privileged, leaving a "genetic underclass" to fend at the most basic level? She bravely calls for bioethicists to speak out publicly.

Unlike Cameron and De Baets, Celia Deane-Drummond accepts that humans may move beyond their natures. Using understandings of freedom, conscience and virtue that go back to Augustine and Aquinas, she admits limited use of inherited genetic modification for lethal diseases, but rules against human cloning or embryonic stem cell technology. Interventions need always to be made in a context of wisdom and prudence.

This is the thrust of the book. Germline modification is mainly accepted but with moral conditions. One is that it is limited to therapy and not enhancement, a distinction that critics such as John Harris have declared to be impractical or even meaningless. Many of the contributors gloss over this problem. Another condition concerns social justice. As Cole-Turner points out, it is hard to see how germline modification "is a moral priority compared with the more urgently pressing health needs around the world".

11. Charles Darwin on the *Origin of Species*: The Illustrated Edition, edited by David Quammen (New York, London, Sterling Publishing, 2008).

2009 is of course the bicentenary of the birth of Charles Darwin and it is 150 years since the appearance of his epoch-making *Origin of Species*. To mark the occasion Sterling have produced a sumptuous illustrated edition of the *Origin*, edited by David Quammen, author of *The Reluctant Mr. Darwin*. The text is the first edition of November 1859, chosen because it was "the freshest, the most dramatic and daring and consequential, of all the versions that came from Darwin's pen". Maybe. The choice seems sensible, anyway, because later editions are readily available to scholars. They contain important revisions and additions but the logistical problems of incorporating them into this version would have been difficult and the whole thing would have become unwieldy. Quammen's introduction and comments on the illustrations seem aimed at a general audience, often slangy and wryly witty (and occasionally problematical). But is this the audience that will buy such a lavish production?

The illustrations are brilliant, beautifully reproduced and telling as contextual aids in understanding Darwin's achievement. Quammen is associated with *National Geographic* and it shows. He and his researchers have ransacked libraries and collections for their sources. The Thomas Cooper Library of the University of South Carolina was a major contributor but there are materials from the Darwin Heirlooms Trust, the Whipple Museum of the History of Science at Cambridge, the American Museum of Natural History, Down House, the Gray Herbarium at Harvard, the Bridgman Art Library, the Wellcome Library in London, the Bibliothèque Nationale in Paris, Oxford Science Archive, and the National Maritime Museum in London as well as the Image Works and Mary Evans Picture Library.

The pictures are cleverly chosen to reinforce the text but Quammen avoids being too simple or literal. He rightly stresses the central significance of the voyage of the *Beagle* and we find illustrations from the voyage (including Conrad Martens's superb watercolour of Murray Narrow) popping up throughout the book, while useful extracts from

Darwin's journal and his *Zoology of the Voyage of the Beagle* are interspersed throughout the text, as are also extracts from his *Autobiography* and other works. These are "literary side dishes and visual condiments to the main course". Not only are there portraits, sketches and photographs of relevant figures, from Darwin's grandfather Erasmus to T. H. Huxley and Henry Drummond, there are stunning lithographs by the ornithologist Elizabeth Gould and much else in this genre, with state of the art present day camera work (including satellite) on plants and creatures, many unknown to Darwin but adding perspective to his views. (He would not have been surprised at this, given his emphasis on the rise of new types and constant extinction of others.) The book succeeds in its aim of offering glimpses into the "settings, institutions and locales" that were important in Darwin's life and the people "who were close to him personally and scientifically". These include Linnaeus, de Candolle, members of the Lunar Society of Birmingham (I'm glad it got a spot as the Lunar Society was very significant), Henslow, Haeckel, Lyell, Cuvier, Lamarck (Quammen is misleadingly harsh about Lamarck, who has been considerably rehabilitated lately), Wallace (treated fairly), Hooker, Asa Gray, Agassiz, and Owen. All of the important Darwin likenesses are there, including the sometimes vicious cartoons. The latter offer a tantalizingly brief insight into the complex reception given to Darwin's ideas. The *Vanity Fair* cartoon of 1871 has a seated Darwin giving a cheeky smirk (not a "leer") that says "I've set the cat among the pigeons. Now let's see your reaction". This contrasts with the stereotype of him as a pathologically timid man – he was multi-layered.

12. Darwin Loves You: Natural Selection and the Re-enchantment of the World, by George Levine (Princeton University Press, Princeton, Oxford, 2008).

Was Darwin a mindless mechanist who ejected love and wonder from the natural world in favour of scientific rationalism and an alienating meaninglessness? No, says Levine, and his book makes a sophisticated and nuanced case for the defence. He draws a connection with Weber. He saw post-Enlightenment science as one major cause of modern impersonalization, "the narrative of disenchantment… of the disappearance of the sacred and mysterious from this world". Darwin would seem, at least superficially, to fit into Weber's narrative, being both a massive figure in science and one who certainly called upon naturalistic and materialistic laws to explain nature. (Levine's invocation of Weber is idiosyncratic but his general point is most relevant.) Levine is passionately concerned to present an alternative, and more complex, Darwin, who presented "a world 'bereft' of transcendental spirit that is yet laden with value and entails a deeply emotional, a 'visceral', response to the workings of nature". Darwin offered a "secular re-enchantment" that balanced the undeniable brutalities of struggle with an empathetic sense of interconnectedness, altruism and wonderful diversity in nature.

I absolutely agree with Levine's emphasis on the plasticity of Darwin's ideas, "infinitely pliable" in Janet Oppenheimer's phrase. Their multivalence permitted the spawning of an amazing range of "Social Darwinisms", from left to right, from racism and eugenics to their liberal opposites (as I have argued in my book *Darwin's Coat-Tails*[1]). Out of Darwinism could come, certainly, despair, repugnance, anomie but also – as Levine brilliantly shows - an existential sense of enjoyment and celebration of the beauties and plenitude of nature. I also agree with Levine when he says:

> The universe Darwin sought to describe was law-bound, and it is possible to infer from his arguments what he surely never affirmed and, I believe, did not intend to imply, that biology fully determines all human behavior.

Darwin, as rightly emerges in this book, was neither determinist nor reductionist.

Darwin seems to be in need of constant rehabilitation, especially given the negative images of him spread by the religious right in America. Levine pursues his thesis across a range of topics – from philosophy of science; the gap between science and culture (that he tries to bridge); the ideological uses of Darwinism (he focuses, interestingly, on Karl Pearson and Benjamin Kidd in the nineteenth century); modern pathways to reductionism such as sociobiology (he shows a fascinated ambivalence about E. O. Wilson) and evolutionary psychology; samples from Darwin's life (especially his agony over the death of his young daughter Annie); sexual selection (Levine rescues Darwin from the more vacuous charges made by feminists); Darwin's language and use of imagery (his metaphors substantively affected his theory and tellingly exemplified the industrial-imperial context of Victorian Britain). As a distinguished literary scholar, Levine is predictably good value on Darwin's rhetoric. In this he builds on the work of the incomparable Gillian Beer. Levine reveals that Darwin's writings were saturated in Romantic sensibility (an insight offered earlier by Robert Richards who rooted his thought in *Naturphilosophie*); but Levine shows also that there is a lingering Romantic sensibility even in modern scientists (such as Wilson). Ultimately Darwin's Weberian objectivity and his Romantic subjectivity were both necessary in order to deliver "one of the great imaginative and intellectual achievements of modern times".

Levine always writes elegantly. However, his book constantly states and restates his essential theme, dinning you around the head until you feel like saying "Enough! I get it". But it is worth getting.

---

[1] Paul Crook, *Darwin's Coat-Tails: Essays on Social Darwinism* (New York, Peter Lang, 2007).

13. The Passing of Protestant England: Secularisation and Social Change, c.1920-1960. By S. J. D. Green (Cambridge: Cambridge University Press, 2011).

Secularisation discourse is a veritable minefield. It has engaged big names – one has only to mention David Martin, Hugh McLeod and Callum Brown – and evoked a plenitude of theories: eg., secularisation, anti-secularisation and post-secularisation. Simon Green's way around the difficulties in each paradigm is to invoke "a conceptual eclecticism bound by a determined empirical particularism", in this case relating theory to "the very particular dynamics of denominational Christianity from which they began their work in the Britain of 1914, or thereabouts". He wants to reassert what seems axiomatic, but has been much ignored, the inextricable link between social, political, intellectual and religious history. He is trying to rescue religious history from the marginalisation that has in fact come out of the process of secularisation itself.

He brilliantly documents how the political importance of religion declined markedly after 1920, followed by the story of institutional decline of the churches (giving proper regard to sectarian and regional differences). A trifle indulgently, he devotes a chapter to rescuing Dean Inge as a serious thinker (I agree, as argued in my *Darwin's Coat-Tails*).[1] Green gives a careful analysis of the "puritan" (nonconformist) ethic, which underpinned the Victorian nation and Empire. Despite the bohemians of Bloomsbury and rationalists who ridiculed its "killjoy" aspects, it showed surprising survival power up until at least the Second World War. There was an underlying downward trend to religiosity up to 1960, a "seismic" movement in religious culture after 1918, but the graph was erratic. Churches had their revivals as well as decay, ecumenism as well as sectarianism, migrations between sects, morphings into more exotic spiritualisms, resiliences and flexibilities. Green documents an overall falling away from orthodox adherence and doctrine, a loss of knowledge about faith (the decline of Sunday schools was a key factor here), especially as taboos weakened on sex, drink, gambling and Sunday observance, and secular amusements such as the cinema and sport proliferated. The war sped up change (if in complex ways). Green makes the interesting point that the black market legitimised dishonesty among the citizenry much more than "any real or imagined outbreak in collective libidinousness ever did".

He is illuminating on the broader social and cultural changes "that forged within a generation a very different country in which an erstwhile, common Puritanism was increasingly confined to the wider Celtic shores and the madder conceits of utopian radicals". Green's judgment is that religion was virtually dead by 1960. He contends against older views that it declined from (variously) the Enlightenment, the Industrial Revolution or during The Great War; but also against Callum Brown's influential assertion that the turning point was in the permissive 1960s, after revivals in the 40s and 50s. On this matter, it seems, Green has trumped Brown.

Green weaves a fascinating narrative, bolstering his brief with a staggering number of telling case-studies, in the later years including Seebohm Rowntree's *English Life and Leisure* (1951), the 1944 Education Act, the debates of the fifties and early sixties, the changing role of women, sociological models, and "contemporary visions of revival [that] proved to be brief delusions". This is a rich, scholarly book, incorporating a lifetime's work. It focuses unrepentantly on England and thus lacks some of the subtle comparative perspectives that one finds in David Martin's recent writing. And there is at times a touch of overkill. It is nevertheless instructive reading for those who would like to find reasons for the moral turpitude that marks recent English history, from Iraq to the City of London crash.

---

[1] Paul Crook, *Darwin's Coat-Tails: Essays on Social Darwinism* (New York, Peter Lang, 2007).

14. The Story of America: Essays on Origins. By Jill Lepore (Princeton and Oxford: Princeton University Press, 2012).

As Jill Lepore states early on, this is not a narrative history of America, but the story of stories about America, or illuminating themes in American history, stories that were often flawed or downright lies but have shown great resilience in the national memory. She shows wonderfully well how such narratives were shaped by the culture and interests of the time, and how they were constantly reinterpreted in later times, according to prevailing circumstances. Historians, she warns, beware of your sources. There is no deeply profound unifying thesis here that will revolutionise American history, but the book is imaginative, highly instructive and compellingly readable. Her themes vary wildly, from iconic to forgotten personages, from voting and constitutions to dictionaries and dime novels. Her cast includes Captain John Smith, Washington, Jefferson, Franklin, Paine, Jackson, Garfield, Dickens, Kit Carson, Longfellow, Noah Webster, Clarence Darrow and Charlie Chan.

Lepore is a Harvard historian and a meticulous researcher, but also an upper echelon journalist. These are essays, all but one written for the *New Yorker*. Her intention is to show how origin stories demonstrate how American democracy has been bound up with "the political culture of ink and type". But one thing emerges inescapably from all this. A searchlight is beamed upon the seamy side of American society, then and now. The sinister, the violent and the corrupt are deeply embedded in the national psyche. Did you know that hundreds of people were killed trying to vote in the nineteenth century? (89 Americans died at the polls on Election Day between 1828 and 1861, most shot. America was awash with guns then, as now.) The United States has the highest homicide rate of any affluent democracy and a jail rate that is four times the world average.

Lepore gives us much on racism, lynchings, burnings of blacks, segregation, the Great Migration of blacks to the North from 1918 to 1930 ("the most underreported story of the twentieth century", as Isabel Wilkerson complained), misery, poverty and despair. Slavery was entrenched even at the time of the Founding Fathers. Jefferson had children by his slave mistress, but it took Annette Gordon-Reed's 1997 book *Thomas Jefferson and Sally Hemmings* to convince some historians. The real scandal, for Gordon-Reed, "was how far historians, and especially the clan of Jefferson biographers, had been willing to go to ignore evidence right in front of them". White-washing of "great men" (and lesser people) has been a national pastime. An entertaining essay on campaign biographies traces this tainted genre – grotesquely slanted and full of balderdash - back to John Eaton's life of General Jackson.

I found two essays of especial significance. "We the Parchment" is an intriguing analysis of the ways in which the constitution has been interpreted and reinterpreted across time, according to the political culture of the day. "Rap Sheet" subtly places the issue of crime and punishment into a proper historical context. Sociologists would be well advised to follow up some of Lepore's original suggestions and insights. She has an unerring knack of picking weak spots in the academic-speak of experts and theorists. She is also a lively writer and story teller. I'll give you just one example of her style. This is on Thomas Paine:

> In the comic book version of history that serves as America's national heritage, where the Founding Fathers are like the Hanna-Barbera Super Friends, Paine is Aquaman to Washington's Superman and Jefferson's Batman: we never find out how he got his super powers and he only shows up when they need someone who can swim.

15. The Colours of Our Memories. By Michel Pastoureau, translated by Janet Lloyd (Cambridge, Polity, 2012).

Why review a book on the history of colours? This response is typical, as Pastoureau justly complains, of academe when dealing with the whole subject of colours. Despite the centrality of colour in human life, it has routinely been dismissed as unworthy of serious scholarly analysis, as petty, peripheral, pointless or frivolous. Thick volumes on the history of art, for example, made no mention of colour: "300 or 500 pages without formulating a single remark, a single word about colours, not even a mention of terms such as 'blue', 'red' or 'yellow': that was quite an achievement!". Ditto with the history of clothing. The author, now a distinguished French medievalist, had encountered similar hostility to subject matter when in the 1960s he embarked on a thesis on heraldic bestiary, when heraldry was despised and animals were deemed unworthy of study. Animals were embraced by a rights movement, and are now studied, but colour less so, only slowly becoming legitimised by scholars such as Pastoureau, a world authority on the history of colours.

This is hardly a systematic treatise, but rather an idiosyncratic collection of personal memories, tangential thoughts, hypotheses, fantasies and even prophecies combined with serious analysis (as he says, part philosophy, sociology and journalism), all connected with colour. This connection is sometimes tenuous, but always the writing is informative, often amusing, and delightfully readable. The book "comprises many fields of observation, encompassing vocabulary and other linguistic factors, fashion and clothing, the objects and practices of daily life, emblems and flags, sport, literature, painting, museums and artistic creation".

There are many insights here that are original, or at least hardly ever incorporated into mainstream commentary. Here are a few. The lighting conditions in which people first viewed the works of the great masters such as Michelangelo were vastly different to that of today's evenly lit galleries. Images were viewed by the light of flickering flames, candles or oil-lamps, "making them vibrate, even lending them a kinetic quality.... For eyes today, colours no longer move, or hardly do; they seem immobile: the difference in perception is immense". The effects of chiaroscuro were much more effective then.

> For nearly four centuries, "black-and-white" documentation was all that was available for reproducing, studying and making known figurative evidence from the past, painting included. In consequence the modes of thought and sensibilities of historians seem likewise to have been converted to black-and-white.

There are other nuggets. Why was green for centuries regarded as unlucky? Historical figures who had phobias range from Le Tellier (the war minister who banned the use of green in all regiments fighting for Louis XIV) to Schubert and Queen Victoria. Green was a cursed colour in the theatre world, just possibly because toxic pigments such as verdigris and even arsenic (nineteenth century), used to "green" costumes, causing cases of poisoning.

Did you know that yellow – in medieval times the colour of cowardice, also associated for long with sickness, madness or the alien (yellow stars for Jews) – was rescued by the Tour de France? The yellow jersey was invented in 1919 by a newspaper sponsoring the Tour, which just happened to be printed on pale yellow paper. It was to become the colour of excellence. Did "Mitterand beige" cost the Left votes because their leader insisted on cladding himself in suits of that unbecoming colour? Pastoureau pursues many such themes: "turbulent stripes", "subversive trousers", "historians without colour", "furling the colours", "playing chess", 1950s "bling", "whims of memory", "spelling and grammar", Scott's *Ivanhoe*, and Stendhals's *The Red and the Black* (does anyone yet know why he chose that title?).

16. G.K. Chesterton: A Biography. By Ian Ker (Oxford, Oxford University Press, 2011).

Corpulent, humorous and witty, perceptive and paradoxical, likeable and larger than life, G. K. Chesterton was a major public intellectual of the early twentieth century. Yet today he is largely unread and forgotten, except by a band of Catholic followers, especially in America. (There is even a *Chesterton Review*.) Ian Ker sets out to redress this situation, claiming that Chesterton was a worthy successor to the great Victorian sages Newman, Carlyle, Arnold and Ruskin. In a sense Ker follows Shaw, who called GK "a man of colossal genius".

This is a biography in the nineteenth century tradition. It is leisurely in pace, a massive tome, full of big chunks from Chesterton's (and other people's) letters and from his voluminous writings, following his life almost day-to-day in great (too often tedious) detail. The book should have been cut by at least two hundred pages. Despite the slow going, the reader is gradually caught up in the mesmerising web of GK's varied career. Ker writes well and from a sound scholarly basis. As is to be expected from a distinguished biographer of Newman, and author of *The Catholic Revival in English Literature* (2003), he is totally at home in the religious and cultural milieu of Chesterton's lifetime (1874-1936). Sources for the life are a problem. Many of his papers were destroyed or lost (including papers available to earlier biographers). Ker has ransacked archives to recover whatever is available. Although there are valuable recent studies on aspects of Chesterton's work, especially William Oddie on his early religious development, Ker's is the best single-volume life since Maisie Ward's classic biography of 1944.

Having said that, I find Ker's claim that Chesterton ranks with the great sages deeply problematic. He is simply not a systematic religious thinker of the class of Newman, for example. Despite GK's elaborate defence of paradox, it ultimately blocks any achievement of a coherent and logical body of thought (not that he ever attempted such a thing). Also, it must be said, his relentless paradox, humour and optimism can be wearing. One longs at times for the doom-laden gloom of a Malcolm Muggeridge. (T. S. Eliot found

Chesterton's style "exasperating to the last point of endurance" and his cheerfulness depressing. I sympathise.)

Nevertheless, Chesterton offered a host of original ideas on a range of topics, from religion and social analysis to politics and economics. They include: free will and determinism; original sin; ritual, dogma and faith; the Trinity and Incarnation; heresy; the religion of mystery and paradox; his theology of development (with interesting parallels to Newman); his philosophy of limitations, wonder, humour and the grotesque. And on the more secular side his searching critiques of capitalism, socialism, imperialism and eugenics; and his theory of distributism (the more equal distribution of property).

In his chief works *Orthodoxy* and *The Everlasting Man* (and one might add his *Aquinas*), he gave fresh insights into the nature of faith, Christ and the Gospels. In numerous works after his conversion to Catholicism (1922), he overturned conventional views on Catholicism, Anglicanism and Protestantism. Coming from a family climate of Unitarianism/pantheism, he was less subject (he said) to the usual prejudices on these subjects. He stood up for (if romanticising) "common and simple people" and their popular culture against the onslaughts of elitism, Nietzschean pessimism and Supermanism.

He had his blindspots (women, Jews, Buddhism, Islam, Fascism) - areas where his deeply embedded values seem to blinker him from really informed understanding (he was a lazy researcher, relying on his prodigious memory). Nevertheless, Ker's biography portrays a magnificent Renaissance man, from journalist to quasi-theologian, novelist and critic. He was a truly heroic figure, warring against the modernist currents of his age, including aestheticism, art-for-art's sake and decadence. When many Christians were timid, he doughtily championed his faith, pugnaciously taking the fight to the secular enemy.

17. Egypt and the Origin of Civilization: The British School of Culture Diffusion, 1890s -1940s. By Joshua D. Smith (Lexington, Kentucky, Vindication Press, 2011).

"The British School of Culture Diffusion" was neither British – the leading light Elliot Smith was Australian – nor was it really a school, rather a group of independent and tough-minded scholars, who nevertheless interacted with and influenced each other enormously. Elliot Smith was a world renowned neuro-anatomist and expert on human evolution; W. H. R. Rivers was a pioneer in the fields of psychotherapy, neurology, physiology and ethnology; and W. J. Perry taught university courses in comparative religion and cultural anthropology at Manchester and London universities. Despite their credentials, their theories on cultural diffusion have been treated with cruel derision in the profession of archaeology and anthropology since the Second World War. Joshua Smith rightly seeks to redress this situation by placing their ideas in an historical context, examining non-epistemic reasons why the profession dismissed such ideas, and returning to primary sources to analyse what they in fact wrote rather than "what is claimed by their detractors". (Modern textbooks tend simply to repeat the negative comments of critics such as Glyn Daniel.) I have put similar revisionist views in my book *Grafton Elliot Smith, Egyptology and the Diffusion of Culture*,[1] in press unfortunately at the time Smith's volume appeared.

A useful account of the theoretical antecedents of Egyptocentric, and more generally, concepts of diffusion covers a range of thinkers, including Kircher, Stukeley, Prichard,Lacouperie, Humboldt, Bastian, Ratzel, Tylor, Graebner, Kroeber and many others; and in the early twentieth century Flinders Petrie, Peake, Fleure, Childe, and even Boas. Diffusionism entailed a diversity of conceptual positions, but it was a contending paradigm in the formative years of anthropology (as historians such as Trigger and Kuklick have shown – historians often do better than the profession in this area). The "British School" was making wide-ranging claims about culture change at a time of interdisciplinary fluidity, gathering information "from the fields of archaeology, linguistics, physical anthropology, comparative mythology and religion,

Egyptology, ethnography, ethnology, and prehistory". When Elliot Smith set up his anatomy department at University College in 1919, he tried to make it an interdisciplinary centre. He was a lifelong foe of narrow specialisms that encouraged tunnel vision and also territorial jealousies that rebuffed the ideas of "outsiders" such as himself. When UC lost out to Malinowski at LSE in a fight for Rockefeller funding, this presaged the eclipse of diffusionism by functionalist-structural paradigms, which were more relevant to colonialist interests. New questions were asked, older issues ignored. Patriotic factors also intruded, especially in America, where what Smith calls "nativist isolationism" ruled (theories of exclusive indigenous development that admitted of no transoceanic cultural contacts).

In his detailed analysis, Smith dispels many still current misconceptions. To give examples, they include the charge that Elliot Smith's heliolithic theory was anti-Darwinian or racist; or that it had Egyptians directly carrying their culture traits across the world, when he postulated indirect mitigated contacts, "wherein the receiving culture adapted the ideas to their pre-existing beliefs and made their own modifications". With respect to America: "He postulated multiple Asiatic and/or Indian diffusionary waves that took place in the Pre-Columbian context". Smith makes admirable use of primary sources on his main topic, but relies heavily upon standard secondary sources for related themes, such as the transition to structural-functionalism (Stocking, Urry, Langham et al). He makes the point that British functionalism was "ahistorical to a fault because it failed to offer any resolution to the omnipresent question of origins that always comes with the study of anthropology", an opinion shared by Evans-Pritchard. Smith nicely broadens the "diffusionist milieu" to include lesser figures such as Meek, Rattray, Fox and Armstrong; and treats the diachronic versus synchronic debate (the diffusionists being allied with the former). Despite being theoretically problematic in places, this book is an important contribution in a contested area.

[1] Paul Crook, *Grafton Elliot Smith, Egyptology and the Diffusion of Culture: A Biographical Perspective* (Brighton, Sussex Academic Press, 2012).

18. The Habsburgs: The History of a Dynasty. By Benjamin Curtis (London, New York, Bloomsbury, 2013).

If you are looking for a concise yet comprehensive history of the famous Habsburg dynasty this is the book for you. Curtis performs a miracle of concision as he deals with a bewildering array of personalities, territories, changing times and events. The dynasty lasted over a millennium, from hazy beginnings under Guntram the Rich in the Swiss canton of Aargau in the 900s, and a conventional starting point under the first important founding father Rudolph I (1218-1291), right up until the long reign of Franz Joseph and the composite monarchy's death throes of 1918. At its height it covered the heartlands of Europe:

> From England to Serbia, Portugal to Poland, in the early modern period the dynasty's dominions extended still further, encompassing nearly all of the Americas [under its Spanish branch], touching territories in Africa and Asia as well.

Holy Roman Emperors as well, the Habsburgs aspired to almost global rule. Their ups and downs, truly great achievements and grievous failures and disappointments, are subtly traced by Curtis. Narrative is balanced by analytical scrutiny of the various phases of Habsburg history according to success in four key dynastic strategies: "1. How the dynasty produced and reproduced itself, which includes succession and marriage politics and territorial acquisition. 2. How the dynasty created legitimacy and loyalty for itself and its political system. 3. How the image and function of the ruler changed, which involves the evolution from the sacralised medieval warrior king to the demystified constitutional monarchy. 4. How the dynasty institutionalized and improved its government structures".

The rulers themselves range, predictably, from magnificent to imbecilic (Habsburg in-breeding contributing to the latter trait). Curtis gives vivid, often revisionist, pen portraits of them. The cast includes Rudolph I, Maximilian I, Charles V ("the last great Western emperor"), Felipe II, Leopold I, Maria Theresia (the most able, to my mind), Joseph II and Franz Joseph I. Curtis is forced to deal in relatively few pages with massive events such as the Ottoman threat to Europe, expulsion of the Moors from Spain, the Reformation and Counter-Reformation, the Thirty Years' War, the Enlightenment, the wars against Revolutionary and Napoleonic France, the Austro-Prussian conflict and the Great War. He does so with impressive competence and succinct analysis.

Nationalistic history has tended to be consistently negative about supranational dynasties such as the Habsburgs. This book is a much needed corrective. Curtis is realistic about the weaknesses and failures of the dynasty, but he is generous too in recognising their real achievements and the advantages of an overarching and cosmopolitan system. Inevitably there were challenges to a transnational state with the nineteenth century rise of nationalisms and liberal constitutionalism. But the dynasty was not fated to die. As Curtis argues, the challenges were potentially containable in many respects, given the widespread loyalty to Franz Joseph and the monarchy, and the dynasty's relatively solid performance in bureaucracy and the economy, which delivered tangible benefits to the middle classes, and helped keep a "loose-limbed bundle of realms" together. The containability was ultimately undermined by self-inflicted strategic mistakes, such as the expansionist push into the Balkans, a misguided reaction against Austria's loss of hegemony to Prussia in Germany, and the spark for World War 1. As Curtis concludes:

> The Habsburgs' employment of the old strategies of dynastic aggrandizement may have few lessons to offer most people in the twenty-first century. But their aspirations to a multinational political order, transcending the small minds and restrictive confines of nationalism, is not only still relevant – it is worthwhile.

19. The Intellectual World of C. S. Lewis. By Alister E. McGrath (Oxford, Wiley-Blackwell, 2014).

C. S. Lewis (1898-1963) is most famous for his Narnia stories. But at the time of his death he was also regarded as a leading Christian apologist in the Anglo-American world, through his wartime broadcasts for the BBC and books such as *Mere Christianity* (1952) and his autobiographical *Surprised by Joy* (1955). However his reputation took a nosedive during the swinging sixties. This was largely, according to McGrath, because of rising secularism and philosophical movements like logical positivism. By the 1980s however Lewis had resurged: his Narnia books became enormously popular, logical positivism was shoved aside by newer fashions, and there was a religious revival in America. He was the right man at the right time. McGrath contends this was because he had a knack, amounting almost to genius, for putting Christian essentials into accessible language using his remarkable literary talents and insights into a broad western cultural tradition, "offering an imaginative and rhetorical rendering of some core themes of the Christian faith that were superbly adapted to the cultural geography of his own age". This set of richly scholarly essays explores in detail these themes. McGrath's acclaimed biography *C. S. Lewis – A Life: Eccentric Genius, Reluctant Prophet* (2013) was not the place for extended analysis of many aspects of Lewis's worldview. Here we have a more sustained intellectual engagement. The aim is "to set Lewis in the greater context of the western literary and theological tradition, exploring how he appropriated and modified its narratives, ideas, and images".

How does Lewis's use of myth and metaphors of light, sun and sight locate him within both classical and contemporary debate on these themes? Why should *Surprised by Joy* be used with caution as a source? Did he have a covert agenda in writing it? How did the now neglected philosophical movement "Oxford Realism" impact upon the impressionable Lewis during his early years at Oxford after his personal trauma during World War 1? How does this influence illuminate his concepts of idealism and realism, as well as his complex transition to theism and later conversion to Christianity? How did

Lewis's restatement of the traditional "argument from desire" lead him to "a rich and complex way of exploring and affirming the rationality and existential appeal of the Christian faith"? How innovative was Lewis's approach to apologetics? What was his relationship to Anglicanism? Can he be regarded as a theologian? McGrath gives deeply thoughtful and quite revisionist answers to these questions.

I found particularly interesting the penetrating section on myth. Spurred on by his fellow Inkling Tolkien, Lewis came to see that Greek and Nordic myths were not incompatible with Christianity. They were anticipations of the full truth, the grand narrative or "big picture" that was offered by Christian faith. As Lewis said, we should expect to find "in the imagination of great Pagan teachers and myth-makers some glimpse of that theme which we believe to be the very plot of the whole cosmic story - the theme of incarnation, death and rebirth".

Indeed humanity's sense of supra-rational reality, the subject of poetry, Romantic literature, Idealistic philosophy, yearnings, imaginings, questings for meaning, sense of awe and the eternal, all these were but tastes of Divine reality. Dry theology and logically ordered statements of Christian belief were inadequate expressions of the vibrancy of true religion, best told "in the form of imaginative narrative transposition of the Christian story". Theology needed to be "remythologized". It was his ability to do this that was the key to Lewis's popular success. McGrath contextualises all this with copious (even over-copious) referencing to classical and modern literature and scholarship. In a shortish chapter he mentions Justin Martyr, Clement of Alexandria, Plato, Keats, Schlegel, Wagner, Yeats, Joyce, Bohr and Heisenberg, Bultman, Habermas and Bruce Lincoln, to cite a few.

20. Malthus: The Life and Legacy of an Untimely Prophet. By Robert J. Mayhew (Cambridge, MA and London, Belknap, 2014).

Robert Mayhew writes stylishly, wittily, lucidly about a much misunderstood Malthus. He puts Malthus in proper historical context, acutely analyses his writings, and follows the convoluted trail of historical responses to Malthus and that distorted and maligned Behemoth "Malthusianism". A rationalist realist about poverty and disease in eighteenth century Britain, Malthus set the swarming of population against the finitude of food resources. He became the age's greatest critic of Panglossian Enlightenment ideas of human perfectibility as embodied by Rousseau and Godwin (his father's heroes). As he also attacked the French Revolution, he became a despised target of radicals like Paine and Cobbett, and Romantics from Wordsworth to Byron. Southey accused him of writing "the political bible of the rich, the selfish and the sensual", and put the Romantic counter-claim that poverty was the product of social arrangements not nature. Such anti-Malthusian arguments have ramified down to the present day "via writers such as Marx and, in a very different idiom, Julian Symon".

The picture is inevitably more complex. Malthus, in Marx's view "the lackey of capitalism", was in fact no comforter of the establishment, his ambiguity on this perhaps due to his ambivalent social position between the gentry and Burke's "swinish multitude". As Mayhew warns:

> The tracks of intellectual history are not so straight and simple as to lead from Wordsworth to the Green Party, and from Malthus to capitalism and climate change [...] Two centuries later, we would be better advised to see the merits in both strands of work rather than merely to re-enact their hostility.

During the time of extensive travels and research that Malthus conducted in his progression to the more nuanced and less bleak second and following editions of his *Essay*, he explored the greater possibilities of humans using "preventive" checks to curb population (social curbs such as later marriages — contraception was crude and anyway he disapproved of it on religious grounds). This was rather than the "positive checks" of war, famine and disease: although, as we know even today these constantly lurk as spectres in the offing. In the process he established himself as a pioneer of environmental economics, examining the nexus between population, economy and environment. This included climate change, a factor almost totally neglected by economists.

He was also a pioneering social statistician. Against stereotypes of him as anti-poor, he wanted a more accurate factual history of them. He collected, but was also methodologically sceptical about the fallibilities of, social, economic and demographic data. This led him to turn his back "on the simplicity and sensationalism that his abstract mathematical argument of 1789 had relied upon and that had made his name" (the famous AP and GP ratios). He now preferred "a cautious and careful empiricism". Mayhew shows how the later editions of Malthus's *Essay* and *Principles of Political Economy* analyse the links between "land, sustenance and resources on one hand, and population, wealth and its allocation on the other".

Malthus, like Darwin, generated a myriad of opinions and agendas, deriders, defenders and in-betweeners, apostles of the right and left, neo-cons and utopians, eugenists, euthanists, Fabians, Fascists. Mayhew follows these intricacies through the Victorian age, the era of world wars and Depression, the post-war years to the present. We encounter "some of the most abhorrent moments in twentieth-century history". They include Hitler's use of Malthusianism to justify genocide. But also don't forget obscenities like Churchill's "Malthusian mentality" in refusing aid during the 1942 Bengal famine. Mayhew documents (in too much detail at times) more recent controversies over the population explosion on "Spaceship Earth" to today's challenges of climate change and environmental insecurity. He concludes that future global uncertainty "will certainly keep Malthus and Malthusian reasoning at the heart of the debates about the interrelationships between population, environmental change, and sociopolitical responses".

21. The Life of R. H. Tawney: Socialism and History. By Lawrence Goldman (London, New York: Bloomsbury, 2014).

Generally regarded as British Labour's greatest theorist, author of those twentieth century classics *The Acquisitive Society* (1921), *Religion and the Rise of Capitalism* (1926), and *Equality* (1931), R. H. Tawney has been much written about. Ross Terrill's 1973 book on Tawney and his times is a particularly fine study. Goldman is thus treading familiar territory. He thoroughly researches Tawney's life, using new materials, and with fine discrimination analyses every aspect of his thought. Tawney's faith is in a morally based, communalist, voluntarist and free socialism, and he puts perhaps the best modern argument for it. His emphasis on grass-roots democracy and faith in the essential virtue and capacity for self-improvement of ordinary people, given the proper opportunities through education and a just social system, is inspiring, if at times verging (like Chesterton) on the romantic (although Tawney had his moments of sceptical realism – this had its roots in his experience of fellow Tommies at the Somme, where he was wounded). Goldman shows the influence upon Tawney of Charles Gore's social Christianity and Ruskin's ethical economics. In one sense Tawney was merely elaborating Ruskin's dictum that "there is no wealth but life", redefining rather than redistributing wealth.

Tawney attacked the amoral profiteering basis of classical capitalism and put an older alternative of communal service, calling for "a reform of the economy to meet collective needs and for a re-ordering of human values that would make economic activity a means to life rather than an end in itself". Goldman is good on the "quasi-religious" milieu that spawned the organised Labour movement from the 1880s. Tawney became something of a lone wolf in continuing this tradition well into the next century. Goldman rightly recognises the undoctrinaire religious foundation of Tawney's thought and analyses it acutely. Chapter 7 on "Socialism and Christianity" is rewarding reading. Goldman shows how Tawney's early idealistic and radical personal socialism evolved into a more instrumentalist, less original, variety. Goldman feels, with reason, that the "authentic" Tawney (who kept re-appearing to the end) was "the Christian egalitarian rather than the secular state socialist".

Goldman, unlike some Tawney admirers, recognises the failings in Tawney, the thinker and the man. He lacked philosophical rigour, avoided definitions, was selective in his subject matter, impatient of alternative ideas and perspectives, while his economics was vulnerable to attack as narrow on class differentiation, ignoring consumption, and flawed on human psychology. He was weak on women's rights and race. A workaholic, he found difficulty in giving out warmth and love, which resulted in an unfulfilling (and possibly sexless) marriage to his loyal supporter and wife Jeanette. Many however attested to his essential nobility of character: "The best man I have ever known" said Hugh Gaitskell.

He was hero-worshipped by his numerous working class students and followers. His pioneering work in adult education was amazing; and he "became the most vocal and persistent advocate of the reform of the British secondary education system". Tawney was an enormously influential historian. Goldman stoutly defends his scholarship against the charges of conservative historians who accused him of political bias: "he left a remarkably coherent and stimulating picture of English society between about 1500 and 1700 – the period from 1540 to 1640 was often referred to as 'Tawney's century' – which is a fixed point of reference to this day in historical discussion". Elton and Trevor-Roper were misguided (if not worse, vindictive) in branding Tawney a Marxist, when he was "a thorough-going historical idealist rather than a historical materialist", and was openly critical of Soviet communism.

In a brilliant concluding assessment, Goldman agrees that he was "the most representative of Labour's twentieth-century intellectuals", but best fitting into a line of social prophets: "Tawney belongs with Carlyle, Ruskin and Morris among others in a tradition of ethical anti-capitalists".

22. We Are Amphibians: Julian and Aldous Huxley on the Future of Our Species. By R. S. Deese (Oakland, University of California Press, 2015).

The Boston historian Richard Deese has written a splendidly readable and analytically rigorous study of a fascinating topic, and one that is of continuing relevance in today's world of endangered species, climate change and global violence. Deese focusses on the world-view, but especially on the ecological ideas, of the Huxley brothers, the biologist Julian and the novelist Aldous, grandsons of the famous Thomas Henry Huxley, whose influence upon them was both inspiring and bedevilling. Deese examines their lives and prolific writings, showing how their views about the human future and our place in nature evolved with life-events and under the influence of a particularly vibrant intellectual/cultural milieu. From Victorian roots in love of science and the ideal of human subjugation of nature, they ultimately foreshadowed movements such as genetic "enhancement", Transhumanism (Julian invented the term) and conservation. Julian was a major player, founding UNESCO and the World Wildlife Fund, but Aldous had an even wider cultural influence. Both were aware of the dangerous potential of science, Julian remaining the more enduringly optimistic (even in the age of the Bomb), Aldous the more despairing, witness his satirical attack on consumerism and a technocratic state that controlled breeding in *Brave New World.* Yet even the "iconoclastic" novelist Aldous spurned the amoralism of modernism (too obsessed with sex). Both rejected the absolutist morality of TH (which denied that evolution, or nature, could provide a basis for ethics), and dabbled in "naturalistic ethics". The hope was that, through psycho/cultural self-directed human evolution, Darwin's hopes for a more altruistic future could be achievable.

I found the chapter on "Spiritual Biology" stimulating (especially as I have dissected Julian's "new religion", Evolutionary Humanism, in my *Darwin's Coat-Tails*).[1] As Deese says: "Both Julian and Aldous saw the void left by traditional religion as a major challenge for the future of humanity, and they saw many of the passions that rushed in to fill it as not only foolish but dangerous", including totalitarian ideologies of right and left, as well as utopian and naturist cults. Such unease was commonplace in the thoughts of Middleton Murry, R. H. Tawney and a host of others at the time. Aldous reflected much on pseudo-religions, mysticism and cults, and experimented in alternative living and mind-expanding drugs in his later Californian life (see his *Doors of Perception*, 1954). Julian's *Religion Without Revelation* (1927) tried to construct an evolutionary-based religion, at times verging on mysticism. Biologists dismissed Julian's purposive evolution as heretical, while there was little popular appeal in what seemed an ersatz religion incorporating Christian values minus the fundamentals of Christian faith. Although they took differing paths, "both of the Huxley brothers tried to integrate the science of evolutionary biology with their own deepest religious intuitions".

"Apes and Essences" shows in rich detail how, in the aftermath of the Great War, Depression and World War 2, Julian was the more pro-science and pro-war (even approving the Manhattan Project), and more centralist (the means to a fairer welfarist society). Aldous feared that science and centralism were the seedbeds of militaristic totalitarianism. He favoured Gandhian pacifism and an economically decentralised, self-sufficient democratic society. Deese gives an intriguing account of the significant legacy that the Huxleys – in their contrasting ways - bequeathed to a whole range of modern movements: global environmentalism and "Deep Ecology", preservation of endangered species and habitats, national parks and wilderness, population control, renewable energy, counterculture and New Ageism, reconnecting Snow's two cultures, and much more. Having only recently, in Julian's words, "emerged from the biological to the psychosocial area of evolution, from the earthly biosphere into the freedom of the atmosphere", we as humans - capable of self-aware evolution have a duty to preserve the beauty and the delicate equilibrium of nature, indeed of our planet.

---

[1] Paul Crook, *Darwin;s Coat-Tails: Essays on Social Darwinism* (New York, Peter Lang, 2007), pp. 315-335.